THE BEST TEST PREPARATION FOR THE
ADVANCED PLACEMENT EXAMINATION

Mathematics
CALCULUS AB

Donald E. Brook
Mathematics Instructor
Mount San Antonio College, Walnut, California

Donna M. Smith
Mathematics Instructor
American River College, Sacramento, California

Tefera Worku
Mathematics Instructor
SUNY-Albany, Albany, New York

 Research & Education Association
61 Ethel Road West • Piscataway, New Jersey 08854

The Best Test Preparation for the
ADVANCED PLACEMENT EXAMINATION
IN MATHEMATICS: CALCULUS AB

Printed in the United States of America

Library of Congress Control Number 2001099116

International Standard Book Number 0-87891-282-7

Research & Education Association
61 Ethel Road West
Piscataway, New Jersey 08854

 REA supports the effort to conserve and protect environmental resources by printing on recycled papers.

CONTENTS

ADVANCED PLACEMENT CALCULUS AB EXAM V

ADVANCED PLACEMENT CALCULUS AB EXAM VI

ANSWER SHEETS

ABOUT RESEARCH & EDUCATION ASSOCIATION

Research & Education Association (REA) is an organization of educators, scientists, and engineers specializing in various academic fields. Founded in 1959 with the purpose of disseminating the most recently developed scientific information to groups in industry, government, and universities, REA has since become a successful and highly respected publisher of study aids, test preps, handbooks, and reference works.

REA's Test Preparation series includes study guides for all academic levels in almost all disciplines. Research & Education Association publishes test preps for students who have not yet completed high school, as well as high school students preparing to enter college. Students from countries around the world seeking to attend college in the United States will find the assistance they need in REA's publications. For college students seeking advanced degrees, REA publishes test preps for many major graduate school admission examinations in a wide variety of disciplines, including engineering, law, and medicine. Students at every level, in every field, with every ambition can find what they are looking for among REA's publications.

Whereas most test preparation books present only a few practice tests that bear little resemblance to the actual exams, REA's series presents tests that accurately depict the official exams in both degree of difficulty and types of questions. REA's practice tests are always based upon the most recently administered exams, and include every type of question that can be expected on the actual exams.

REA's publications and educational materials are highly regarded and continually receive an unprecedented amount of praise from professionals, instructors, librarians, parents, and students. Our authors are as diverse as the subject matter represented in the books we publish. They are well-known in their respective disciplines and serve on the faculties of prestigious high schools, colleges, and universities throughout the United States and Canada.

ACKNOWLEDGMENTS

In addition to our authors, we would like to thank Dr. Max Fogiel, President, for his overall guidance, which brought this publication to completion; Larry B. Kling, Quality Control Manager, for his supervision of revisions; David Bordeau, Editorial Assistant, and Michael Tomolonis, Assistant Managing Editor for Production, for coordinating revisions; Mel Friedman and Penny Luczak for their editorial contributions; and Michael C. Cote for typesetting the manuscript.

Advanced Placement Examination in Calculus AB

INDEPENDENT STUDY SCHEDULE

ADVANCED PLACEMENT CALCULUS AB
INDEPENDENT STUDY SCHEDULE

The following study schedule allows for thorough preparation for the AP Calculus AB Examination. Although it is designed for six weeks, it can be reduced to a three-week course by collapsing each two-week period into one. Be sure to set aside enough time (at least two hours each day) to study. But no matter which study schedule works best for you, the more time you spend studying, the more prepared and relaxed you will feel on the day of the exam.

It is important for you to discover the time and place for studying that works best for you. Some students may set aside a certain number of hours every morning to study, while others may choose to study at night before going to sleep. Other students may study during the day—say, while waiting in line—or they may find another unusual way to do their studying. Only you will be able to know when and where your studying is most effective. Keep in mind that the most important factor is consistency. Use your time wisely. Work out a study routine and stick to it!

Week	Activity
Week 1	Take Exam I to determine your strengths and weaknesses. You can then determine the areas in which you need to strengthen your skills.
Week 2	Carefully read and study the AP Calculus AB Review included in this book.
Week 3	Take Exams II & III, and after scoring your exams, review carefully all incorrect answer explanations. If there are any types of questions or particular subjects that seem difficult to you, review those subjects by studying again the appropriate section of the AP Calculus AB Review.
Week 4	Take Exams IV & V, and after scoring your exams, review carefully all incorrect answer explanations. If there are any types of questions or particular subjects that seem difficult to you, review those subjects by studying again the appropriate section of the AP Calculus AB Review.

Week 5	Take Exam VI, and after scoring your exam, review carefully all incorrect answer explanations. If there are any types of questions or particular subjects that seem difficult to you, review those subjects by studying again the appropriate section of the AP Calculus AB Review.
Week 6	Study any areas you consider to be your weaknesses by using the AP Calculus AB Review and any other study resources you have on hand. Review the practice tests one more time to be sure you understand the problems that you originally answered incorrectly.

Advanced Placement Examination in Calculus AB

INTRODUCTION

ABOUT THIS BOOK

This book provides an accurate and complete representation of the Advanced Placement Examination in Mathematics: Calculus AB. The six practice tests provided are based on the format of the most recently administered Advanced Placement Calculus AB Exams. Each test is three hours and 15 minutes in length and includes every type of question that can be expected on the actual exam. Following each test is an answer key complete with detailed explanations designed to clarify the material for the student. By completing all six tests and studying the explanations which follow, students will discover their strengths and weaknesses and become well prepared for the actual exam.

ABOUT THE TEST

The Advanced Placement Calculus AB Examination is offered each May at participating schools and multi-school centers throughout the world.

The Advanced Placement Program is designed to allow high school students to pursue college-level studies while attending high school. The participating colleges, in turn, grant credit and/or advanced placement to students who do well on the examinations.

The Advanced Placement Calculus courses cover college-level mathematics; they are intended for students with a strong background in college-preparatory mathematics, including algebra, axiomatic geometry, trigonometry, and analytic geometry. The courses cover graphical, numerical, analytic, and verbal calculus, along with overarching concepts like derivatives, integrals, limits, applications and modeling, and approximation.

The AP Calculus AB exam has two sections:

Section I) **Multiple-choice**: composed of 45 multiple-choice questions, designed to measure the student's abilities in a wide range of mathematical topics. These questions vary in difficulty and complexity. This section is broken into two parts. Part A consists of 28 questions for which a calculator *cannot* be used. Part B contains 17 questions, some of which will *require* the use of a graphing calculator. One hour and forty-five minutes is allowed for this section of the exam.

Section II) **Free-response**: tests how well and how accurately the student is able to recall and utilize knowledge of calculus. Section II is also divided into two parts. Part A contains 3 questions which will *require* the use of a graphing calculator. Part B contains 3 questions for which a calculator *cannot* be used. Between 0 and 9 points are awarded for each question based on the work shown and whether or not the solution given is correct. Partial credit is given for answers that are correct in format, yet incorrect in the solution. Therefore, REA strongly recommends that examinees show all their work. Each of these two sections counts for 50% of the student's total exam grade. Because the exam contains such a vast array of material, it is a foregone conclusion that all students will not be able to answer all questions correctly.

These calculators have been approved by the College Board for use on the AP Calculus AB exam; bring one with you when you take the test:

Casio
fx-6000 series
fx-6200 series
fx-6300 series
fx-6500 series
fx-7000 series
fx-7300 series
fx-7400 series
fx-7500 series
fx-7700 series
fx-7800 series
fx-8000 series
fx-8500 series
fx-8700 series
fx-8800 series
fx-9700 series
fx-9750 series
cfx-9800 series
cfx-9850 series
cfx-9950 series
cfx-9970 series
Algebra fx 2.0 series

Sharp
EL-5200
EL-9200 series
EL-9300 series
EL-9600 series

Texas Instruments
TI-73
TI-80
TI-81
TI-82
TI-83/TI-83 Plus
TI-85
TI-86
TI-89

Radio Shack
EC-4033
EC-4034
EC-4037

Other
Micronta
Smart[2]

Hewlett-Packard
HP-28 series
HP-48 series
HP-49 series
HP-38G
HP-39G
HP-40G

The sample tests in this book provide calculator questions with explanations that include the steps necessary with the calculator. These steps are illustrated after the word *calculator,* listing the keystrokes that should be used.

ABOUT THE REVIEW SECTION

This book contains review material that students will find useful as a study aid while preparing for the AP Calculus AB Examination. This review—in a handy outline format—provides information that will most likely appear on the actual test. Included in this section are the following topics:

Elementary Functions — Covers the Properties of Functions, the Properties of Particular Functions, and Limits.

Differential Calculus — Covers Derivatives and Application of the Derivative.

Integral Calculus — Covers Anti-Derivatives, Applications of Anti-Derivatives, the Law of Exponential Change, Techniques of Integration, the Definite Integral, and Applications of the Integral.

SCORING THE TEST

SCORING THE MULTIPLE-CHOICE SECTION

For the multiple choice section, use this formula to calculate your raw score:

$$\underline{\hspace{1cm}} - (\ \underline{\hspace{1cm}} \times 1/4) = \underline{\hspace{1cm}}$$

number   number   raw score (round to nearest whole #)
right   wrong*

* DO NOT INCLUDE UNANSWERED QUESTIONS

SCORING THE FREE-RESPONSE SECTION

For the free-response section, use this formula to calculate your raw score:

$$\underline{\hspace{0.6cm}} + \underline{\hspace{0.6cm}} + \underline{\hspace{0.6cm}} + \underline{\hspace{0.6cm}} + \underline{\hspace{0.6cm}} + \underline{\hspace{0.6cm}} = \underline{\hspace{0.8cm}}$$

problems one through six   raw score

The score for each problem should reflect how completely the question was answered, that is, the solution that was produced and the steps taken. You should gauge at what point a mistake was made, and determine whether any use of calculus or mathematics was incorrect. Each problem is given a score of between 0 and 9 points. More points should be given for correct answers that include all work in the answer explanation, and fewer points should be given for incorrect answers and necessary work that was not written down. It would be helpful to have a teacher or an impartial person knowledgeable in calculus decide on how points should be awarded.

THE COMPOSITE SCORE

To obtain your composite score, use the following method:

$$1.200 \times \underline{\hspace{1.5cm}} = \underline{\hspace{1.5cm}} \text{ (weighted multiple-choice score)}$$

multiple-choice   round to the nearest whole number
raw score

NOW ADD:

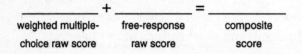

weighted multiple-	free-response	composite
choice raw score	raw score	score

Compare your score with this table to approximate your grade:

AP GRADE	COMPOSITE SCORE
5	78–102
4	64–77
3	45–63
2	30–44
1	0–29

The overall scores are interpreted as follows: 5–extremely well qualified; 4–well qualified; 3–qualified; 2–possibly qualified; and 1–no recommendation. Most colleges will grant students who earn a 3 or above either college credit or advanced placement. Check with your school guidance office about specific school requirements.

CONTACTING THE AP PROGRAM

For registration bulletins or more information about the Calculus AB exam, contact:

AP Services
P.O. Box 6671
Princeton, NJ 08541-6671
Phone: (609) 771-7300

Website: www.collegeboard.org/ap

Advanced Placement Examination in Calculus AB

REVIEW

Chapter 1

Elementary Functions: Algebraic, Exponential, Logarithmic, and Trigonometric

A. Properties of Functions

Definition: A function is a correspondence between two sets—the domain and the range—such that for each value in the domain there corresponds exactly one value in the range.

A function has three distinct features:

a) the set x which is the domain,

b) the set y which is the co-domain or range,

c) a functional rule, f, that assigns only one element $y \in Y$ to each $x \in X$. We write $y = f(x)$ to denote the functional value y at x.

Consider Figure 1. The "machine" f transforms the domain X, element by element, into the co-domain Y.

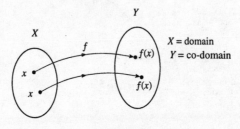

FIGURE 1

Parametric Equations

If we have an equation $y = f(x)$, and the explicit functional form contains an arbitrary constant called a parameter, then it is called a parametric equation. A function with a parameter represents not one but a family of curves.

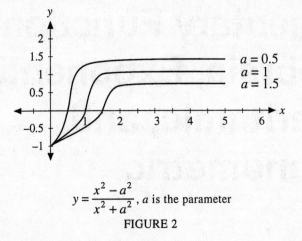

$$y = \frac{x^2 - a^2}{x^2 + a^2}, \; a \text{ is the parameter}$$

FIGURE 2

Often the equation for a curve is given as two functions of a parameter t, such as

$$X = x(t) \text{ and } Y = y(t).$$

Corresponding values of x and y are calculated by solving for t and substituting.

Vectors

A vector (AB) is denoted $\overrightarrow{AB}$, where B represents the head and A represents the tail. This is illustrated in Figure 3.

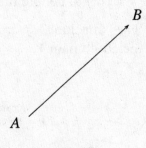

FIGURE 3

The length of a line segment is the magnitude of a vector. If the magnitude and direction of two vectors are the same, then they are equal.

Vectors which can be translated from one position to another without any change in their magnitude or direction are called free vectors.

The unit vector is a vector with a length (magnitude) of one.

The zero vector has a magnitude of zero.

The unit vector, $\vec{i}$, is a vector with magnitude of one in the directions of the x–axis.

The unit vector $\vec{j}$ is a vector with magnitude of one in the direction of the y–axis.

When two vectors are added together, the resultant force of the two vectors produce the same effect as the two combined forces. This is illustrated in Figure 4.

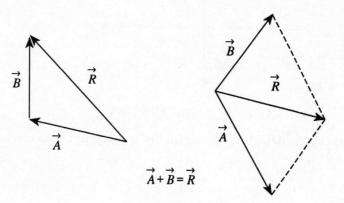

$$\vec{A} + \vec{B} = \vec{R}$$

FIGURE 4

In these diagrams, the vector $\vec{R}$ is called the resultant vector.

Combination of Functions

Let f and g represent functions, then

a)   the sum $(f + g)(x) = f(x) + g(x)$,

b)   the difference $(f - g)(x) = f(x) - g(x)$,

c)   the product $(fg)(x) = f(x)\,g(x)$,

d)   the quotient $\left(\dfrac{f}{g}\right)(x) = \dfrac{f(x)}{g(x)}$, $g(x) \neq 0$,

e)   the composition function $(g \circ f)(x) = g(f(x))$ where $f(x)$ must be in the domain of g.

Graphs of a Function

If (x, y) is a point or ordered pair on the coordinate plane R then x is the first coordinate and y is the second coordinate.

To locate an ordered pair on the coordinate plane simply measure the distance of x units along the x–axis, then measure vertically (parallel to the y–axis) y units.

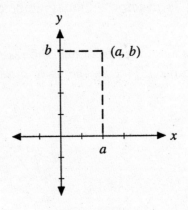

FIGURE 5

This graph illustrates the origin, the x–intercept, and the y–intercept.

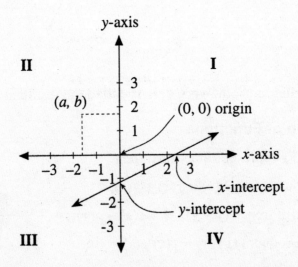

I, II, III, IV are called quadrants in the COORDINATE PLANE.
(a, b) is an ordered pair with x–coordinate a and y–coordinate b.
FIGURE 6 – Cartesian Coordinate System

The following three graphs illustrate symmetry.

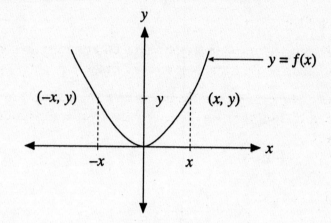

a) Symmetric about the y-axis

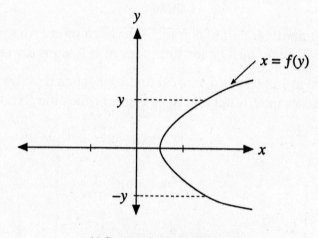

b) Symmetric about the x-axis
Note: This is not a function of x.

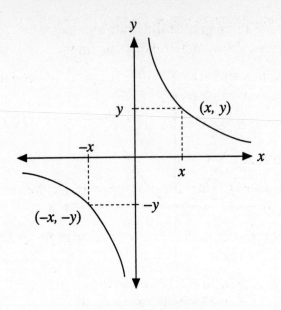

c) Symmetric about the origin.
FIGURE 7

Another important part of a graph is the asymptote. An asymptote is a line which will never be touched by the curve as it tends toward infinity.

A vertical asymptote is a vertical line $x = a$, such that the functional value $|f(x)|$ grows indefinitely large as x approaches the fixed value a.

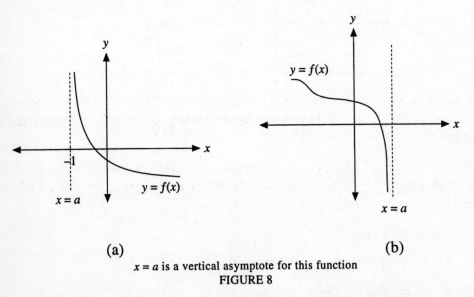

(a)   (b)

$x = a$ is a vertical asymptote for this function
FIGURE 8

The following steps encapsulate the procedure for drawing a graph:

a)   Determine the domain and range of the function.

b)   Find the intercepts of the graph and plot them.

c)   Determine the symmetries of the graph.

d)   Locate the vertical asymptotes and plot a few points on the graph near each asymptote.

e)   Plot additional points as needed.

Polar Coordinates

Polar coordinates is a method of representing points in a plane by the use of ordered pairs.

The polar coordinate system consists of an origin (pole), a polar axis and a ray of specific angle.

The polar axis is a line that originates at the origin and extends indefinitely in any given direction.

The position of any point in the plane is determined by its distance from the origin and by the angle that the line makes with the polar axis.

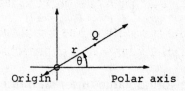

FIGURE 9

The coordinates of the polar coordinate system are (r, θ).

The angle (θ) is positive if it is generated by a counterclockwise rotation of the polar axis, and is negative if it is generated by a clockwise rotation.

The graph of an equation in polar coordinates is a set of all points, each of which has at least one pair of polar coordinates, (r, θ), which satisfies the given equation.

To plot a graph:

1.   Construct a table of values θ and r.

2.   Plot these points.

3.   Sketch the curve.

Inverse of a Function

Assuming that f is a one-to-one function with domain X and range Y, then a function g having domain Y and range X is called the inverse function of f if:

$$f(g(y)) = y \text{ for every } y \in Y \text{ and}$$

$$g(f(x)) = x \text{ for every } x \in X.$$

The inverse of the function f is denoted f^{-1}.

To find the inverse function f^{-1}, you must solve the equation $y = f(x)$ for x in terms of y.

Be careful: This solution must be a function.

Even and Odd Functions

A function is even if

$$f(-x) = f(x) \quad \text{or} \quad f(x) + f(-x) = 2f(x).$$

A function is said to be odd if

$$f(-x) = -f(x) \quad \text{or} \quad f(x) + f(-x) = 0.$$

Absolute Value

Definition: The absolute value of a real number x is defined as

$$|x| = \begin{cases} x & \text{if } x \geq 0 \\ -x & \text{if } x < 0 \end{cases}$$

For real numbers a and b:

a) $|a| = |-a|$

b) $|ab| = |a| \cdot |b|$

c) $-|a| \leq a \leq |a|$

d) $ab \leq |a| |b|$

e) $|a + b|^2 = (a + b)^2$

Periodicity

A function f with domain X is periodic if there exists a positive real number p such that $f(x + p) = f(x)$ for all $x \in X$.

The smallest number p with this property is called the period of f.

Over any interval of length p, the behavior of a periodic function can be completely described.

Zeroes of a Function

To locate an ordered pair on the coordinate plane simply measure the distance of x units along the x-axis, then measure vertically (parallel to the y-axis) y units.

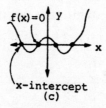

Zeroes of a function
FIGURE 10

B. Properties of Particular Functions

In order to graph a trigonometric function, it is necessary to identify the amplitude and the period of the function.

For example, to graph a function of the form

$$y = a \sin (bx + c)$$

$$a = \text{amplitude and } \frac{2\pi}{b} = \text{period}.$$

Let us graph the function $y = 2 \sin(2x + \frac{\pi}{4})$. Amplitude $= 2$, period $=$ $\frac{2\pi}{2} = \pi$, phase $\angle = \frac{\pi}{8}$.

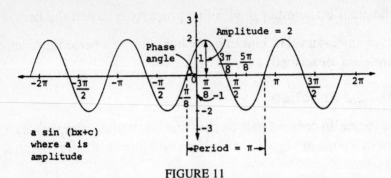

FIGURE 11

The following graphs represent the functions $y = \sin x$ and $y = \cos x$. The amplitude of each is one, while the period of each is 2π.

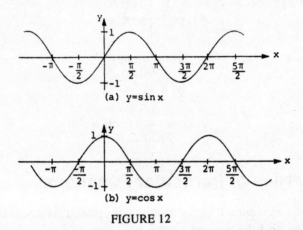

FIGURE 12

Identities and Formulas for Trigonometric Functions

Provided the denominators are not zero, the following relationships exist:

$$\sin t = \frac{1}{\csc t} \qquad\qquad \tan t = \frac{\sin t}{\cos t}$$

$$\cos t = \frac{1}{\sec t} \qquad\qquad \cot t = \frac{\cos t}{\sin t}$$

$$\tan t = \frac{1}{\cot t}$$

If PQR is an angle t and P has coordinates (x, y) on the unit circle, then by joining PR we get angle $PRQ = 90°$ and then we can define all the trigonometric functions in the following way:

sine of t, $\sin t = y$

cosine of t, $\cos t = x$

tangent of t, $\tan t = \dfrac{y}{x}$, $x \neq 0$

cotangent of t, $\tan t = \dfrac{x}{y}$, $y \neq 0$

secant of t, $\sec t = \dfrac{1}{x}$, $x \neq 0$

cosecant of t, $\csc t = \dfrac{1}{y}$, $y \neq 0$.

$\cos^2 x + \sin^2 x = 1$

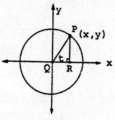

FIGURE 13

Therefore,

$\sec^2 = 1 + \tan^2\theta$, $\csc^2\theta = 1 + \cot^2\theta$

$\sin(A + B) = \sin A \cos B + \cos A \sin B$

$\sin(A - B) = \sin A \cos B - \cos A \sin B$

$\cos(A + B) = \cos A \cos B - \sin A \sin B$

$\cos(A - B) = \cos A \cos B + \sin A \sin B$

$\sin^2\theta = \dfrac{1 - \cos 2\theta}{2}$

$\cos^2\theta = \dfrac{1 + \cos 2\theta}{2}$

Sine law: $\quad \dfrac{a}{\sin\theta} = \dfrac{b}{\sin\phi} = \dfrac{c}{\sin\psi}$

Cosine law: $\quad a^2 = b^2 + c^2 - 2bc\cos\theta$

$$b^2 = c^2 + a^2 - 2ca \cos \phi$$
$$c^2 = a^2 + b^2 - 2ab \cos \psi$$

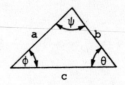

FIGURE 14

Exponential and Logarithmic Functions

If f is a nonconstant function that is continuous and satisfies the functional equation $f(x+y) = f(x) \cdot f(y)$, then $f(x) = a^x$ for some constant a. That is, f is an exponential function.

Consider the exponential function a^x, $a > 0$ and the logarithmic function $\log_a x$, $a > 0$. Then a^x is defined for all $x \in R$, and $\log_a x$ is defined only for positive $x \in R$.

These functions are inverses of each other,

$$a^{\log_a x} = x; \; \log_a(a^y) = y.$$

Let a^x, $a > 0$ be an exponential function. Then for any real numbers x and y

a) $a^x \times a^y = a^{x+y}$

b) $(a^x)^y = a^{xy}$

Let $\log_a x$, $a > 0$ be a logarithmic function. Then for any positive real numbers x and y

a) $\log_a(xy) = \log_a(x) + \log_a(y)$

b) $\log_a(x^y) = y \log_a(x)$

C. Limits

The following are important properties of limits: Consider

$$\lim_{x \to a} f(x) = L \text{ and } \lim_{x \to a} g(x) = K, \text{ then}$$

A)   Uniqueness—If $\lim_{x \to a} f(x)$ exists then it is unique.

B) $\lim\limits_{x \to a} [f(x) + g(x)] = \lim\limits_{x \to a} f(x) + \lim\limits_{x \to a} g(x) = L + K$

C) $\lim\limits_{x \to a} [f(x) - g(x)] = \lim\limits_{x \to a} f(x) - \lim\limits_{x \to a} g(x) = L - K$

D) $\lim\limits_{x \to a} [f(x) \times g(X)] = \lim\limits_{x \to a} f(x) \times \lim\limits_{x \to a} g(x) = L \times K$

E) $\lim\limits_{x \to a} \dfrac{f(x)}{g(x)} = \dfrac{\lim\limits_{x \to a} f(x)}{\lim\limits_{x \to a} g(x)} = \dfrac{L}{K}$ provided $K \neq 0$

Special Limits

A) $\lim\limits_{x \to 0} \dfrac{\sin x}{x} = 1$,

B) $\lim\limits_{x \to \infty} \left(1 + \dfrac{1}{n}\right)^{n} = e$,

Some nonexistent limits which are frequently encountered are:

A) $\lim\limits_{x \to 0} \dfrac{1}{x^2}$, as x approaches zero, x^2 gets very small and also becomes zero, therefore, $\dfrac{1}{0}$ is not defined and the limit does not exist.

B) $\lim\limits_{x \to 0} \dfrac{|x|}{x}$ does not exist.

Continuity

A function f is continuous at a point a if

$\lim\limits_{x \to a} f(x) = f(a)$.

This implies that three conditions are satisfied:

A) $f(a)$ exists, that is, f is defined at a.

B) $\lim\limits_{x \to a} f(x)$ exists, and

C) the two numbers are equal.

To test continuity at a point $x = a$ we test whether

$$\lim_{x \to a^+} M(x) = \lim_{x \to a^-} M(x) = M(a)$$

Theorems on Continuity

A) A function defined in a closed interval $[a, b]$ is continuous in $[a, b]$ if and only if it is continuous in the open interval (a, b), as well as continuous from the right at "a" and from the left at "b."

B) If f and g are continuous functions at a, then so are the functions $f + g$, $f - g$, fg, and $\dfrac{f}{g}$ where $g(a) \neq 0$.

C) If $\lim\limits_{x \to a} g(x) = b$ and f is continuous at b, $\lim\limits_{x \to a} f(g(x)) = f(b) = f[\lim\limits_{x \to a} g(x)]$.

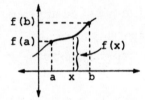

FIGURE 15

D) If g is continuous at a and f is continuous at $b = g(a)$, then

$$\lim_{x \to a} f(g(x)) = f[\lim_{x \to a} g(x)] = f(g(a)).$$

E) Intermediate Value Theorem. If f is continuous on a closed interval $[a, b]$ and if $f(a) \neq f(b)$, then f takes on every value between $f(a)$ and $f(b)$ in the interval $[a, b]$.

Chapter 2

Differential Calculus

A. The Derivative

The Definition and Δ-Method

The derivative of a function expresses its rate of change with respect to an independent variable. The derivative is also the slope of the tangent line to the curve.

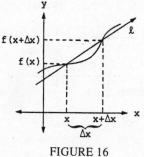

FIGURE 16

Consider the graph of the function f in Figure 16. Choosing a point x and a point $x + \Delta x$ (where Δx denotes a small distance on the x-axis) we can obtain both $f(x)$ and $f(x + \Delta x)$. Drawing a tangent line, l, of the curve through the points $f(x)$ and $f(x + \Delta x)$, we can measure the rate of change of this line. As we let the distance, Δx, approach zero, then

$$\lim_{\Delta x \to 0} \frac{f(x + \Delta x) - f(x)}{\Delta x}$$

becomes the instantaneous rate of change of the function or the derivative.

We denote the derivative of the function f to be f'. So we have

$$f'(x) = \lim_{\Delta x \to 0} \frac{f(x + \Delta x) - f(x)}{\Delta x}$$

17

If $y = f(x)$, some common notations for the derivative are

$$y' = f'(x)$$

$$\frac{dy}{dx} = f'(x)$$

$$D_x y = f'(x) \quad \text{or} \quad Df = f'$$

Rules for Finding Derivatives

General Rule:

A) If f is a constant function, $f(x) = c$, then $f'(x) = 0$.

B) If $f(x) = x$, then $f'(x) = 1$.

C) If f is differentiable, then $(cf(x))' = cf'(x)$

D) Power Rule:

   If $f(x) = x^n$, $n \in$ Z, then

   $f'(x) = nx^{n-1}$; if $n \leq 0$ then x^n is not defined at $x = 0$.

E) If f and g are differentiable on the interval (a, b) then:

   a) $(f + g)'(x) = f'(x) + g'(x)$

   b)   Product Rule:

   $$(fg)'(x) = f(x)g'(x) = g(x)f'(x)$$

Example:

Find $f'(x)$ if $f(x) = (x^3 + 1)(2x^2 + 8x - 5)$.

$$f'(x) = (x^3 + 1)(4x + 8) + (2x^2 + 8x - 5)(3x^2)$$

$$= 4x^4 + 8x^3 + 4x + 8 + 6x^4 + 24x^3 - 15x^2$$

$$= 10x^4 + 32x^3 - 15x^2 + 4x + 8$$

   c)   Quotient Rule:

   $$\left(\frac{f'}{g}\right)(x) = \frac{g(x)f'(x) - f(x)g'(x)}{[g(x)]^2}$$

Example:

Find $f'(x)$ if $f(x) = \dfrac{3x^2 - x + 2}{4x^2 + 5}$

$$f'(x) = \frac{-(3x^2 - x + 2)(8x) + (4x^2 + 5)(6x - 1)}{(4x^2 + 5)^2}$$

$$= \frac{-(24x^3 - 8x^2 + 16x) + (24x^3 - 4x^2 + 30x - 5)}{(4x^2 + 5)^2}$$

$$= \frac{4x^2 + 14x - 5}{(4x^2 + 5)^2}$$

F)   If $f(x) = x^{\frac{m}{n}}$, then

$$f'(x) = \frac{m}{n} x^{\frac{m}{n} - 1}$$

where $m, n \in Z$ and $n \neq 0$.

G)   Polynomials.

If $f(x) = (a_0 + a_1 x + a_2 x^2 + \ldots + a_x x^n)$ then

$f'(x) = a_1 + 2a_2 x + 3a_3 x^2 + \ldots + na_n x^{n-1}$.

This employs the power rule and rules concerning constants.

The Chain Rule

Chain Rule: Let $f(u)$ be a composite function, where $u = g(x)$. Then $f'(u) = f'(u)\, g'(x)$ or if $y = f(u)$ and $u = g(x)$ then $D_x y = (D_u y)\,(D_x u) = f'(u) g'(x)$.

Example:

Find the derivative of: $y = (2x^3 - 5x^2 + 4)^5$.

$$Dx = \frac{d}{dx}.$$

This problem can be solved by simply applying the theorem for $d(u^n)$. However, to illustrate the use of the chain rule, make the following substitutions:

$$y = u^5 \quad \text{where} \quad u = 2x^3 - 5x^2 + 4$$

Therefore, by the chain rule,

$$D_x y = D_u y \times D_x u = 5u^4 \, (6x^2 - 10x)$$
$$= 5 \, (2x^3 - 5x^2 + 4)^4 \, (6x^2 - 10x).$$

Implicit Differentiation

An implicit function of x and y is a function in which one of the variables is not directly expressed in terms of the other. If these variables are not easily or practically separable, we can still differentiate the expression.

Apply the normal rules of differentiation such as the product rule, the power rule, etc. Remember also the chain rule which states

$$\frac{du}{dx} \times \frac{dx}{dt} = \frac{du}{dt} \, .$$

Once the rules have been properly applied we will be left with, as in the example of x and y, some factors of $\frac{dy}{dx}$.

We can then algebraically solve for the derivative $\frac{dy}{dx}$ and obtain the desired result.

Example:

Find y' in terms of x and y, using implicit differentiation, where

$$y' = \frac{dy}{dx},$$

in the expression:

$$y^3 + 3xy + x^3 - 5 = 0.$$

The derivative of y^3 is $3y^2 y'$. The term $3xy$ must be treated as a product. The derivative of $3xy$ is $3xy' + 3y$. The derivative of x^3 is $3x^2$. The derivative of -5 is 0. Therefore,

$$3y^2y' + 3xy' + 3y + 3x^2 = 0.$$

We can now solve for y':

$$y' = -\frac{y + x^2}{y^2 + x}.$$

Trigonometric Differentiation

The three most basic trigonometric derivatives are:

$$\frac{d}{dx}(\sin x) = \cos x,$$

$$\frac{d}{dx}(\cos x) = -\sin x,$$

$$\frac{d}{dx}(\tan x) = \sec^2 x.$$

Given any basic trigonometric function, it can be differentiated by applying these basics in combination with the general rules for differentiating algebraic expressions.

The following will be most useful if committed to memory:

$$D_x \sin u = \cos u \, D_x u$$

$$D_x \cos u = -\sin u \, D_x u$$

$$D_x \tan u = \sec^2 u \, D_x u$$

$$D_x \sec u = \tan u \sec u \, D_x u$$

$$D_x \cot u = -\csc^2 u \, D_x u$$

$$D_x \csc u = -\csc u \cot u \, D_x u$$

Inverse Trigonometric Differentiation

Inverse trigonometric functions may be sometimes handled by inverting the expression and applying rules for the direct trigonometric functions.

For example, $y = \sin^{-1}x$

$$D_x y = D_x \sin^{-1}x = \frac{1}{\cos y} = \frac{1}{\sqrt{1 - x^2}}, \ |x| < 1.$$

Here are the derivatives for the inverse trigonometric functions which can be found in a manner similar to the above function:

$$D_x \sin^{-1} u = \frac{1}{\sqrt{1-u^2}} D_x u, \qquad |u| < 1$$

$$D_x \cos^{-1} u = \frac{-1}{\sqrt{1-u^2}} D_x u, \qquad |u| < 1$$

$$D_x \tan^{-1} u = \frac{1}{1+u^2} D_x u, \qquad \text{where } u = f(x) \text{ differentiable}$$

$$D_x \sec^{-1} u = \frac{1}{|u|\sqrt{u^2-1}} D_x u, \qquad u = f(x), |f(x)| > 1$$

$$D_x \cot^{-1} u = \frac{-1}{1+u^2} D_x u, \qquad u = f(x) \text{ differentiable}$$

$$D_x \csc^{-1} u = \frac{-1}{|u|\sqrt{u^2-1}} D_x u, \qquad u = f(x), |f(x)| > 1$$

High Order Derivatives

The derivative of any function is also a legitimate function which we can differentiate. The second derivative can be obtained by:

$$\frac{d}{dx}\left[\frac{d}{dx}u\right] = \frac{d^2}{dx^2}u = u'' = D^2 u,$$

where $u = g(x)$ is differentiable.

The general formula for higher orders and the nth derivative of u is,

$$\underbrace{\frac{d}{dx}\frac{d}{dx}\cdots\frac{d}{dx}}_{n \text{ times}} u = \frac{d^{(n)}}{dx^{(n)}}u = u^{(n)} = D_x^{(n)} u .$$

The rules for first order derivatives apply at each stage of higher order differentiation (e.g., sums, products, chain rule).

A function which satisfies the condition that its nth derivative is zero, is the general polynomial

$$P_{n-1}(x) = a_{n-1}x^{n-1} + a_{n-2}x^{n-2} + \dots + a_0.$$

Derivatives of Vector Functions

A) Continuity

Let $f(x)$ be a function defined for all values of x near $t = t_0$ as well as at $t = t_0$. Then the function $f(x)$ is said to be continuous at t_0 if

$$\lim_{t \to t_0} f(t) = f(t_0)$$

if and only if for all $\varepsilon > 0$, there exists a $\delta > 0$, such that $|f(t) - f(t_0)| < \varepsilon$, if $|t - t_0| < \delta$.

B) Derivative

The derivative of the vector valued function $V(t)$ with respect to $t \in R$ is defined as the limit

$$\frac{dV(t)}{dt} = \lim_{\Delta t \to 0} \frac{V(t + \Delta t) - V(t)}{\Delta t}$$

If a vector is expressed in terms of its components along the fixed coordinate axes,

$$V = V_1(t)i + V_2(t)j + V_3(t)k,$$

there follows

$$\frac{dV(t)}{dt} = \frac{dV_1}{dt}i + \frac{dV_2}{dt}j + \frac{dV_3}{dt}k .$$

For the derivative of a product involving two or more vectors the following formulae are used:

$$\frac{d}{dt}(A \cdot B) = A \cdot \frac{dB}{dt} + \frac{dA}{dt} \cdot B$$

$$\frac{d}{dt}(A \times B) = A \times \frac{dB}{dt} + \frac{dA}{dt} \times B$$

$$\frac{d}{dt}(A \cdot B \times C) = \frac{dA}{dt} \cdot (B \times C) + A \cdot \left(\frac{dB}{dt} \times C \right) + A \cdot \left(\frac{dC}{dt} \times B \right).$$

Parametric Formula for $\dfrac{dy}{dx}$

According to the chain rule,

$$\frac{dy}{dt} = \frac{dy}{dx} \cdot \frac{dx}{dt} .$$

Since $\dfrac{dx}{dt} \neq 0$, we can divide through $\dfrac{dx}{dt}$ to solve for $\dfrac{dy}{dx}$. We then obtain the equation

$$\frac{dy}{dx} = \frac{dy}{dt} \div \frac{dx}{dt} .$$

Example:

Find $\dfrac{dy}{dx}$ from

$$y = x^3 - 3x^2 + 5x - 4,$$

where $x = t^2 + t$.

From these equations, we find

$$\frac{dy}{dx} = 3x^2 - 6x + 5$$

$$= 3(t^2 + t)^2 - 6(t^2 + t) + 5,$$

$$\frac{dx}{dt} = 2t + 1.$$

Since

$$\frac{dy}{dt} = \frac{dy}{dx} \cdot \frac{dx}{dt}$$

from the chain rule,

$$\frac{dy}{dt} = [3(t^2 + t)^2 - 6(t^2 + t) + 5]\,(2t + 1).$$

We can also first substitute the value of x in terms of t into the equation for y. We then have:

$$y = (t^2 + t)^3 - 3(t^2 + t)^2 + 5(t^2 + t) - 4 \,.$$

When we differentiate this with respect to t, we obtain:

$$\frac{dy}{dt} = 3(t^2 - t)^2 \, (2t + 1) - 6 \, (t^2 + t) \, (2t + 1) + 5(2t + 1)$$

$$= [3(t^2 + t)^2 - 6(t^2 + t) + 5] \, (2t + 1),$$

which agrees with the previous answer.

The first method using the chain rule, however, often results in the simpler solution when dealing with problems involving parametric equations.

Exponential and Logarithmic Differentiation

The exponential function e^x has the simplest of all derivatives. Its derivative is itself.

$$\frac{d}{dx} e^x = e^x \text{ and } \frac{d}{dx} e^u = e^u \frac{du}{dx}$$

Since the natural logarithmic function is the inverse of $y = e^x$ and $\ln e = 1$, it follows that

$$\frac{d}{dx} \ln y = \frac{1}{y} \frac{dy}{dx} \text{ and } \frac{d}{dx} \ln u = \frac{1}{u} \frac{du}{dx}$$

If x is any real number and a is any positive real number, then

$$a^x = e^{x \ln a}$$

From this definition we obtain the following:

a) $\quad \dfrac{d}{dx} a^x = a^x \ln a$ and $\dfrac{d}{dx} a^u = a^u \ln a \, \dfrac{du}{dx}$

b) $\quad \dfrac{d}{dx} (\log_a x) = \dfrac{1}{x \ln a}$ and $\dfrac{d}{dx} \log_a |u| = \dfrac{1}{u \ln a} \dfrac{du}{dx}$

Sometimes it is useful to take the logs of a function and then differentiate since the computation becomes easier (as in the case of a product).

Steps in Logarithmic Differentiation

1. $y = f(x)$ given

2. $\ln y = \ln f(x)$ take logs and simplify

3. $D_x(\ln y) = D_x(\ln f(x))$ differentiate implicitly

4. $\dfrac{1}{y} D_x y = D_x(\ln f(x))$

5. $D_x y = f(x) D_x(\ln f(x))$ multiply by $y = f(x)$

To complete the solution it is necessary to differentiate $\ln f(x)$. If $f(x) < 0$ for some x then step 2 is invalid and we should replace step 1 by $|y| = |f(x)|$, and then proceed.

Example:

$$y = (x + 5)(x^4 - 1)$$

$$\ln y = \ln[(x + 5)(x^4 - 1)] = \ln(x + 5) + \ln(x^4 + 1)$$

$$\frac{d}{dx}\ln y = \frac{d}{dx}\ln(x + 5) + \frac{d}{dx}\ln(x^4 + 1)$$

$$\frac{1}{y}\frac{dy}{dx} = \frac{1}{x + 5} + \frac{4x^3}{x^4 + 1}$$

$$\frac{dy}{dx} = (x + 5)(x^4 + 1)\left[\frac{1}{x + 5} + \frac{4x^3}{x^4 + 1}\right]$$

$$= (x^4 + 1) + 4x^3(x + 5)$$

This is the same result as obtained by using the product rule.

The Mean Value Theorem

If f is continuous on $[a, b]$ and has a derivative at every point in the interval (a, b), then there is at least one number c in (a, b) such that

$$f'(c) = \frac{f(b) - f(a)}{b - a}$$

Notice in Figure 17 that the secant has slope

$$\frac{f(b)-f(a)}{b-a}$$

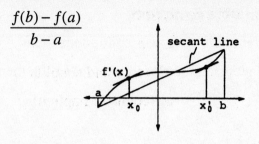

FIGURE 17

and $f'(x)$ has slope of the tangent to the point $(x, f(x))$. For some x_0 in (a, b) these slopes are equal.

Example:

If $f(x) = 3x^2 - x + 1$, find the point x_0 at which $f'(x)$ assumes its mean value in the interval $[2, 4]$.

Recall the mean value theorem. Given a function $f(x)$ which is continuous in $[a, b]$ and differentiable in (a, b), there exists a point x_0 where $a < x_0 < b$ such that:

$$\frac{f(b)-f(a)}{b-a} = f'(x_0),$$

where x_0 is the mean point in the interval.

In our problem, $3x^2 - x + 1$ is continuous, and the derivative exists in the interval $(2, 4)$. We have:

$$\frac{f(4)-f(2)}{4-2} = \frac{\left[3(4)^2 - 4 + 1\right] - \left[3(2)^2 - 2 + 1\right]}{4-2}$$

$$= f'(x_0),$$

or

$$\frac{45-11}{2} = 17 = f'(x_0) = 6x_0 - 1$$

$$6x_0 = 18$$

$$x_0 = 3 .$$

$x_0 = 3$ is the point where $f'(x)$ assumes its mean value.

Theorems of Differentiable Functions

A) If $f(x)$ is differentiable at x_0, it is continuous there.

B) If $f(x)$ is continuous on the closed interval $[a, b]$, then there is a point $x' \in [a, b]$ for which

$$f(x') < f(x) \, (x : x \in [a, b])$$

C) If $f(x)$ is continuous on the closed interval $[a, b]$, then there is a point x_0 in $[a, b]$ for which

$$f(x_0) \geq f(x) \, (x : x \in [a, b])$$

D) If $f(x)$ is an increasing function on an interval, then at each point x_0, where x is differentiable we have

$$f'(x_0) \geq 0$$

E) If $f(x)$ is strictly increasing on an interval, and suppose also that $f'(x_0) > 0$ for some x_0 in the interval, then the inverse function $f^{-1}(x)$ if it exists, is differentiable at the point $y_0 = f(x_0)$.

F) If $f(x)$ is differentiable on the interval $[a, b]$, and $g(x)$ is a differentiable function in the range of f, then the composed function $h = g \circ f$ $(h(x) = g[f(x)])$ is also differentiable on $[a, b]$.

G) Suppose that $f(x)$, $g(x)$ are differentiable on the interval $[a, b]$ and that $f'(x) = g'(x)$ for all $x \in [a, b]$, then there is a constant c such that $f(x) = g(x) + C$.

H) Rolle's Theorem

If $f(x)$ is continuous on $[a, b]$, differentiable on (a, b), and $f(a) = f(b) = 0$, then there is a point δ in (a, b) such that $f'(\delta) = 0$.

I) Mean Value Theorem

a) f is continuous on $[a, b]$

b) f is differentiable on (a, b) then there exists some point $\delta \in (a, b)$, such that

$$f'(\delta) = \frac{f(b) - f(a)}{b - a} .$$

L'Hôpital's Rule

An application of the Mean Value Theorem is in the evaluation of

$$\lim_{x \to a} \frac{f(x)}{g(x)} \text{ where } f(a) = 0 \text{ and } g(a) = 0.$$

L'Hôpital's Rule states that if the

$$\lim_{x \to a} \frac{f(x)}{g(x)}$$

is an indeterminate form (i.e., $\frac{0}{0}$ or $\frac{\infty}{\infty}$), then we can differentiate the numerator and the denominator separately and arrive at an expression that has the same limit as the original problem.

Thus,

$$\lim_{x \to a} \frac{f(x)}{g(x)} = \lim_{x \to a} \frac{f'(x)}{g'(x)}$$

In general, if $f(x)$ and $g(x)$ have properties

1) $f(a) = g(a) = 0$

2) $f^{(k)}(a) = g^{(k)}(a) = 0$ for $k = 1, 2, \ldots n$; but

3) $f^{(n+1)}(a)$ or $g^{(n+1)}(a)$ is not equal to zero, then

$$\lim_{x \to a} \frac{f(x)}{g(x)} = \lim_{x \to a} \frac{f^{(n+1)}(x)}{g^{(n+1)}(x)}$$

B. Application of the Derivative

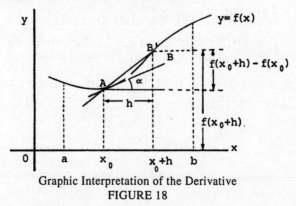

Graphic Interpretation of the Derivative
FIGURE 18

Graphically the derivative represents the slope of the tangent line AB to the function at the point $(x_0, f(x_0))$.

Tangents and Normals

Tangents

A line which is tangent to a curve at a point "a", must have the same slope as the curve. That is, the slope of the tangent is simply

$$m = \lim_{h \to 0} \frac{f(a+h) - f(a)}{h}$$

Therefore, if we find the derivative of a curve and evaluate for a specific point, we obtain the slope of the curve and the tangent line to the curve at that point.

A curve is said to have a vertical tangent at a point $(a, f(a))$ if f is continuous at a and

$$\lim_{x \to a} |f'(x)| = \infty \ .$$

Normals

A line normal to a curve at a point must have a slope perpendicular to the slope of the tangent line. If $f'(x) \neq 0$ then the equation for the normal line at a point (x_0, y_0) is

$$y - y_0 = \frac{-1}{f'(x_0)} (x - x_0).$$

Example:

Find the slope of the tangent line to the ellipse $4x^2 + 9y^2 = 40$ at the point $(1, 2)$.

The slope of the line tangent to the curve $4x^2 + 9y^2 = 40$ is the slope of the curve and can be found by taking the derivative, $\frac{dy}{dx}$ of the function and evaluating it at the point $(1, 2)$. We could solve the equation for y and then find y'. However it is easier to find y' by implicit differentiation. If

$$4x^2 + 9y^2 = 40,$$

then

$$8x + 18y(y') = 0.$$

$$18y(y') = -8x$$

$$y' = \frac{-8x}{18y} = \frac{-14x}{9y} \ .$$

At the point $(1, 2), x = 1$ and $y = 2$. Therefore, substituting these points into $y' = \dfrac{4x}{9y}$, we obtain:

$$y' = \frac{-4(1)}{9(2)} = -\frac{2}{9}$$

The slope is $-\dfrac{2}{9}$.

Minimum and Maximum Values

If a function f is defined at an interval I, then

A) f is increasing on I if $f(x_1) < f(x_2)$ whenever x_1, x_2 are in I and $x_1 < x_2$.

B) f is decreasing on I if $f(x_1) > f(x_2)$ whenever $x_1 < x_2$ in I.

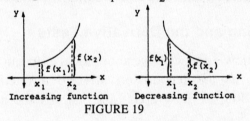

Increasing function   Decreasing function
FIGURE 19

C) f is constant if $f(x_1) = f(x_2)$ for every x_1, x_2 in I.

Suppose f is defined on an open interval I and C is a number in I then,

a) $f(c)$ is a local maximum value if $f(x) \le f(c)$ for all X in I.

b) $f(c)$ is a local minimum value if $f(x) \ge f(c)$ for all x in I.

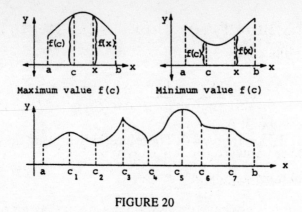

FIGURE 20

Solving Maxima and Minima Problems

Step 1. Determine which variable is to be maximized or minimized (i.e., the dependent variable y).

Step 2. Find the independent variable x.

Step 3. Write an equation involving x and y. All other variables can be eliminated by substitution.

Step 4. Differentiate with respect to the independent variable.

Step 5. Set the derivative equal to zero to obtain critical values.

Step 6. Determine maxima and minima.

Curve Sketching and the Derivative Tests

Using the knowledge we have about local extrema and the following properties of the first and second derivatives of a function, we can gain a better understanding of the graphs (and thereby the nature) of a given function.

A function is said to be smooth on an interval (a, b) if both f' and f'' exist for all $x \in (a, b)$.

The First Derivative Test

Suppose that c is a critical value of a function f, in an interval (a, b), then if f is continuous and differentiable we can say that,

A) if $f'(x) > 0$ for all $a < x < c$ and $f'(x) < 0$ for all $c < x < b$, then $f(c)$ is a local maximum.

B) if $f'(x) < 0$ for all $a < x < c$ and $f'(x) > 0$ for all $c < x < b$, then $f(c)$ is a local minimum.

C) if $f'(x) > 0$ or if $f'(x) < 0$ for all $x \in (a, b)$ then $f(c)$ is not a local extrema.

Concavity

If a function is differentiable on an open interval containing c, then the graph at this point is

A) concave upward (or convex) if $f''(c) > 0$;

B) concave downward if $f''(c) < 0$.

If a function is concave upward then f' is increasing as x increases. If the function is concave downward, f' is decreasing as x increases.

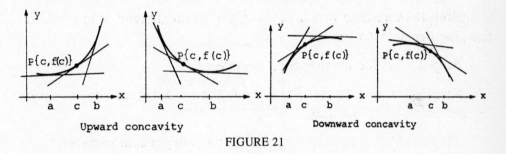

Upward concavity   Downward concavity

FIGURE 21

Points of Inflection

Points which satisfy $f'(x) = 0$ may be positions where concavity changes. These points are called the points of inflection. It is the point at which the curve crosses its tangent line.

Graphing a Function Using the Derivative Tests

The following steps will help us gain a rapid understanding of a function's behavior.

A) Look for some basic properties such as oddness, evenness, periodicity, boundedness, etc.

B) Locate all the zeroes by setting $f(x) = 0$.

C) Determine any singularities, $f(x) = \infty$.

D) Set $f'(x)$ equal to zero to find the critical values.

E) Find the points of inflection by setting $f''(x) = 0$.

F) Determine where the curve is concave, $f'' < 0$, and where it is convex, $f''(x) > 0$.

G) Determine the limiting properties and approximations for large and small |x|.

H) Prepare a table of values x, $f(x)$, $f'(x)$ which includes the critical values and the points of inflection.

I) Plot the points found in Step H and draw short tangent lines at each point.

J) Draw the curve making use of the knowledge of concavity and continuity.

Example:

Determine the maxima and minima of $f(x) = x^3 - x$ in the interval from $x = -1$ to $x = 2$.

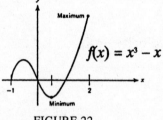

FIGURE 22

To determine the extreme points, we find $f'(x)$, equate it to 0, and solve for x to obtain the critical points. We have:

$$f'(x) = 3x^2 - 1 = 0. \qquad x^2 = \frac{1}{3}.$$

Therefore, critical values are $x = \pm \dfrac{1}{\sqrt{3}}$. Now

$$f\left(\frac{1}{\sqrt{3}}\right) = -\frac{2}{3\sqrt{3}} \quad \text{and} \quad f\left(-\frac{1}{\sqrt{3}}\right) = \frac{2}{3\sqrt{3}}.$$

Evaluating f at the end points of the interval we have $f(-1) = 0$ and $f(2) = 6$. Therefore, $x = 2$, an end point, is the maximum point for f, and $x = \dfrac{1}{\sqrt{3}}$ is the minimum point as can be seen in $[-1, 2]$ are 6 and $-\dfrac{2}{3\sqrt{3}}$.

The point $\left(-\dfrac{1}{\sqrt{3}}, \dfrac{2}{3\sqrt{3}}\right)$ is not an absolute maximum, but it is a relative maximum.

Rectilinear Motion

When an object moves along a straight line we call the motion rectilinear motion. Distance s, velocity v, and acceleration a, are the chief concerns of the study of motion.

Velocity is the proportion of distance over time.

$$v = \frac{s}{t}$$

$$\text{Average velocity} = \frac{f(t_2) - f(t_1)}{t_2 - t_1}$$

where t_1, t_2 are time instances and $f(t_2) - f(t_1)$ is the displacement of an object.

Instantaneous velocity at time t is defined as

$$v - D\, s(t) = \lim_{h \to 0} \frac{f(t+h) - f(t)}{h}$$

We usually write

$$v(t) = \frac{ds}{dt} \ .$$

Acceleration, the rate of change of velocity with respect to time is

$$a(t) = \frac{dv}{dt} \ .$$

It follows clearly that

$$a(t) = v'(t) = s''(t) \ .$$

When motion is due to gravitational effects, $g = 33.2$ ft/sec^2 or $g = 9.81$ m/sec^2 is usually substituted for acceleration.

Speed at time t is defined as $|v(t)|$. The speed indicates how fast an object is moving without specifying the direction of motion.

Example:

A particle moves in a straight line according to the law of motion:

$$s = t^3 - 4t^2 - 3t.$$

When the velocity of the particle is zero, what is its acceleration?

The velocity, v, can be found by differentiating this equation of motion with respect to t. Further differentiation gives the acceleration. Hence, the velocity, v, and acceleration, a, are:

$$v = \frac{ds}{dt} = 3t^2 - 8t - 3,$$

$$a = \frac{dv}{dt} = 6t - 8.$$

The velocity is zero when

$$3t^2 - 8t - 3 = (3 + 1)(t - 3) = 0,$$

from which

$$t = -\frac{1}{3} \text{ or } t = 3.$$

The corresponding values of the acceleration are

$$a = -10 \text{ for } t = -\frac{1}{3}, \quad \text{and}$$

$$a = +10 \text{ for } t = 3.$$

Rate of Change and Related Rates

Rate of Change

In the last section we saw how functions of time can be expressed as velocity and acceleration. In general, we can speak about the rate of change of any function with respect to an arbitrary parameter (such as time in the previous section).

For linear functions $f(x) = mx + b$, the rate of change is simply the slope m.

For nonlinear functions we define the

1) average rate of change between points c and d to be (see Figure 23)

$$\frac{f(d) - f(c)}{d - c}$$

2) instantaneous rate of change of f at the point x to be

$$f'(x) = \lim_{h \to 0} \frac{f(x+h) - f(x)}{h}$$

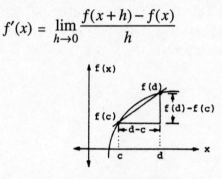

FIGURE 23

If the limit does not exist, then the rate of change of f at x is not defined.

The form, common to all related rate problems, is as follows:

A) Two variables, x and y, are given. They are functions of time, but the explicit functions are not given.

B) The variables, x and y, are related to each other by some equation such as $x^2 + y^3 - 2x - 7y^2 + 2 = 0$.

C) An equation which involves the rate of change $\dfrac{dx}{dt}$ and $\dfrac{dy}{dt}$ is obtained by differentiating with respect to t and using the chain rule.

As an illustration, the previous equation leads to

$$2x \frac{dx}{dt} + 3y^2 \frac{dy}{dt} - 2 \frac{dx}{dt} - 14y \frac{dy}{dt} = 0$$

The derivatives $\dfrac{dx}{dt}$ and $\dfrac{dy}{dt}$ in this equation are called the related rates.

Example:

A point moves on the parabola $6y = x^2$ in such a way that when $x = 6$ the abscissa is increasing at the rate of 2 ft. per second. At what rate is the ordinate increasing at that instant? See Figure 24.

Since

$$6y = x^2,$$

$$6\,\frac{dy}{dt} = 2x\,\frac{dx}{dt}, \quad \text{or}$$

$$\frac{dy}{dt} = \frac{x}{3} \times \frac{dx}{dt}. \tag{1}$$

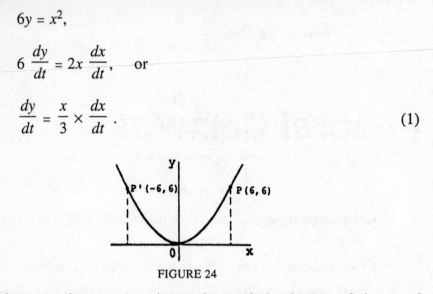

FIGURE 24

This means that, at any point on the parabola, the rate of change of ordinate = $(x/3)$ times the rate of change of abscissa. When $x = 6$, $\dfrac{dx}{dt} = 2$ ft. per second. Thus, substitution gives:

$$\frac{dy}{dt} = \frac{6}{3} \times 2 = 4 \text{ ft/sec.}$$

Chapter 3

Integral Calculus

A. Antiderivatives

Definition

If $F(x)$ is a function whose derivative $F'(x) = f(x)$, then $F(x)$ is called the antiderivative of $f(x)$.

Theorem:

If $F(x)$ and $G(x)$ are two antiderivatives of $f(x)$, then $F(x) = G(x) + c$, where c is a constant.

Power Rule for Antiderivatives

Let "a" be any real number, "r", any rational number not equal to -1, and "c" an arbitrary constant.

$$\text{If } f(x) = ax^r, \text{ then } F(x) = \frac{1}{r+1}x^{r+1} + c.$$

Theorem:

An antiderivative of a sum is the sum of the antiderivatives.

$$\frac{d}{dx}(F_1 + F_2) = \frac{d}{dx}(F_1) + \frac{d}{dx}(F_2) = f_1 + f_2$$

B. Application of Antiderivatives $y = y_0 e^{Kt}$: The Law of Exponential Change.

Example:

In the course of any given year, the number y of cases of a disease is reduced by 10%. If there are 10,000 cases, today, about how many years will it take to reduce the number of cases to less than 1,000?

$$y = y_0 e^{Kt}$$

$y_0 = 10,000$, so $y = 10,000 e^{Kt}$. When $t = 1$, there are 10% fewer cases or 9,000 cases remaining so

$$9,000 = 10,000 \ e^{K}$$

$$e^{K} = 0.9 \quad \text{therefore,} \quad K = \ln 0.9$$

Then $\quad 1,000 = 10,000 e^{(\ln 0.9)t} \Rightarrow$

$$0.1 = e^{(\ln 0.9)t} \Rightarrow \ln 0.1 = \ln 0.9t$$

So $\qquad t = \dfrac{\ln 0.1}{\ln 0.9} \approx 21.9 \text{ years}$

Another application of the antiderivative involves its use with velocity. The following problem illustrates this.

Example:

A body falls under the influence of gravity (gx 32 ft./sec^2) so that its speed is $v = 32t$. Determine the distance it falls in 3 sec. Let $x = $ distance.

$$v = f(t) = 32t$$

The velocity is dependent on time because of the following general relationship:

$$v = gt + v_i$$

where v increases indefinitely as time goes on — neglecting air resistance and some other factors. The initial velocity v_i is zero in this case because the body starts from rest.

Assuming the distance covered is dx in time t, we can represent the velocity in a differential form:

$$\frac{dx}{dt} = v = 32t.$$

Integrating to find the relationship between x and t yields:

$$\int dx = \int 32t\, dt .$$

$$x = \frac{32t^2}{2} + C .$$

$x = 0$ when $t = 0$. Therefore,

$$0 = 16(0)^2 + C, \, C = 0.$$

$$x = 16t^2.$$

The distance the body falls from the reference point,

$$x = 16t^2 = 16(3)^2 = 144 \text{ ft.}$$

C. Techniques of Integration

Table of Integrals

$$\int \alpha\, dx = \alpha x + C.$$

$$\int x^n dx = \frac{1}{n+1} x^{n+1} + C, \, n \neq 1.$$

$$\int \frac{dx}{x} = \ln |x| + C.$$

$$\int e^x dx = e^x + C.$$

$$\int p^x dx = \frac{p^x}{\ln p} + C.$$

$$\int \ln x\, dx = x \ln x - x + C.$$

$$\int \cos x\, dx = \sin x + C.$$

$$\int \sin x\, dx = -\cos x + C.$$

$$\int \sec^2 x\, dx = \tan x + C.$$

$$\int \sec x\, \tan x\, dx = \sec x + C.$$

$$\int \tan x \, dx = \ln |\sec x| + C.$$

$$\int \cot x \, dx = \ln |\sin x| + C.$$

$$\int \sec x \, dx = \ln |\sec x + \tan x| + C.$$

$$\int \csc x \, dx = \ln |\csc x - \cot x| + C.$$

When integrating trigonometric functions, the power rule is often involved. Before applying the fundamental integration formulas, it also may be necessary to simplify the function. For that purpose, the common trigonometric identities are most often applicable as, for example, the half-angle formulas and the double-angle formulas. Again, no general rule can be given for finding the solutions. It takes a combination of experience and trial-and-error to learn what to substitute to arrive at the best solution method.

Example:

Integrate:

$$\int \cos x \, e^{2 \sin x} dx.$$

This problem is best solved by the method of substitution. We let $u = 2 \sin x$. Then $du = 2 \cos x \, dx$. Substituting, we obtain:

$$\int \cos x \, e^{2\sin x} dx = \frac{1}{2} \int e^{2\sin x} (2 \cos x \, dx)$$

$$= \frac{1}{2} \int e^u du = \frac{1}{2} e^u + C$$

$$= \frac{1}{2} \int e^{2\sin x} + C.$$

Integration by Parts

Differential of a production is represented by the formula

$$d(uv) = udv + vdu.$$

Integration of both sides of this equation gives

$$uv = \int u \, dv + \int v \, du \qquad (1)$$

$$\int u \, dv = uv - \int v \, du \qquad (2)$$

Equation (2) is the formula for integration by parts.

Example:

Evaluate $\int x \ln x \, dx$

Let

$$u = \ln x \qquad\qquad dv = xdx$$

$$du = \frac{1}{x}dx \qquad\qquad v = \frac{1}{2}x^2$$

Thus,

$$\int x \ln x \, dx = \frac{1}{2}x^2 \ln x - \int \frac{1}{2}x^2 \, \frac{1}{x}dx$$

$$= \frac{1}{2}x^2 \ln x - \frac{1}{2} \int x \, dx$$

$$= \frac{1}{2}x^2 \ln x - \frac{1}{4}x^2 + c$$

Integration by parts may be used to evaluate definite integrals. The formula is:

$$\int_a^b u \, dv = [uv]_a^b - \int_a^b v \, du$$

Example:

Integrate: $\int x \cdot \cos x \cdot dx$.

In this case we use integration by parts, the rule for which states:

$$\int u \, dv = uv - \int v \, du.$$

Let $u = x$ and $dv = \cos x \, dx$. Then $du = dx$ and

$$v = \int \cos x \cdot dx = \sin x.$$

$$\int u \cdot dv = uv - \int v \cdot du$$

becomes $\int x \cdot \cos x \cdot dx = x \cdot \sin x - \int \sin x \cdot dx.$

To integrate $\int \sin x \, dx$ we use the formula, $\int \sin u \, du = -\cos u + C.$ This gives:

$$\int x \cdot \cos x \cdot dx = x \sin x - (-\cos x) + C$$

$$= x \sin x + \cos x + C.$$

Trigonometric Substitution

If the integral contains expressions of the form

$$\sqrt{a^2 - x^2}, \quad \sqrt{a^2 + x^2} \quad \text{or} \quad \sqrt{x^2 - a^2},$$

where $a > 0$, it is possible to transform the integral into another form by means of trigonometric substitution.

General Rules for Trigonometric Substitutions

1. Make appropriate substitutions.

2. Sketch a right triangle.

3. Label the sides of the triangle by using the substituted information.

4. The length of the third side is obtained by use of the Pythagorean Theorem.

5. Utilize sketch, in order to make further substitutions.

   A. If the integral contains the expression of the form $\sqrt{a^2 - x^2}$, make the substitution $x = a \sin \theta$.

   $$\sqrt{a^2 - x^2} = \sqrt{a^2 - a^2 \sin^2 \theta} = \sqrt{a^2 - (1 - \sin^2 \theta)}$$

   $$= \sqrt{a^2 \cos^2 \theta} = a \cos \theta.$$

   In trigonometric substitution the range of θ is restricted.

   For example, in the sine substitution the range of $\theta = -\dfrac{\pi}{2} \le$

$\theta \le \dfrac{\pi}{2}$. The sketch of this substitution is shown in Figure 25.

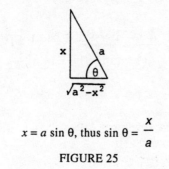

$x = a \sin \theta$, thus $\sin \theta = \dfrac{x}{a}$

FIGURE 25

B. If the integral contains the expression of the form $\sqrt{x^2 - a^2}$, make the substitution $x = a \sec \theta$. The sketch is shown in Figure 26.

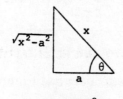

$x = a \sec \theta$

FIGURE 26

C. If the integral contains the expression of the form $\sqrt{a^2 + x^2}$, make the substitution $x = a \tan \theta$. The sketch is shown in Figure 27.

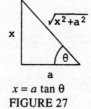

$x = a \tan \theta$

FIGURE 27

Example:

Evaluate $\displaystyle \int \frac{dx}{\sqrt{4 + x^2}}$

Let $x = 2 \tan \theta$; $\qquad dx = 2 \sec^2 \theta \, d\theta$

Thus, $\displaystyle\int \frac{dx}{\sqrt{4+x^2}} = \int \frac{2\sec^2\theta\, d\theta}{\sqrt{4+(2\tan\theta)^2}}$

$$= \int \frac{2\sec^2\theta\, d\theta}{\sqrt{4(1+\tan^2\theta)}}$$

$$= \int \frac{2\sec^2\theta\, d\theta}{2\sqrt{\sec^2\theta}}$$

$$= \int \sec\theta\, d\theta$$

$$= \ln |\sec\theta + \tan\theta| + c\,.$$

FIGURE 28

To convert from θ back to x we use Figure 28 to find:

$$\sec\theta = \frac{\sqrt{4+x^2}}{2} \quad\text{and}\quad \tan\theta = \frac{x}{2}\,.$$

Therefore,

$$\int \frac{dx}{\sqrt{4+x^2}} = \ln\left|\frac{\sqrt{4+x^2}}{2} + \frac{x}{2}\right| + c\,.$$

Summary of Trigonometric Substitutions

Given Expression	Trigonmetric Substitution
$\sqrt{x^2-a^2}$	$x = a \sec\theta$
$\sqrt{x^2+a^2}$	$x = a \tan\theta$
$\sqrt{a^2-x^2}$	$x = a \sin\theta$

D. The Definite Integral

Area

To find the area under a graph of a function f from a to b, we divide the interval $[a, b]$ into n subintervals, all having the same length $\dfrac{b-a}{n}$. This is illustrated in the following figure.

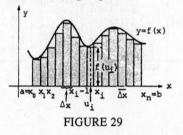

FIGURE 29

Since f is continuous on each subinterval, f takes on a minimum value at some number u_i in each subinterval.

We can construct a rectangle with one side of length $[x_{i-1}, x_i]$, and the other side of length equal to the minimum distance $f(u_i)$ from the x-axis to the graph of f.

The area of this rectangle is $f(u_i)\,\Delta x$. The boundary of the region formed by the sum of these rectangles is called the inscribed rectangular polygon.

The area (A) under the graph of f from a to b is

$$A = \lim_{x \to 0} \sum_{i=1}^{} f(u_i)\Delta x \ .$$

The area A under the graph may also be obtained by means of circumscribed rectangular polygons.

In the case of the circumscribed rectangular polygons the maximum value of f on the interval $[x_{i-1}, x_i]$, v_i, is used.

Note that the area obtained using circumscribed rectangular polygons should always be larger than that obtained using inscribed rectangular polygons.

Definition of Definite Integral

Definition:

Let f be a function that is defined on a closed interval [a, b]. A Riemann Sum of f for P is any expression R_p of the form,

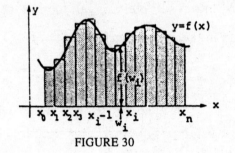

FIGURE 30

$$R_p = \sum_{i=1}^{n} f(w_i)\Delta x_i,$$

where w_i is some number in $[x_{i-1}, x_i]$, for $i = 1, 2, \ldots, n$.

Definition:

Let f be a function that is defined on a closed interval [a, b]. The definite integral of f from a to b, denoted by

$$\int_a^b f(x)\, dx$$

is given by

$$\int_a^b f(x)\, dx = \lim_{P \to 0} \sum_i f(w_i)\Delta x_i,$$

provided the limit exists.

Theorem:

If f is continuous on [a, b], then f is integrable on [a, b].

Theorem:

If $f(a)$ exists, then

$$\int_a^a f(x)\, dx = 0.$$

Properties of the Definite Integral

A) If f is integrable on $[a, b]$ and k is any real number, then kf is integrable on $[a, b]$ and

$$\int_a^b kf(x)\, dx = k \int_a^b f(x)\, dx .$$

B) If f and g are integrable on $[a, b]$, then $f + g$ is integrable on $[a, b]$ and

$$\int_a^b [f(x) + g(x)]\, dx = \int_a^b f(x)\, dx + \int_a^b g(x)\, dx.$$

C) If $a < c < b$ and f is integrable on both $[a, c]$ and $[c, b]$ then f is integrable on $[a, b]$ and

$$\int_a^b f(x)\, dx = \int_a^c f(x)\, dx + \int_c^b f(x)\, dx.$$

D) If f is integrable on a closed interval and if a, b, and c are any three numbers on the interval, then

$$\int_a^b f(x)\, dx = \int_a^c f(x)\, dx + \int_c^b f(x)\, dx.$$

E) If f is integrable on $[a, b]$ and if $f(x) \geq 0$ for all x in $[a, b]$, then

$$\int_a^b f(x)\, dx \geq 0.$$

The Fundamental Theorem of Calculus

The fundamental theorem of calculus establishes the relationship between the indefinite integrals and differentiation by use of the mean value theorem.

Mean Value Theorem for Integrals

If f is continuous on a closed interval $[a, b]$, then there is some number P in the open interval (a, b) such that

$$\int_a^b f(x)\, dx = f(P)\, (b - a)$$

To find $f(P)$ we divide both sides of the equation by $(b - a)$ obtaining

$$f(P) = \frac{1}{b-a} \int_a^b f(x) \, dx.$$

Definition of the Fundamental Theorem

Suppose f is continuous on a closed interval $[a, b]$, then

a)   If the function G is defined by:

$$G(x) = \int_a^x f(t) \, dt,$$

for all x in $[a, b]$, then G is an antiderivative of f on $[a, b]$.

b)   If F is any antiderivative of f, then

$$\int_a^b f(x) \, dx = F(b) - F(a)$$

E. Applications of the Integral

Area

If f and g are two continuous functions on the closed interval $[a, b]$, then the area of the region bounded by the graphs of these two functions and the ordinates $x = a$ and $x = b$ is

$$A = \int_a^b [f(x) - g(x)] \, dx \, .$$

where $f(x) \geq 0$ and $f(x) \geq g(x)$

$a \leq x \leq b$

This formula applies whether the curves are above or below the x-axis.

The area below $f(x)$ and above the x-axis is represented by

$$\int_a^b f(x)$$

The area between $g(x)$ and the x-axis is represented by $\int g(x)$.

Example:

Find the area of the region bounded by the curves

$$y = x^2 \quad \text{and} \quad y = \sqrt{x} \, .$$

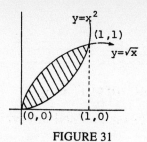

FIGURE 31

$$\text{Area} = A = \int_0^1 \left(\sqrt{x} - x^2\right) dx$$

$$= \int_0^1 \sqrt{x}\, dx = \int_0^1 x^2\, dx$$

$$= \left[\frac{2}{3}x^{\frac{3}{2}} - \frac{1}{3}x^3\right]_0^1 = \left[\frac{2}{3} - \frac{1}{3}\right] = \frac{1}{3}$$

Volume of a Solid of Revolution

If a region is revolved about a line, a solid called a solid of revolution is formed. The solid is generated by the region. The axis of revolution is the line about which the revolution takes place.

There are several methods by which we may obtain the volume of a solid of revolution. We shall now discuss three such methods.

Disk Method

The volume of a solid generated by the revolution of a region about the *x*-axis is given by the formula

$$V = \pi \int_a^b [f(x)]^2\, dx,$$

provided that *f* is a continuous, nonnegative function on the interval [a, b].

Shell Method

This method applies to cylindrical shells exemplified by

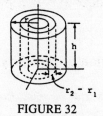

FIGURE 32

03 396

The volume of a cylindrical shell is

$$V = \pi r_2^2 h - \pi r_1^2 h$$

$$= \pi \, (r_2 + r_1) \, (r_2 - r_1) \, h$$

$$= 2 \, \pi \left(\frac{r_2 + r_1}{2} \right) (r_2 - r_1) \, h$$

where r_1 = inner radius

        r_2 = outer radius

        h = height

Let $r = \dfrac{r_2 + r_1}{2}$ and $\Delta r = r_2 - r_1$, then the volume of the shell becomes

$$V = 2\pi r h \Delta r$$

The thickness of the shell is represented by Δr and the average radius of the shell by r.

Thus,

$$V = 2\pi \int_a^b xf(x) \, dx$$

is the volume of a solid generated by revolving a region about the y-axis. This is illustrated by Figure 33.

FIGURE 33

Parallel Cross Sections

A cross section of a solid is a region formed by the intersection of a solid by a plane. This is illustrated by Figure 34.

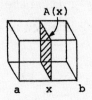

FIGURE 34

If x is a continuous function on the interval $[a, b]$, then the volume of the cross sectional area $A(x)$ is

$$V = \int_a^b A(x)\, dx.$$

Area of Surface of Revolution

A surface of revolution is generated when a plane is revolved about a line.

If f' and g' are two continuous functions on the interval $[a, b]$ where $g(t) = 0$, $x = f(t)$, and $y = g(t)$ then, the surface area of a plane revolved about the x-axis is given by the formula

$$S = \int_a^b 2\pi g(t)\, \sqrt{[f'(t)]^2 + [g'(t)]^2}\, dt$$

Since $x = f(t)$ and $y = g(t)$,

$$S = \int_a^b 2\pi y\, \sqrt{\left(\frac{dx}{dt}\right)^2 + \left(\frac{dy}{dt}\right)^2}\, dt$$

If the plane is revolved about the y-axis, then the surface area is

$$S = \int_a^b 2\pi x\, \sqrt{\left(\frac{dx}{dt}\right)^2 + \left(\frac{dy}{dt}\right)^2}\, dt$$

These formulas can be simplified to give the following:

$$S = 2\pi y \int_a^b ds$$

for revolution about the x-axis, and

$$S = 2\pi x \int_a^b ds$$

for revolution about the y-axis.

In the above equations, ds is given as $ds = \sqrt{1 + f'(x)^2}\, dx$.

Advanced Placement Examination in Calculus AB

EXAM I

ADVANCED PLACEMENT
CALCULUS AB
EXAM I

SECTION I

PART A

Time: 55 minutes
28 questions

DIRECTIONS: Each of the following problems is followed by five choices. Solve each problem, select the best choice, and blacken the correct space on your answer sheet. Calculators may not be used for this section of the exam.

NOTE: Unless otherwise specified, the domain of function f is assumed to be the set of all real numbers x for which $f(x)$ is a real number.

1. $\int_{-2}^{-1} \sqrt{2}\, x^{-2} dx$ is approximately

   (A) -0.707 (D) -2.475

   (B) 0.619 (E) 0.707

   (C) 2.475

2. If $f(x) = \pi^2$, then $f'(1) =$

   (A) 2π (D) 1

   (B) 0 (E) π^2

   (C) π

3. If $y = \dfrac{1}{\sqrt[3]{e^x}}$, then $y'(1)$ is approximately

(A) 0.239

(D) –0.088

(B) 2.150

(E) 0.171

(C) –0.239

4. $\displaystyle\lim_{h \to 0} \dfrac{\sin(\pi + h) - \sin \pi}{h}$

(A) 1

(D) $+ \infty$

(B) 0

(E) $- \infty$

(C) –1

5. The slope of the line tangent to the curve $y^3 + x^2y^2 - 3x^3 = 9$ at $(1, 2)$ is approximately

(A) 0.0625

(D) –2.29

(B) 3.2

(E) –3.2

(C) –11.45

6. If $f'(x) = \sin x$ and $f(\pi) = 3$, then $f(x) =$

(A) $\cos x + 4$

(D) $\cos x + 3$

(B) $-\cos x + 2$

(E) $-\cos x - 2$

(C) $-\cos x + 4$

7. The position of a particle moving along a straight line at any time t is given by $s(t) = 2t^3 - 4t^2 + 2t - 1$. What is the acceleration of the particle when $t = 2$?

(A) 32

(D) 8

(B) 16

(E) 0

(C) 4

8. If $f[g(x)] = \sec(x^3 + 4)$, $f(x) = \sec x^3$, and $g(x)$ is <u>not</u> an integer multiple of $\dfrac{\pi}{2}$, then $g(x) =$

(A) $\sqrt[3]{x+4}$

(D) $\sqrt[3]{x} - 4$

(B) $\sqrt[3]{x-4}$

(E) $\sqrt[3]{x} + 4$

(C) $\sqrt[3]{x^3 + 4}$

9. The horizontal asymptotes of $f(x) = \dfrac{1-|x|}{x}$ are given by

(A) $y = 1$

(D) $y = 0$

(B) $y = -1$

(E) $y = 1, y = -1$

(C) $x = 0, x = 1, x = -1$

10. The acceleration of a particle moving on a line is $a = t^{-\frac{1}{2}} + 3t^{\frac{1}{2}}$. If the particle was at rest at $t = 0$, then what was its velocity at $t = 9.61$?

(A) 65.782

(D) 1

(B) 68.782

(E) 45.782

(C) –1

11. The domain of the function defined by $f(x) = \ln(x^2 - x - 6)$ is the set of all real numbers x such that

(A) $x > 0$

(D) $-2 < x < 3$

(B) $-2 \leq x \leq 3$

(E) $-2 > x$ or $x > 3$

(C) $-2 \leq x$ or $x \geq 3$

12. $\displaystyle\int_{1}^{e^2} \frac{\ln(x^2)}{x}\, dx$ is approximately

   (A) $\dfrac{8}{3}$

   (B) 2

   (C) $\dfrac{16}{3}$

   (D) 4

   (E) $\dfrac{e^4}{2}$

13. If $y = \arccos\,(\cos^4 x - \sin^4 x)$, then $y'' =$

   (A) 2

   (B) 0

   (C) $-2\,(\cos x - \sin x)$

   (D) $-2\,(\sin x + \cos x)$

   (E) -1

14. If $\dfrac{f(x_1)}{f(x_2)} = f\!\left(\dfrac{x_1}{x_2}\right)$ for all real numbers x_1 and x_2, (except those for which $x_2 \neq 0$ and $f(x_2) \neq 0$), which of the following could define f?

   (A) $f(x) = \dfrac{1}{x}$

   (B) $f(x) = x^2 + 3$

   (C) $f(x) = x + 1$

   (D) $f(x) = \ln x$

   (E) $f(x) = e^x$

15. $\dfrac{\ln(x^3 e^x)}{x} =$

   (A) $\dfrac{3(\ln x + e^x)}{x}$

   (B) $\ln(x^3 e^x - x)$

   (C) $\ln x^2 + 1$

   (D) $\dfrac{3\ln x + x}{x}$

   (E) $\dfrac{3\ln x}{x}$

16. $\lim\limits_{x \to 1} \dfrac{\dfrac{1}{x+1} - \dfrac{1}{2}}{x-1} =$

(A) $-\dfrac{1}{4}$

(D) 0

(B) -1

(E) does not exist

(C) $\dfrac{1}{4}$

17. If $\dfrac{r^2}{r-1} \geq r$, then

(A) $r \geq 0$

(D) $r \leq 0$ or $r \geq 1$

(B) $r \leq 0$

(E) $0 \leq r < 1$

(C) $r \leq 0$ or $r > 1$

18. If $f'(C) = 0$ for $f(x) = 3x^2 - 12x + 9$, where $0 \leq x \leq 4$, then $c =$

(A) 2

(D) 1

(B) 3

(E) $\dfrac{1}{3}$

(C) 0

19. $\lim\limits_{x \to 9} \dfrac{x-9}{3-\sqrt{x}} =$

(A) 6

(D) -12

(B) -6

(E) $+\infty$

(C) 0

20. $\int \left(x - \dfrac{1}{x} \right)^2 dx =$

(A) $\dfrac{1}{3}\left(x - \dfrac{1}{x} \right)^3 + C$

(D) $\dfrac{1}{3}x^3 - 2x - \dfrac{1}{x} + C$

(B) $\dfrac{1}{3}\left(x - \dfrac{1}{x} \right)^3 \left(1 + \dfrac{1}{x^2} \right) + C$

(E) $\dfrac{1}{3}(1 - \ln x)^3 + C$

(C) $\dfrac{1}{3}x^3 - 2x - \dfrac{1}{x^2} + C$

21. If $e^{g(x)} = \dfrac{x^x}{x^2 - 1}$, then $g(x) =$

(A) $x \ln x - 2x$

(D) $\dfrac{x \ln x}{\ln(x^2 - 1)}$

(B) $\dfrac{\ln x}{2}$

(E) $x \ln x - \ln (x^2 - 1)$

(C) $(x - 2) \ln x$

22. If $h(x) = \dfrac{x^2 + 1}{x^2}$ where $x > 1$, then $h^{-1}(x) =$

(A) $\dfrac{1}{\sqrt{x - 1}}$

(D) $\dfrac{1}{\sqrt{x - 1} + 1}$

(B) $\sqrt{\dfrac{x}{1 + 2x}}$

(E) $\dfrac{1}{-\sqrt{x - 1}}$

(C) $\dfrac{-1}{\sqrt{x}}$

23. If $f(x) = \begin{cases} \dfrac{2x-6}{x-3} & x \neq 3 \\ 5 & x = 3 \end{cases}$, then $\lim\limits_{x \to 3} f(x) =$

(A) 5

(D) 6

(B) 1

(E) 0

(C) 2

24. If $f(x) = \dfrac{\sqrt{x+2}}{x+2}$ and $g(x) = \dfrac{1}{x} - 2$, then $f[g(x)] =$

(A) $\dfrac{\sqrt{\dfrac{1}{x} - 2}}{\dfrac{1}{x} - 2}$

(D) $\sqrt{x}$

(B) $\sqrt{\dfrac{1-2x}{x}}$

(E) $\dfrac{\sqrt{x}}{x}$

(C) $\dfrac{\sqrt{\dfrac{1}{x-2} + 2}}{\dfrac{1}{x-2} + 2}$

25. If $\tan x = 2$, then $\sin 2x =$

(A) $\dfrac{2}{5}$

(D) $\dfrac{4}{3}$

(B) $\dfrac{4\sqrt{5}}{5}$

(E) $\dfrac{2}{3}$

(C) $\dfrac{4}{5}$

26. Let $f(x) = x^3$. Find the value of x_1 that satisfies the Mean Value Theorem on the closed interval $[1, 3]$.

(A) 1.414

(D) 2.000

(B) 1.732

(E) 2.082

(C) 2.351

27. At what value of x does $f(x) = \dfrac{x^3}{3} - x^2 - 3x + 5$ have a relative minimum?

(A) −1 only

(D) 3 only

(B) 0 only

(E) −1 and 3

(C) +1 only

28. Properties of the definite integral are:

I. $\displaystyle\int_a^b cf(x)\,dx = c\int_a^b f(x)\,dx$

II. $\displaystyle\int_a^b f(x)\,dx = -\int_b^a f(x)\,dx$

III. $\displaystyle\int_b^a [f(x)\cdot g(x)]\,dx = \int_a^b f(x)\,dx \cdot \int_a^b g(x)\,dx$

(A) I only

(D) I, II, and III

(B) II only

(E) I and II only

(C) III only

PART B

Time: 50 minutes

17 questions

DIRECTIONS: Calculators may be used for this section of the test. Each of the following problems is followed by five choices. Solve each problem, select the best choice, and blacken the correct space on your answer sheet.

NOTES:

1. Unless otherwise specified, answers can be given in unsimplified form.

2. The domain of function f is assumed to be the set of all real numbers x for which $f(x)$ is a real number.

29. If $f(x) = \log_b x$, then $f(bx) =$

    (A) $bf(x)$

    (B) $f(b) f(x)$

    (C) $1 + f(x)$

    (D) $x f(b)$

    (E) $f(x)$

30. If $f(x) = \begin{cases} x+1 & x \le 1 \\ 3 + ax^2 & x > 1 \end{cases}$, then $f(x)$ is continuous for all x if $a = ?$

    (A) 1

    (B) -1

    (C) $\dfrac{1}{2}$

    (D) 0

    (E) -2

31. If $g(x) = \dfrac{-x - f(x)}{f(x)}$, $f(1) = 4$ and $f'(1) = 2$, then $g'(1) =$

(A) $-\dfrac{1}{2}$

(D) $\dfrac{1}{8}$

(B) $\dfrac{11}{8}$

(E) $-\dfrac{1}{8}$

(C) $\dfrac{3}{16}$

32. The domain of $f(x) = \sqrt{4 - x^2}$ is

(A) $-2 \le x \le 2$

(D) $-2 < x < 2$

(B) $-2 \le x$ or $x \ge 2$

(E) $x \ge 2$

(C) $-2 < x$ or $x > 2$

33. $\displaystyle\int \dfrac{x + e^x}{xe^x}\, dx =$

(A) $-e^{-x} - \dfrac{1}{x^2} + C$

(D) $-\dfrac{1}{e^{2x}} + \ln |x| + C$

(B) $e^{-x} - \ln |x| + C$

(E) $e^{-x} - \dfrac{1}{x^2} + C$

(C) $-e^{-x} + \ln |x| + C$

34. The area enclosed by the graphs of $y = x^2$ and $y = 2x + 3$ is

(A) $\dfrac{38}{3}$

(D) $\dfrac{16}{3}$

(B) $\dfrac{40}{3}$

(E) $\dfrac{32}{3}$

(C) $\dfrac{34}{3}$

35. The volume of revolution formed by rotating the region bounded by $y = x^3$, $y = x$, $x = 0$ and $x = 1$ about the x–axis is represented by

(A) $\pi \int_0^1 (x^3 - x)^2 \, dx$

(D) $\pi \int_0^1 (x^2 - x^6) \, dx$

(B) $\pi \int_0^1 (x^6 - x^2) \, dx$

(E) $2\pi \int_0^1 (x^6 - x^2) \, dx$

(C) $2\pi \int_0^1 (x^2 - x^6) \, dx$

36. The vertical asymptote and horizontal asymptote for $f(x) = \dfrac{\sqrt{x}}{x+4}$ are

(A) $x = -4$, $y = 0$

(B) no vertical asymptote, $y = 0$

(C) no vertical or horizontal asymptote

(D) $x = -4$, no horizontal asymptote

(E) $x = -4$, $y = 1$

37. If $f(x) = x^3 - x$, then

(A) $\dfrac{\sqrt{3}}{3} = x$ is a local maximum of f

(B) $\dfrac{\sqrt{3}}{3} = x$ is a local minimum of f

(C) $\sqrt{3} = x$ is a local maximum of f

(D) $\sqrt{3} = x$ is a local minimum of f

(E) $-\sqrt{3} = x$ is a local minimum of f

38. If $\int_a^b f(x)\,dx = 0$, then necessarily

    (A) $f(x) = 0$

    (B) $a = b$

    (C) $f(x) = 0$ or $a = b$

    (D) $f(-x) = -f(x)$

    (E) None of these

39. $\int_0^2 x^x dx$ is

    (A) 3.27

    (B) 2.83

    (C) 4.21

    (D) 3.02

    (E) 1.98

40. The position of a particle moving along a straight line at any time t is given by $S(t) = 2t^3 - 4t^2 + 2t - 1$. The least velocity during the time interval $[0, 2]$ is

    (A) 4.25

    (B) 0.5

    (C) −0.67

    (D) −1.5

    (E) 3

41. The acceleration of a particle moving on a line is

    $$a(t) = t^{-\frac{1}{2}} + 3t^{\frac{1}{2}}.$$

    Starting from rest, the distance traveled by the particle from $t = 0$ to $t = 3.61$ is approximately

    (A) 632.15

    (B) 65.78

    (C) 20.21

    (D) 300.1

    (E) 28.95

42. Let $f(x) = 3x^2 - 12x + 7$. If $f(x) = 0$, then x equals

    (A) 1 and 2

    (B) −2.28 and 1

    (C) 3 and 2.5

    (D) 0.71 and 3.28

    (E) 1 and −6

43. Let $f(x) = x^3 - x$. If $f'(-x) = -f'(x)$, find x.

    (A) −1 and 1

    (B) 0 only

    (C) All x

    (D) ± 0.58

    (E) None of these

44. At each point (x, y) on a curve, the slope of the curve is $3x^2 (y - 6)$. If the curve contains the point $(0, 7)$, then its equation is:

    (A) $y = 6e^{x^3}$

    (B) $y = x^3 + 7$

    (C) $y = 6e^{x^3} + 7$

    (D) $y^2 = x^3 + 6$

    (E) $y = e^{x^3} + 6$

45. The coefficient of x^3 in the Taylor series for $f(x) = \ln x$ about $x = 1$ is

    (A) $\dfrac{1}{6}$

    (B) $\dfrac{2}{3}$

    (C) $\dfrac{1}{2}$

    (D) $\dfrac{1}{3}$

    (E) $\dfrac{1}{4}$

SECTION II

Time: 1 hour and 30 minutes
6 problems*

DIRECTIONS: Show all your work. Grading is based on the methods used to solve the problems as well as the accuracy of your final answers. Please make sure all procedures are clearly shown. For some problems or parts of problems it will be necessary to use a calculator.

NOTES:

1. Unless otherwise specified, answers can be given in unsimplified form.

2. The domain of function f is assumed to be the set of all real numbers x for which $f(x)$ is a real number.

---

1. Let f be the function given by $f(x) = 1 + \dfrac{1}{x} + \dfrac{1}{x^2}$.

   (A) Find the x and y intercepts.

   (B) Write an equation for each vertical and each horizontal asymptote for the graph of f.

   (C) Find the intervals on which f is increasing and decreasing.

   (D) Find the maximum and minimum value of f.

---

*The practice tests in this book incorporate Section II free-response solutions that approximate the content breakdown you will encounter on the AP exam. The overall timing and formatting of the practice tests in this book mirror the actual test; examinees should note, however, that this section is split into two parts on the AP exam. Furthermore, prospective examinees should pay attention to restrictions on calculator use. For details, consult current official College Board materials in print or on the Web.

2. (A) Find the slope of the line $2x + y - 7 = 0$.

   (B) Find the slope of the tangent line to the semicircle

   $x^2 + y^2 = 5$, $y \geq 0$.

   (C) Find the point on this semicircle having the tangent that is perpendicular to the line $2x + y - 7 = 0$ in part (A).

   (D) Find the intercepts of the tangent line in part (C).

3. (A) Let f have the properties described below

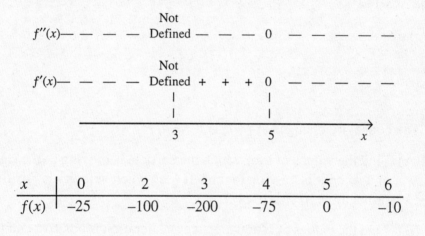

x	0	2	3	4	5	6
$f(x)$	-25	-100	-200	-75	0	-10

$\lim\limits_{x \to -\infty} f(x) = 0$

   (A) Find the intervals where f is concave down.

   (B) Find the equation of each vertical tangent line.

   (C) Find each point of inflection of f.

   (D) Sketch the graph of f.

4. Let the graph of $s(t)$, the position function (in feet) of a moving particle, be as given below. Let t be time measured in seconds.

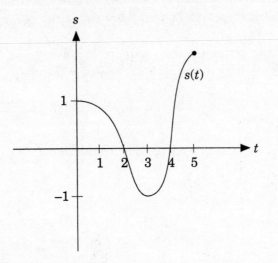

The concavity changes at $t = 2$ and $t = 4$.

(A) Find the values of t for which the particle is moving to the right and when it is moving to the left (i.e., when velocity is positive or negative, respectively).

(B) Find the values of t for which the acceleration is positive and for which it is negative.

(C) Find the values of t for which the particle is speeding up (i.e., when $|v|$ is increasing).

5. Function $f(x) = 2x^2 + x^3$.

(A) Find the local maximum of $f(x)$.

(B) Find the local minimum of $f(x)$.

(C) Evaluate $\int_{-2}^{1} f(x)$.

6. A flood light is on the ground 45 meters from a building. A thief 2 meters tall runs from the floodlight directly towards the building at 6 meters/sec. How rapidly is the length of his shadow on the building changing when he is 15 meters from the building?

FIGURE

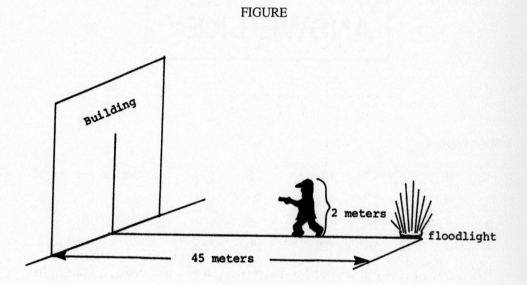

ADVANCED PLACEMENT CALCULUS AB EXAM I

ANSWER KEY

Section I

1.	(E)	12.	(D)	23.	(C)	34.	(E)
2.	(B)	13.	(B)	24.	(D)	35.	(D)
3.	(C)	14.	(A)	25.	(C)	36.	(B)
4.	(C)	15.	(D)	26.	(E)	37.	(B)
5.	(A)	16.	(A)	27.	(D)	38.	(E)
6.	(B)	17.	(C)	28.	(E)	39.	(B)
7.	(B)	18.	(A)	29.	(C)	40.	(C)
8.	(C)	19.	(B)	30.	(B)	41.	(E)
9.	(E)	20.	(D)	31.	(E)	42.	(D)
10.	(A)	21.	(E)	32.	(A)	43.	(D)
11.	(E)	22.	(A)	33.	(C)	44.	(E)
						45.	(D)

Section II

See Detailed Explanations of Answers.

ADVANCED PLACEMENT
CALCULUS AB
EXAM I

DETAILED EXPLANATIONS
OF ANSWERS

SECTION I

1. **(E)**

$$\int_{-2}^{-1} \sqrt{2}x^{-1}dx = \sqrt{2}\int_{-2}^{-1} x^{-1}dx. \text{ Since } \int \frac{1}{x^2}dx = -\frac{1}{x}, \text{ we have}$$

$$\sqrt{2}\left[-x^{-1}\right]_{-2}^{-1} = \sqrt{2}\left\{-\left[\frac{1}{(-1)} - \frac{1}{(-2)}\right]\right\}$$

$$= \sqrt{2}\left\{1 - \frac{1}{2}\right\}$$

$$= \frac{\sqrt{2}}{2}$$

$$\approx 0.707\ldots$$

2. **(B)**

$f(x) = \pi^2$. The value of $f(x)$ is constant, therefore its derivative is zero.

3. **(C)**

$$y = (e^x)^{-\frac{1}{3}} = e^{-\frac{x}{3}}$$

$$\therefore \ y' = e^{-\frac{x}{3}}\left(-\frac{1}{3}\right)$$

$$= -\frac{1}{3}e^{-\frac{x}{3}}$$

$$y'(1) = -\frac{1}{3e^{\frac{1}{3}}}$$

Since $3e^{\frac{1}{3}} = (27e)^{\frac{1}{3}} \approx (73)^{\frac{1}{3}} \approx 4, \ y'(1)$ must be near $-\frac{1}{4}$.

4. **(C)**

$$\lim_{h \to 0} \frac{\sin(\pi + h) - \sin \pi}{h}$$

This expression is the definition of the derivative of the function sin x, when the derivative is evaluated at $x = \pi$. Since $\dfrac{d(\sin x)}{dx} = \cos x$, and $\cos \pi = -1$, the answer is (C).

5. **(A)**

$$\frac{d}{dx}(y^3 + x^2 y^2 - 3x^3) = \frac{d}{dx}(9)$$

$$3y^2 y' + 2xy^2 + 2yy'x^2 - 9x^2 = 0$$

Note: the product rule must be used when differentiating $x^2 y^2$. Factor y' from the first and third terms.

$$y'(3y^2 + 2yx^2) = 9x^2 - 2xy^2$$

$$y' = \frac{9x^2 - 2xy^2}{3y^2 + 2x^2 y}$$

$\dfrac{dy}{dx}$ at (1.5, 2) is $\dfrac{9(1.5)^2 - 2(1.5)(2)^2}{3(2)^2 + 2(1.5)^2(2)} \approx \dfrac{8.25}{21} \approx 0.39$

6. **(B)**

$f(x) = \displaystyle\int f'(x)dx = \int \sin x \, dx = -\cos x + C.$

Since $f(\pi) = 3$ and $\cos \pi = -1$, $C = 2$

Therefore, $f(x) = -\cos x + 2.$

7. **(B)**

$a(t) = s''(t) = \dfrac{d}{dt}(6t^2 - 8t + 2) = 12t - 8$

$a''(2) = 24 - 8 = 16$

8. **(C)**

Let $y = g(x)$, then $f[g(x)] = f(y) = \sec y^3$.

Since $f[g(x)] = \sec(x^3 + 4)$ then $\sec(y^3) = \sec(x^3 + 4)$

$$y^3 = x^3 + 4$$

$$y = g(x) = \sqrt[3]{x^3 + 4}$$

9. **(E)**

For large positive values of x, the function $f(x)$ behaves as

$$\lim_{x \to +\infty} \frac{1 - |x|}{x} = \lim_{x \to +\infty} \frac{1 - x}{x}$$

$$= \lim_{x \to +\infty} \frac{1}{x} - 1 = -1$$

Likewise, as $x \to -\infty$,

$$\lim_{x \to -\infty} \frac{1 - |x|}{x} = \lim_{x \to -\infty} \frac{1 + x}{x}$$

$$= \lim_{x \to -\infty} \frac{1}{x} + 1 = 1$$

The horizontal asymptotes are $y = -1$ and $y = 1$.

10. **(A)**

$$\text{velocity} = \int_0^{9.61} \left(t^{-\frac{1}{2}} + 3t^{\frac{1}{2}} \right) dt$$

$$= \left(2t^{\frac{1}{2}} + 2t^{\frac{3}{2}} \right) \Big|_0^{9.61}$$

$$= 2(3.1 - 0) + 2(3.1^3 - 0)$$

$$= 65.782$$

11. **(E)**

The domain is all reals such that $x^2 - x - 6 > 0$

$$\text{or } (x - 3)(x + 2) > 0$$

$$\text{or } x < -2 \text{ or } x > 3.$$

12. **(D)**

Since $\ln (x^2) = 2 \ln x$, we have

$$\int_1^{e^2} \frac{\ln(x^2)}{x} dx = 2 \int_1^{e^2} \frac{\ln x}{x} dx.$$

This integral can be evaluated by using the substitution $u = \ln x$. The integrand becomes u, with $du = \dfrac{dx}{x}$, and the limits of integration change to

$$u(1) = \ln 1 = 0$$
$$u(e^2) = \ln(e^2) = 2.$$

We get

$$\int_0^2 u \, du = u^2 \Big|_0^2$$

$$= 2^2 - 0 = 4$$

13. **(B)**

$y = \arccos (\cos^4 x - \sin^4 x)$

$= \arccos [(\cos^2 x + \sin^2 x)(\cos^2 x - \sin^2 x)]$

$= \arccos [(1)(\cos 2x)]$

$= \arccos [\cos 2x]$

$= 2x + 2\pi m$

$-2x + 2\pi m$

$y' = \pm 2, \ y'' = 0$

14. **(A)**

$$\frac{f(x_1)}{f(x_2)} = \frac{\dfrac{1}{x_1}}{\dfrac{1}{x_2}} = \frac{x_2}{x_1}$$

Likewise $f\left(\dfrac{x_1}{x_2}\right) = \dfrac{1}{\left(\dfrac{x_1}{x_2}\right)} = \dfrac{x_2}{x_1}$.

15. **(D)**

$$\frac{\ln(x^3 e^x)}{x} = \frac{\ln x^3 + \ln e^x}{x} = \frac{3\ln x + x}{x}$$

16. **(A)**

$$\lim_{x \to 1} \frac{\dfrac{1}{x+1} - \dfrac{1}{2}}{x-1}$$

Obtain a common denominator in the main numerator.

$$\lim_{x \to 1} \frac{\dfrac{2-(x+1)}{2(x+1)}}{x-1} = \lim_{x \to 1} \frac{1-x}{2(x+1)(x-1)}$$

$$= \lim_{x \to 1} \frac{-1}{2(x+1)}$$

$$= \frac{-1}{2(1+1)} = -\frac{1}{4}$$

<u>Note:</u> $\dfrac{1-x}{x-1} = -1$ for $x \neq 1$

17. **(C)**

$\dfrac{r^2}{r-1} \geq r$ is equivalent to

$\dfrac{r^2}{(r-1)} - r \geq 0$. The lefthand side can be rewritten as

$$\frac{r^2 - r(r-1)}{r-1} = \frac{r}{(r-1)} = \frac{r(r-1)}{(r-1)^2}$$

Express r with a denominator of $r - 1$.

Thus the original problem is the same as $\left\{\dfrac{r(r-1)}{(r-1)^2}\right\} \geq 0$

Then $r = 0$ when the numerator and denominator are both positive or both negative.

Three cases:

1. $\{\ \} = 0$. Then $r = 0$ or $r = 1$. However, the lefthand side is undefined for $r = 1$, therefore $r = 0$.

2. r and $r - 1$ are both positive, therefore $r > 1$.

3. r and $r - 1$ are both negative, therefore $r < 0$, therefore $\{\ \} \geq 0$ for $r \leq 0$ or $r > 1$.

18. **(A)**

$$f'(x) = 6x - 12$$

$$f'(c) = 0$$

$$6c - 12 = 0$$

$$c = 2$$

19. **(B)**

$$\lim_{x \to 9} \frac{x-9}{3-\sqrt{x}}$$

Rationalize the denominator by multiplying by $\dfrac{3+\sqrt{x}}{3+\sqrt{x}}$

$$= \lim_{x \to 9} \frac{(x-9)(3+\sqrt{x})}{(3-\sqrt{x})(3+\sqrt{x})}$$

$$= \lim_{x \to 9} \frac{(x-9)(3+\sqrt{x})}{9-x}$$

$$\underline{\text{Note:}} \quad \frac{x-9}{9-x} = -1 \text{ for } x \neq 9$$

$$= \lim_{x \to 9} -(3+\sqrt{x})$$

$$= -6$$

20. **(D)**

$$\int \left(x - \frac{1}{x} \right)^2 dx = \int \left(x^2 - 2x\frac{1}{x} + \frac{1}{x^2} \, dx \right)$$

$$\int \left(x^2 - 2 + x^{-2} \right) dx = \frac{1}{3}x^3 - 2x - \frac{1}{x} + C$$

21. **(E)**

$$e^{g(x)} = \frac{x^x}{x^2 - 1} \quad \text{Take the natural logarithm of both sides.}$$

$$\ln e^{g(x)} = \ln\left(\frac{x^x}{x^2 - 1}\right)$$

$$g(x) = \ln x^x - \ln\left(x^2 - 1\right)$$

$$= x \ln x - \ln\left(x^2 - 1\right)$$

22. **(A)**

Suppose $y = h(x)$. If we can solve for x as a function of y, i.e., find $x = g(y)$, then the function $g(x)$ is the inverse function of h, that is $g = h^{-1}$.

Starting with $y = \dfrac{x^2 + 1}{x^2} = 1 + \dfrac{1}{x^2}$, we have $x^2 = \dfrac{1}{y-1}$. Since $x > 1$, we take

the positive square root to get $x = \dfrac{1}{\sqrt{y-1}}$, therefore, $x - g(y) = \dfrac{1}{\sqrt{y-1}}$.

Finally, $h^{-1}(x) = g(x) = \dfrac{1}{\sqrt{x-1}}$.

23. **(C)**

$$\lim_{x \to 3} f(x) = \lim_{x \to 3} \frac{2x - 6}{x - 3} = \lim_{x \to 3} \frac{2(x - 3)}{x - 3} = 2$$

24. **(D)**

$$f[g(x)] = f\left(\frac{1}{x} - 2\right) = \frac{\sqrt{\left(\frac{1}{x} - 2\right) + 2}}{\left(\frac{1}{x} - 2\right) + 2}$$

$$= \sqrt{\frac{\frac{1}{x}}{\frac{1}{x}}} = \frac{\frac{1}{\sqrt{x}}}{\frac{1}{x}} = \frac{1}{\sqrt{x}} \times \frac{x}{1}$$

Rationalize the denominator

$$= \frac{x}{\sqrt{x}} \times \frac{\sqrt{x}}{\sqrt{x}}$$

$$= \sqrt{x}$$

25. **(C)**

If $\tan x = 2 = \frac{2}{1}$, we have the following diagram. The hypotenuse

is $C = \sqrt{1^2 + 2^2} = \sqrt{5}$.

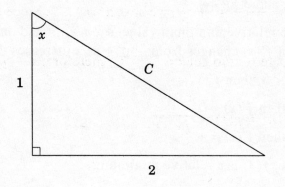

$$\sin 2x = 2\sin x \cos x$$

$$= 2\left(\frac{2}{\sqrt{5}}\right)\left(\frac{1}{\sqrt{5}}\right)$$

$$= \frac{4}{5}$$

26. **(E)**

$$f(x) = x^3 \qquad\qquad f(b) = f(3) = 27$$

$$f'(x_1) = 3x_1^2 \qquad\quad f(a) = f(1) = 1$$

$$f(b) - f(a) = (b - a) f'(x_1)$$

$$27 - 1 = (3 - 1) (3x_1^2)$$

$$x = \sqrt{\frac{13}{3}} = 2.082$$

27. **(D)**

$$f'(x) = x^2 - 2x - 3 = (x + 1) (x - 3)$$

$(x + 1) (x - 3) = 0 \Rightarrow x = -1$ and 3 are critical values.

The numbers -1 and 3 divide the x-axis into 3 intervals, from $-\infty$ to -1, -1 to 3, and 3 to $-\infty$.

$f(x)$ has a relative minimum value at $x = x_1$, if and only if $f'(x_1) = 0$ and the sign of $f'(x)$ changes from $-$ to $+$ as x increases through x_1.

If $-1 < x < 3$, then $f'(x) = -$

If $x = 3$, then $f'(x) = 0$

If $x > 3$, then $f'(x) = +$

Therefore, $f(3)$ is a relative minimum.

28. **(E)**

III is not a property of the definite integral. For example, let $f(x) = x$, $g(x) = \dfrac{1}{x}$. Then

$$\int_a^b f(x) \cdot g(x) \, dx = \int_a^b x \cdot \frac{1}{x} dx$$

$$= \int_a^b dx = b - a ,$$

but

$$\int_a^b f(x)\,dx \cdot \int_a^b g(x)\,dx = \int_a^b x\,dx \cdot \int_a^b \frac{1}{x}\,dx$$

$$= \frac{x^2}{2}\Big|_a^b \cdot \ln|x|\Big|_a^b$$

$$= \left(\frac{b^2}{2} - \frac{a^2}{2}\right)\cdot \ln\left|\frac{b}{a}\right|$$

$$\neq b - a$$

29. **(C)**

$$f(bx) = \log_b(bx)$$

$$= \log_b b + \log_b x$$

$$= 1 + \log_b x$$

$$= 1 + f(x)$$

30. **(B)**

$f(x)$ is continuous for $x < 1$ and $x > 1$ because polynomials are continuous for all reals. We must determine "a" such that $f(x)$ is continuous at $x = 1$.

(i) $f(1) = 1+1 = 2$, thus $f(1)$ is defined.

(ii) $\lim\limits_{x\to 1} f(x)$ exists if $\lim\limits_{x\to 1+} f(x) = \lim\limits_{x\to 1-} f(x)$

$$\lim_{x\to 1+} f(x) = \lim_{x\to 1+}\left(3 + ax^2\right) = 3 + a(1)^2 = 3 + a$$

$$\lim_{x\to 1-} f(x) = \lim_{x\to 1-}(x+1) = 1+1 = 2$$

If $\lim\limits_{x\to 1+} f(x) = \lim\limits_{x\to 1-} f(x)$, then $3 + a = 2$

$$a = -1$$

Hence, $\lim\limits_{x\to 1} f(x) = 2$ if $a = -1$.

(iii) Since $\lim\limits_{x \to 1} f(x) = f(1)$ the nf is continuous when $a = -1$

The graph of $f(x)$ with $a = -1$ is sketched below:

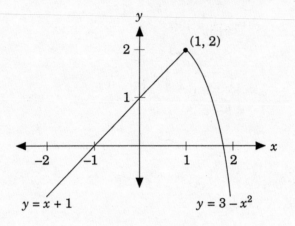

31. **(E)**

$$g(x) = -\frac{(x + f(x))}{f(x)} \qquad f(1) = 4, \, f'(1) = 2$$

$$g'(x) = -\left[\frac{(1 + f'(x))f(x) - f'(x)(x + f(x))}{[f(x)]^2}\right]$$

$$g'(1) = -\left[\frac{(1 + f'(1))f(1) - f'(1)(1 + f(1))}{(f(1))^2}\right]$$

$$= -\left[\frac{(1 + 2)4 - 2(1 + 4)}{16}\right]$$

$$= -\left[\frac{12 - 10}{16}\right]$$

$$= -\frac{1}{8}$$

32. **(A)**

$4 - x^2 \geq 0$

$(2 - x)(2 + x) \geq 0$

Consider the following sign diagram:

x					-2			2		
$2 - x$	+	+	+	+	+	0	−	−	−
$2 + x$	−	−	0	+	+	+	+	+	+
$(2 - x)(2 + x)$	−	−	0	+	+	0	−	−	−

Since $(2 - x)(2 + x) \geq 0$ when $-2 \leq x \leq 2$, the domain is $-2 \leq x$

33. **(C)**

$$\int \frac{x + e^x}{xe^x}\,dx = \int \left(\frac{x}{xe^x} + \frac{e^x}{xe^x} \right) dx$$

$$= \int \left(e^{-x} + x^{-1} \right) dx$$

$$= -e^{-x} + \ln x + C$$

34. **(E)**

First determine where the graphs $y = x^2$ and $y = 2x + 3$ intersect.

$$x^2 = 2x + 3$$

$$x^2 - 2x - 3 = 0$$

$$(x - 3)(x + 1) = 0$$

$$x = 3, -1$$

$$A = \int_{-1}^{3} \left(2x+3-x^2\right)dx$$

$$= \int_{-1}^{3} \left\{(2x+3)-x^2\right\}dx$$

$$= \left(x^2 + 3x - \frac{1}{3}x^3\right)\Bigg|_{-1}^{3}$$

$$= 3^2 - (-1)^2 + 3(3-(-1)) - \frac{1}{3}\left(3^3 - (-1)^3\right)$$

$$= 9 - 1 + 3(4) - \frac{1}{3}(27+1)$$

$$= 20 - \frac{28}{3}$$

$$= \frac{32}{3}$$

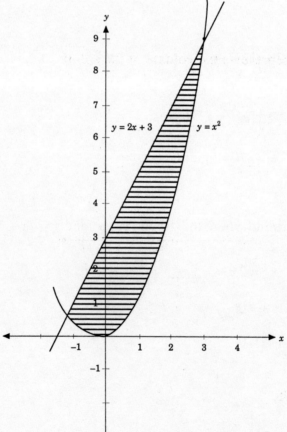

35. **(D)**

$\pi \int_0^1 x^2 dx$ represents the volume of the solid:

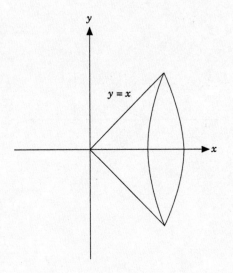

$\pi \int_0^1 x^6 dx$ represents the volume of the solid:

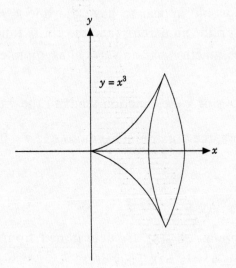

Subtracting

$$\pi \int_0^1 x^2 dx - \pi \int_0^1 x^6 dx$$

$\pi \int_0^1 \left(x^2 - x^6 \right) dx$, we have the solid of revolution:

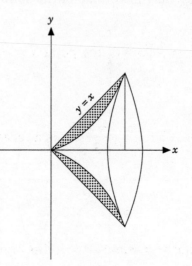

with $V = \pi \int_0^1 \left(x^2 - x^6 \right) dx$

36. **(B)**

The function would appear to have the line $x = -4$ as a vertical asymptote. However, the numerator (and the entire function) are defined only for $x \geq 0$. This function has no vertical asymptote.

For large values of x the function tends to the value $y \approx \dfrac{\sqrt{x}}{x} \rightarrow 0$, as $x \rightarrow \infty$. Therefore, the horizontal asymptote is $y = 0$.

37. **(B)**

$$f'(x) = 3x^2 - 1.$$

The critical points of $f(x)$ are determined from the roots of this equation, i.e., from $3x^2 - 1 = 0$. They are:

$$x = \pm \frac{1}{\sqrt{3}} = \pm \frac{\sqrt{3}}{3}$$

The nature of each critical point is dictated by a higher order derivative:

$$f''(x) = 6x$$

Since $f''\left(\dfrac{\sqrt{3}}{3}\right) = 2\sqrt{3} > 0$, the point $x = \dfrac{\sqrt{3}}{3}$, $y = \dfrac{-2\sqrt{3}}{9}$ is a local minimum.

$f''\left(-\dfrac{\sqrt{3}}{3}\right) = -2\sqrt{3} < 0$, $-\dfrac{\sqrt{3}}{3} = x$ is a local maximum (not listed as an answer).

38. **(E)**

$\displaystyle\int_{-1}^{1} x^3 dx = 0$ but $x^3 \neq 0$ and $-1 \neq 1$; this eliminates answers (A), (B), and (C).

$\displaystyle\int_{0}^{\pi} \cos x \, dx = 0$, but $\cos x$ is not an odd function; this eliminates answer (D), and leaves only answer (E).

39. **(B)**

Use the calculator to solve the problem directly. For example,

$fnInt$ $(X\wedge x, x, 0, 2)$.

Pressing ENTER, gives 2.83.

40. **(C)**

The rate of movement of the particle is the velocity $s'(t)$. Use your graphic calculator to draw both $s(t)$ and $s'(t)$.

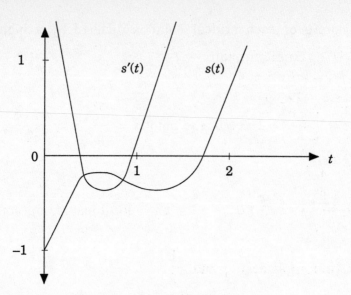

The velocity is given by $v(t) = 6t^2 - 8t + 2$.

The acceleration $a(t) = 12t - 8$ vanishes at $t = \dfrac{2}{3}$; at this time the velocity has reached its minimum. This occurs during the interval $[0,2]$.

Therefore, the minimum velocity of $v = -\dfrac{2}{3}$ occurs at $t = \dfrac{2}{3}$.

41. **(E)**

Since the particle starts from rest, the distance it travels can be found by integrating twice: first to find the velocity as a function of time, and then to find the distance as a function of time. We have:

$$a(t) = \frac{1}{\sqrt{t}} + 3\sqrt{t}.$$

Therefore, $\quad v(t) = 2\sqrt{t} + 2t^{\frac{3}{2}}$ (since $v(0) = 0$)

and $\qquad d(t) = \dfrac{4}{3}t^{\frac{3}{2}} + \dfrac{4}{5}t^{\frac{5}{2}}$

Distance travelled is $d(3.61) - d(0) = 28.95 - 0 = 28.95$

42. **(D)**

    Use the quadratic formula:

    $$x = \frac{12 \pm \sqrt{144 - 84}}{6}$$

    $$= 2 \pm \sqrt{\frac{15}{3}}$$

    $$\approx 2 \pm \frac{4}{3}$$

    Therefore, roots near $\frac{2}{3}$ and $3\frac{1}{3}$.

43. **(D)**

    $$f(x) = x^3 - x$$

    $f'(x) = 3x^2 - 1$, an *even* function.

    $f'(x)$ can satisfy $f'(x) = -f'(-x)$, which is the defining characteristic of an *odd* function, at $x = 0$ but *only* if $f'(x) =$ passes through the origin. It does not. Therefore, the answer is (E).

44. **(E)**

    Solve the differential equation $\frac{dy}{dx} = 3x^2(y - 6)$

    Separate variables: $3x^2 dx = \frac{dy}{(y - 6)}$, and integrate

    $$3\int x^2 dx = \int \frac{dy}{(y - 6)}$$

    $$x^3 = \ln(y - 6) + C$$

    $$\ln(y - 6) = x^3 - C$$

    $$y - 6 = e^{x^3 - C}$$

    $$y = e^{x^3 - C} + 6$$

Let $A = e^{-C}$, then $y = Ae^{x^3} + 6$

Substitute in $(0, 7)$: $7 = A + 6$

$A = 1 = e^{-C} \Rightarrow c = 0$

Therefore, $y = e^{x^3} + 6$.

45. **(D)**

The coefficients for the power series of $f(x)$ about $x = b$ are given by:

$$a_n = \frac{f^{(n)}}{n!}$$

$f(x) = \ln x \qquad\qquad f(1) = 0$

$f'(x) = \dfrac{1}{x} \qquad\qquad f'(1) = 1$

$f''(x) = -\dfrac{1}{x^2} \qquad\qquad f''(1) = -1$

$f'''(x) = \dfrac{2}{x^3} \qquad\qquad f'''(1) = 2$

$a_3 = \dfrac{f'''(1)}{3!} = \dfrac{2}{3!} = \dfrac{1}{3}$

$$\boxed{\textbf{SECTION II}}$$

1. (A)

If $x = 0$, $f(x)$ is undefined, so there is no y-intercept.

If $y = f(x) = 0$, then

$$0 = 1 + \frac{1}{x} + \frac{1}{x^2}$$

$$\Rightarrow 0 = \frac{x^2 + x + 1}{x^2}$$

$$\Rightarrow x^2 + x + 1 = 0$$

$$\Rightarrow x = \frac{-1 \pm \sqrt{1-4}}{2}$$

which gives non-real solutions, so there is no x-intercept.

(B)

$$y = \frac{x^2 + x + 1}{x^2}$$

As $x \to \pm\infty$, we see $f(x) \to 1$, so $y = 1$ is a horizontal asymptote. As $x \to 0$, the function tends to $y \approx \frac{1}{x^2}$, which has the vertical asymptote $x = 0$.

(C)

$$f'(x) = -\frac{1}{x^2} - \frac{2}{x^3}, \quad f \text{ is increasing when}$$

$$f'(x) = -\frac{1}{x^2} - \frac{2}{x^3} > 0$$

$$\Rightarrow -x - 2 > 0 \text{ if } x > 0$$

$$\Rightarrow x < -2 \text{ if } x > 0; \text{ impossible.}$$

OR $-2 < x$ if $x < 0$, so $-2 < x < 0$ and the interval on which $f(x)$ increases is $(-2, 0)$

$f(x)$ is decreasing if $f'(x) = -\dfrac{1}{x^2} - \dfrac{2}{x^3} < 0$.

If $x > 0$, then $-\dfrac{1}{x^2} - \dfrac{2}{x^3} < 0$

$$\Rightarrow -x - 2 < 0 \Rightarrow -2 < x, \text{ and } x > 0$$

so one interval of decreasing $f(x)$ is $(0, \infty)$.

If $x < 0$, then $-\dfrac{1}{x^2} - \dfrac{2}{x^3} < 0$

$$\Rightarrow -x - 2 < 0 \Rightarrow -2 < x \text{ and } x > 0$$

so, another interval on which $f(x)$ is decreasing is $(-\infty, -2)$.

(D)

Since $y' = \dfrac{-(x+2)}{x^3}$ and $y'' = \dfrac{2(x+3)}{x^4}$

We see that $\left(-2, \dfrac{3}{4}\right)$ is a local minimum. In fact, it is *the* minimum of the function.

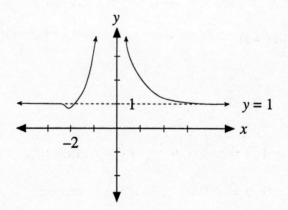

2. (A)

$2x + y - 7 = 0$, $y = 7 - 2x$, slope $= -2$

(B)

By implicit differentiation,

$2x + 2yy' = 0$

$$\Rightarrow y' = -\frac{2x}{2y} = -\frac{x}{y} = -\frac{x}{\sqrt{5 - x^2}}$$

(C)

The slope of the perpendicular must be the negative reciprocal of -2, namely, $\frac{1}{2}$. Now,

$$-\frac{x}{y} = \frac{1}{2} \Rightarrow y = -2x.$$

Since, $x^2 + y^2 + 5$, we see $x^2 + (-2x)^2 = 5$

$$\Rightarrow x^2 + 4x^2 = 5, \; 5x^2 = 5, \; x = \pm 1$$

If $x = 1$, $y = -2x = -2$

If $x = -1$, $y = -2x = 2$

Since $y \geq 0$ was specified, the point is $(-1, 2)$

(D)

The tangent line has equation

$$y - 2 = \frac{1}{2}(x + 1)$$

$$\Rightarrow y = \frac{x}{2} + \frac{5}{2}$$

When $x = 0$, $y = \frac{5}{2}$ so $\left(0, \frac{5}{2}\right)$ is the y-intercept.

When $y = 0$, $x = -5$ so $(-5, 0)$ is the x-intercept.

3. (A)

$f(x)$ is concave down where $f''(x) < 0$ namely on the intervals $(-\infty, 3)$, $(3, 5)$ and $(5, \infty)$.

(B)

Vertical tangent at $x = 3$.

(C)

No inflection point exists because the concavity (sign of the second derivative) never changes.

(D)

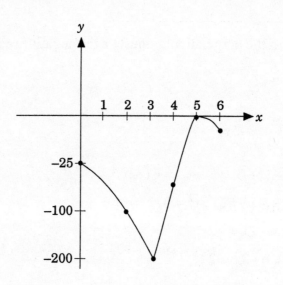

4. (A)

$s(t)$ is increasing (particle is moving to the right) when $3 < t \leq 5$.

The particle is moving to the left when $s(t)$ is decreasing, namely when $1 \leq t < 3$.

(B)

The acceleration is positive when $s''(t) > 0$ which is when the graph is concave up. This occurs for $2 < t < 4$.

The acceleration is negative when the graph is concave down, namely when $0 \leq t < 2$ or $4 < t < 5$.

(C)

The particle is speeding up when the velocity and acceleration are both positive or both negative. This occurs when $3 \leq t < 4$ or $1 < t < 2$.

5.   (A)

Draw the graph of $f(x)$.

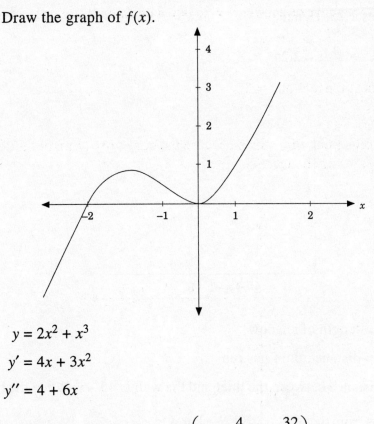

$y = 2x^2 + x^3$

$y' = 4x + 3x^2$

$y'' = 4 + 6x$

Roots of y' at $(x = 0, y = 0)$; $\left(x = -\dfrac{4}{3},\ y = \dfrac{32}{27} \right)$

Use y'' to show that the point $(0,0)$ is local minimum while $\left(-\dfrac{4}{3},\ \dfrac{32}{27} \right)$ is local maximum.

$f(x)$ has a local maximum in $-2 < t < -1$. By using viewing window $[-2, 0]$ $[0, 2]$, the value of this maximum can be found to be 1.19 at $x = -1.35$.

(B)

In the graph, it can be easily seen that $f(x)$ has a local minimum at $x = 0$; its value equals 0.

(C)

By using your calculator, $\displaystyle\int_{-2}^{1} f(x)$ can easily be solved by

$$fnInt\ (2x\char`^2 + x\char`^3, x, -2, 1)$$

which gives 2.25. Hence,

$$\int_{-2}^{1} 2x^2 + x^3 dx = 2.25$$

6.

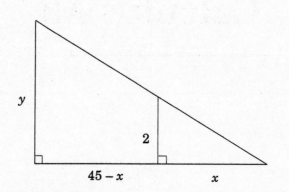

Let y = length of shadow

x = distance thief has run

The distance between the thief and the wall is $45 - x$. When the thief is 15 meters from the wall, $x = 30$. We know $\dfrac{dx}{dt} = 6m/sec$. We want to find $\dfrac{dy}{dt}$.

By similar triangles,

$$\frac{y}{2} = \frac{45}{x} \Rightarrow y = \frac{90}{x}, \text{ so} \frac{dy}{dx} = -\frac{90}{x^2}$$

By the chain rule,

$$\frac{dy}{dt} = \frac{dy}{dx}\frac{dx}{dt}. \quad \text{At } x = 30, \quad \frac{dy}{dt} = -\frac{90}{30^2} \times 6$$

$$= -\frac{540}{900} = -\frac{3}{5} \text{ m/sec.}$$

Advanced Placement Examination in Calculus AB

EXAM II

ADVANCED PLACEMENT
CALCULUS AB
EXAM II

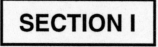

PART A

Time: 55 minutes
28 questions

DIRECTIONS: Each of the following problems is followed by five choices. Solve each problem, select the best choice, and blacken the correct space on your answer sheet. Calculators may not be used for this section of the exam.

NOTE: Unless otherwise specified, the domain of function f is assumed to be the set of all real numbers x for which $f(x)$ is a real number.

1. $\int_1^2 \dfrac{x^3 + 1}{x^2}\, dx =$

   (A) 0　　　　　　　　　　　　　(D) 1

   (B) $\dfrac{3}{2}$　　　　　　　　　　　(E) 3

   (C) 2

2. If $f(x) = \sqrt{1 - x^2}$, which of the following is NOT true?

   (A) Domain of $f = [-1, 1]$

   (B) $[f(x)]^2 + x^2 = 1$

(C) Range of f is $[0, 1]$

(D) $f(x) = f(-x)$

(E) The line $y = 1$ intersects the graph of f at two points.

3. $\lim\limits_{x \to \infty} \left(1 + \dfrac{1}{n}\right)^{n+2} =$

(A) e^2 (D) e

(B) $e + 2$ (E) $e + e^2$

(C) $2e$

4. $\lim\limits_{x \to 0} \dfrac{\cos^2 x - 1}{2x \sin x} =$

(A) -1 (D) $\dfrac{1}{2}$

(B) $-\dfrac{1}{2}$ (E) 0

(C) 1

5. If $y = \dfrac{1}{\sqrt{2x+3}}$, then $y'(0)$ is approximately

(A) 0.193   (D) 5.196

(B) -0.096 (E) -140.296

(C) -0.193

6. If $f(x) = |x|$, then

(A) Domain of $f' =$ Domain of f.

(B) $f'(x) = \dfrac{|x|}{x}$ for every real number x.

(C) $(f'(x))(f(x)) = f(x)$ for every real number x.

(D) Range of f' is the set $\{-1,1\}$.

(E) The graph of f' is

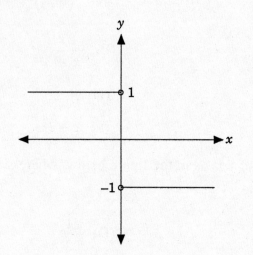

7. $\int_0^1 (2x + 1)^{-3} \, dx$ is approximately

(A) 0.888   (D) –1.500

(B) –1.111   (E) 0.222

(C) –0.277

8. If $f(x+c) = f(x) \cdot f(c)$ for every real number x and c and $f(0) \neq 1$, then $f(0) =$

(A) 1   (D) –1

(B) 0   (E) $\sqrt{2}$

(C) 0 and 1

9. If $y = \dfrac{x-1}{x+1}$, then $\dfrac{dy}{dx} =$

(A) $\dfrac{2x}{(x+1)^2}$

(D) $-\dfrac{2}{(x+1)^2}$

(B) $\dfrac{2}{x+1}$

(E) $\dfrac{2x}{x+1}$

(C) $\dfrac{2}{(x+1)^2}$

10. If the graph of f is as in the figure below, where slope of $L_1 = 2$, then $f'(x_0)$ is

(A) $\dfrac{1}{2}$

(D) $-\dfrac{1}{2}$

(B) -2

(E) 0

(C) 2

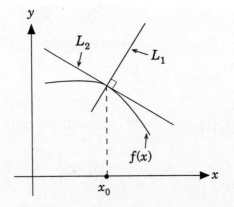

11. If $f(x) = \dfrac{1}{x-2}$ and $\displaystyle\lim_{x \to (-k+1)} f(x)$ does not exist, then $k =$

(A) 2

(D) -2

(B) 3

(E) -1

(C) 1

12. If $f(x) = \dfrac{1}{10 - \sqrt{x^2 + 64}}$ is not continuous at c, then $c =$

(A) 6

(B) –6

(C) ±6

(D) ±4

(E) 5

13. If $f(x) = \dfrac{1}{x-2}$, $(fg)'(1) = 6$, and $g'(1) = -1$, then $g(1) =$

(A) –5

(B) 5

(C) –7

(D) 7

(E) 8

14. If $f'(x) = \dfrac{(x^4 + 5x + 1)(12x) - (6x^2 - 1)(4x^3 + 5)}{(x^4 + 5x + 1)^2}$ and $f(0) = 2$, then $f(1)$ is approximately

(A) 0.102

(B) 0.714

(C) 3.714

(D) 3.102

(E) 0.857

15. $\displaystyle\int_0^1 (\sec^2 x - \tan^2 x)\, dx =$

(A) 3

(B) 5

(C) 2

(D) 4

(E) 1

16. Suppose $2 \le f(x) \le (1-x)^2 + 2$ for all $x \ne 1$ and that $f(1)$ is undefined. What is $\lim_{x \to 1} f(x)$?

    (A) 3

    (B) 2

    (C) 4

    (D) $\dfrac{5}{2}$

    (E) 1

17. If f is differentiable at 0, and $g(x) = [f(x)]^2$, $f(0) = f'(0) = -1$, then $g'(0) =$

    (A) -2

    (B) -1

    (C) 1

    (D) 4

    (E) 2

18. $\dfrac{dy}{dx} = x \cot(3x^2)$, then $y =$

    (A) $\ln |\sin 3x^2| + c$

    (B) $6 \ln |\sin 3x^2| + c$

    (C) $6 \ln c |\sin 3x^2|$

    (D) $\dfrac{1}{6} \ln |\sin 3x^2| + c$

    (E) $\ln c |\sin 3x^2|$

19. If the k–th derivative of $(3x - 2)^3$ identically is zero, then k is necessarily

    (A) 4

    (B) 3

    (C) ≥ 4

    (D) 2

    (E) 5

20. If arctan $(x) = \ln (y^2)$, then, in terms of x and y, $\dfrac{dy}{dx} =$

(A) $\dfrac{1}{1-x^2}$ (D) $\dfrac{y}{1+x^2}$

(B) $\dfrac{-1}{1-x^2}$ (E) $\dfrac{y}{2(1+x^2)}$

(C) $\dfrac{y}{1-x^2}$

21. The volume $V(\text{in}^3)$ of unmelted ice remaining from a melting ice cube after t seconds is $V = 2{,}000 - 40t + 0.2t^2$. How fast is the volume changing when $t = 40$ seconds?

(A) $-26 \text{ in}^3/\text{sec}$ (D) $0 \text{ in}^3/\text{sec}$

(B) $24 \text{ in}^3/\text{sec}$ (E) $-24 \text{ in}^3/\text{sec}$

(C) $120 \text{ in}^3/\text{sec}$

22. If $\displaystyle\int_a^b f(x)\, dx = 8$, $a = 2$, f is continuous, and the average value of f on $[a, b]$ is 4, then $b =$

(A) 0   (D) 3

(B) 2   (E) 5

(C) 4

23. If $0 \le x \le 1$, then $\dfrac{d}{dx}\displaystyle\int_x^0 \dfrac{dt}{2+t} =$

(A) $\dfrac{1}{x+2}$ (D) $\ln |2 + x| + c$

(B) $-\dfrac{1}{x+2}$ (E) $-\ln |2 + x| + c$

(C) $\ln |2 + x|$

24. $\lim\limits_{x \to -1} \dfrac{x + x^2}{x^2 - 1} =$

(A) $-\dfrac{1}{2}$

(D) $\dfrac{1}{2}$

(B) 1

(E) Does not exist

(C) −1

25. For $x \neq 0$, $\lim\limits_{h \to 0} \dfrac{1}{h}\left(\dfrac{1}{x + h} - \dfrac{1}{x}\right) =$

(A) $\dfrac{1}{x^2}$

(D) $-\dfrac{2}{x^2}$

(B) $-\dfrac{2}{x}$

(E) 0

(C) $-\dfrac{1}{x^2}$

26. If $2x^3 + 3xy + e^y = 6$, what is y' when $x = 0$?

(A) −0.896

(D) − 1.792

(B) 0.896

(E) 0

(C) 1.792

27. The area between the line $y = x$ and the curve $y = \dfrac{1}{2}x^2$ is

(A) 1

(D) $\dfrac{3}{2}$

(B) $\dfrac{1}{2}$

(E) 2

(C) $\dfrac{2}{3}$

28. An ellipse with semiaxes a and b has area πab. If the area is 9π (held constant), how fast is b increasing when $a = 1$ and a is decreasing at $\dfrac{1}{2}$ units/minute?

(A) $4\dfrac{1}{2}$ units/minute

(D) 3 units/minute

(B) $\dfrac{2}{9}$ units/minute

(E) Cannot tell

(C) 3π units/minute

PART B

Time: 50 minutes
17 questions

DIRECTIONS: Calculators may be used for this section of the test. Each of the following problems is followed by five choices. Solve each problem, select the best choice, and blacken the correct space on your answer sheet.

NOTES:

1. Unless otherwise specified, answers can be given in unsimplified form.

2. The domain of function f is assumed to be the set of all real numbers x for which $f(x)$ is a real number.

---

29. Let $f(x) = 2\sqrt{x}$. If $f(c) = f'(c)$, then c equals

   (A) 0   (D) 0.5

   (B) 0.82   (E) 2.1

   (C) 1.2

30. A particle moves along the x–axis. Its velocity is given by

$$V(t) = \begin{cases} t^2 & \text{for } 0 \le t \le 2 \\ t+2 & \text{for } t > 2 \end{cases}$$

   If it starts at the origin, its position after 4 seconds is $x =$

   (A) $37\dfrac{1}{3}$ (D) $\dfrac{8}{3}$

   (B) $12\dfrac{2}{3}$ (E) 6

   (C) 10

31. If $f'(x) = g'(x)$, $f'(x)$ and $g'(x)$ are continuous in $[-1, 1]$, and $f(0) - g(0) = 2$, then

   (A) $f(x) - g(x) = -2$

   (B) $\int_{-1}^{1} (f(x) - g(x)) \, dx = 4$

   (C) $\int_{-1}^{1} (f(x) - g(x)) = 0$

   (D) The graphs of $f(x)$ and $g(x)$ intersect in $[-1, 1]$.

   (E) $\int_{-1}^{1} (g(x) - f(x)) \, dx = 4$

32. An antiderivative of $\dfrac{x}{\sqrt{16 + x^2}}$ is

   (A) $x\sqrt{16 + x^2}$

   (B) $x\,(16 + x^2)$

   (C) $\ln\left|16 + x^2\right|$

   (D) $\sqrt{16 + x^2}$

   (E) $\left(\dfrac{1}{2} \ln\left|16 + x^2\right|\right) (\ln x)$

33. $\displaystyle\lim_{x \to \infty} \dfrac{(1 - 2x^2)^3}{(x^2 + 1)^3}$

   (A) 8

   (B) 1

   (C) 0

   (D) ∞

   (E) -8

34. The function f defined by $f(x) = x + \dfrac{1}{x}$ has relative minimum at $x =$

    (A) −1   (D) 1

    (B) $-\dfrac{1}{2}$ (E) $\dfrac{1}{2}$

    (C) 0

35. The area of a region bounded by the parabola $8 + 2x - x^2$ and the x-axis is:

    (A) $41\dfrac{1}{3}$ (D) $9\dfrac{1}{3}$

    (B) 36   (E) 24

    (C) 20

36. $\displaystyle\int_{-1}^{1} |x^2 - 1|\, dx =$

    (A) $\dfrac{4}{3}$ (D) $\dfrac{2}{3}$

    (B) 0   (E) $\dfrac{5}{3}$

    (C) $-\dfrac{4}{3}$

37. Let $f(x) = x^3 - 2x$. The relationship between its local minimum and local maximum is

    (A) $f_{min} = 2f_{max}$ (D) $f_{min} = 1.5f_{max}$

    (B) $f_{min} = f_{max}$ (E) $f_{min} = \sqrt{f_{max}}$

    (C) $f_{min} = -f_{max}$

38. Which of the following functions is not symmetric with respect to the origin?

    (A) tan x

    (D) sin x

    (B) $\dfrac{1}{x}$

    (E) cos x

    (C) cot x

39. Estimate the largest value of $|y'(x)|$ for $y = \sqrt{1-x}$ inside $0 \le x \le 0.8$.

    (A) −1.12

    (D) 3

    (B) 5.00

    (E) 2

    (C) 0

40. If $f(x) = x^{\frac{1}{2}} \ln x$, then $f'(2)$ equals

    (A) −0.75

    (D) 0

    (B) 0.95

    (E) 0.75

    (C) 0.25

41. Which of the following statements is/are true?

    I.   If f is continuous everywhere, then f is differentiable everywhere.

    II. If f is differentiable everywhere, then f is continuous everywhere.

    III. If f is continuous and $f(x) \ge 2$ for every x in [3, 7], then $\int_3^7 f(x)\, dx > 8$.

    (A) I only

    (D) I and III only

    (B) II only

    (E) II and III only

    (C) III only

42. Let $g(x)$ be the inverse of $f(x)$, i.e., $f(g(x)) = x = g(f(x))$. If $f'(x) = g'(x)$, then $f'(1)$ is necessarily

    (A) 1

    (D) ± 1

    (B) -1

    (E) $\dfrac{1}{2}$

    (C) 0

43. Which of the following is NOT true about $y = \cos(-x + \pi)$?

    (A) y has the same period as $\cos(x - \pi)$.

    (B) y has the same period as $\tan(2 - \dfrac{x}{2})$.

    (C) y has only one inflection point in $(-\pi, \pi)$.

    (D) $\dfrac{d^2y}{dx^2} + y = 0$.

    (E) y has minimum at $x = 0$.

44. $\displaystyle\lim_{x \to 0} \dfrac{\sin 2x - 2x}{x^3} =$

    (A) Does not exist

    (D) ∞

    (B) 1

    (E) $-\infty$

    (C) $-\dfrac{4}{3}$

45. If a is a constant, then $\displaystyle\int_0^\infty xe^{ax}\, dx$

    (A) always diverges

    (D) converges if $a < 0$

    (B) always converges

    (E) None of these

    (C) converges if $a > 0$

SECTION II

Time: 1 hour and 30 minutes
6 problems*

DIRECTIONS: Show all your work. Grading is based on the methods used to solve the problems as well as the accuracy of your final answers. Please make sure all procedures are clearly shown. For some problems or parts of problems it will be necessary to use a calculator.

NOTES:
1. Unless otherwise specified, answers can be given in unsimplified form.

2. The domain of function f is assumed to be the set of all real numbers x for which $f(x)$ is a real number.

---

1. Show that, if f is continuous and $0 \leq f(x) \leq 1$ for every x in $[0, 1]$, then there exists at least one point c such that $f(c) = c$. (Hint: Apply the intermediate value theorem to $g(x) = x - f(x)$, or try to answer it by sketching graphs which represent the possible cases of the graph of f).

2. Let $f(x) = \ln (x^2 - x - 6)$

    (A) The domain of $f(x)$ is $x < b$ or $x > a$. Find a and b.

    (B) Find $f(5)$.

    (C) Find $f'(-3)$.

---

* The practice tests in this book incorporate Section II free-response solutions that approximate the content breakdown you will encounter on the AP exam. The overall timing and formatting of the practice tests in this book mirror the actual test; examinees should note, however, that this section is split into two parts on the AP exam. Furthermore, prospective examinees should pay attention to restrictions on calculator use. For details, consult current official College Board materials in print or on the Web.

3. If $f(x) = \dfrac{1-x^2}{x^2+1}$, then

   (A) Find the domain of f.

   (B) Find $\lim\limits_{x \to \infty} f(x)$ and $\lim\limits_{x \to -\infty} f(x)$.

   (C) Find the intervals where f increases and where it decreases. Justify your answer.

   (D) Find the equation of the tangent line that is parallel to the x-axis.

4. A conical silver cup 8 inches across the top and 12 inches deep is leaking water at the rate of 2 inches³ per minute. (Figure below.) At what rate is the water level dropping:

   (A) when the water is 6 inches deep?

   (B) when the cup is half full?

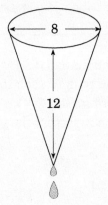

5. $y = f(x)$ is a function where f' and f'' exist and have the following characteristics:

x	$x < -2$	$x = -2$	$-2 < x < 0$	$0 < x < 2$	$x = 2$	$x > 2$
$f'(x)$	+	0	–	–	0	+
$f''(x)$	–	–	–	+	+	+

If $f(-2) = 8$, $f(0) = 4$ and $f(2) = 0$, then

    (A) Find all inflection points of $-2f$

    (B) Find all relative minimum and relative maximum values of $-2f$

    (C) Discuss the concavity of $-2f$

    (D) Sketch the graph of $-2f$

6.   (A) At what values of x do $y = x$ and $y = x^3$ intersect?

    (B) Find the area of the region bounded by $y = x$ and $y = x^3$

    (C) Find the volume obtained by rotating the region in (B) about the x-axis.

ADVANCED PLACEMENT CALCULUS AB EXAM II

ANSWER KEY

Section I

1.	(C)	12.	(C)	23.	(B)	34.	(D)
2.	(E)	13.	(A)	24.	(D)	35.	(B)
3.	(D)	14.	(C)	25.	(C)	36.	(A)
4.	(B)	15.	(E)	26.	(A)	37.	(C)
5.	(C)	16.	(B)	27.	(C)	38.	(E)
6.	(D)	17.	(E)	28.	(A)	39.	(A)
7.	(E)	18.	(D)	29.	(D)	40.	(B)
8.	(B)	19.	(C)	30.	(B)	41.	(B)
9.	(C)	20.	(E)	31.	(B)	42.	(D)
10.	(D)	21.	(E)	32.	(D)	43.	(C)
11.	(E)	22.	(C)	33.	(E)	44.	(C)
						45.	(D)

Section II

See Detailed Explanations of Answers.

ADVANCED PLACEMENT
CALCULUS AB
EXAM II

DETAILED EXPLANATIONS
OF ANSWERS

$$\boxed{\textbf{SECTION I}}$$

1. **(C)**

$$\frac{x^3+1}{x^2} = \frac{x^3}{x^2} + \frac{1}{x^2}$$

$$= x + \frac{1}{x^2}$$

Therefore,

$$\int_1^2 \frac{x^3+1}{x^2}\,dx = \int_1^2 \left(x + x^{-2}\right) dx$$

$$= \left(\frac{x^2}{2} - \frac{1}{x}\right)\Big|_1^2$$

$$= \left(2 - \frac{1}{2}\right) - \left(\frac{1}{2} - 1\right)$$

$$= 2$$

Remark: Use parentheses as on the previous page to avoid computational errors like: $2 - \dfrac{1}{2} - \dfrac{1}{2} - 1 = 0$.

2. **(E)**

(i) $y = \sqrt{1 - x^2}$ is defined $\Leftrightarrow 1 - x^2 \geq 1$

$$\Leftrightarrow x^2 \leq 1$$

$$\Leftrightarrow |x| \leq 1$$

Therefore, domain $= [-1, 1]$

(ii) $y \geq 0$ for every x in $[-1, 1]$ and its graph is as follows:

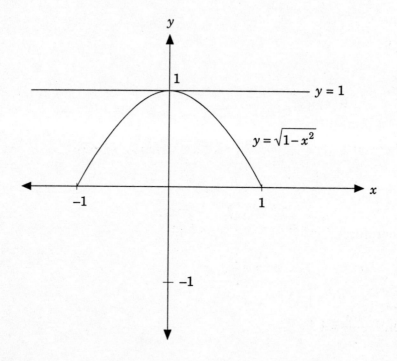

Moreover, its range is $[0, 1]$.

Finally, $f(x)$ is 1 only when $x = 0$. Hence, (E) is not true.

3. **(D)**

$$\left(1+\frac{1}{n}\right)^{n+2} = \left(1+\frac{1}{n}\right)^{n}\left(1+\frac{1}{n}\right)^{2} \tag{i}$$

Therefore,

$$\lim_{n\to\infty}\left(1+\frac{1}{n}\right)^{n+2} = \lim_{n\to\infty}\left(1+\frac{1}{n}\right)^{n} \times \lim_{n\to\infty}\left(1+\frac{1}{n}\right)^{2}, \quad \text{from (i).}$$

$$= (e)\times(1)^{2}$$

$$= e$$

Note: $\left(1+\dfrac{1}{n}\right)^{n+2} \neq \left(\left(1+\dfrac{1}{n}\right)^{n}\right)^{2}$ and therefore, e^{2} is incorrect.

4. **(B)**

$$\cos^{2}x - 1 = -(1 - \cos^{2}x) \tag{i}$$

$$= -\sin^{2}x$$

Therefore, $\displaystyle\lim_{x\to0}\frac{\cos^{2}x-1}{2x\sin x}$ becomes, using substitution (i)

$$\lim_{x\to0}\frac{-\sin^{2}x}{2x\sin x} = \lim_{x\to0}\left(-\frac{1}{2}\right)\frac{\sin x}{x}$$

$$= -\frac{1}{2},$$

since $\displaystyle\lim_{x\to0}\frac{\sin x}{x} = 1$.

You can also use L'Hôpital's rule.

Also see from (i) above that $\cos^{2}x - 1 \neq \sin^{2}x$. Thus $\dfrac{1}{2}$ is not the limit.

5. **(C)**

$$y = \frac{1}{\sqrt{2x+3}} = (2x+3)^{-\frac{1}{2}}$$

Using chain rule,

$$\frac{dy}{dx} = \left[-\frac{1}{2}(2x+3)^{-\frac{1}{2}-1} \right] \times \left[\frac{d}{dx}(2x+3) \right]$$

$$= \left[-\frac{1}{2}(2x+3)^{-\frac{3}{2}} \right] \times 2$$

$$= -\frac{1}{(2x+3)^{\frac{3}{2}}}$$

So, $y^1(0) = \dfrac{1}{\sqrt{(0+3)^3}} = -\dfrac{1}{\sqrt{27}} \approx -0.193$

6. **(D)**

$$|x| = \begin{cases} x & \text{for } x > 0 \\ -x & \text{for } x < 0 \end{cases}$$

$$\Rightarrow f'(x) = \begin{cases} 1 & \text{for } x > 0 \\ -1 & \text{for } x < 0 \end{cases}$$

But f is not differentiable at 0.

As a result, Domain of $f' = \{x \in R \mid x \neq 0\}$, while Domain of $f = R$. Consequently, A, B, and C are false. Moreover, the graph of f' is:

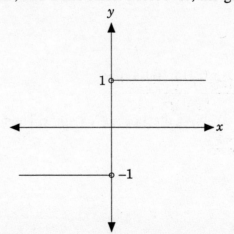

7. **(E)**

Let $u = 2x + 1$. Then, $du = 2dx$, i.e., $dx = \dfrac{du}{2}$. Also, when $x = 0$, $u = 1$ and when $x = 1$, $u = 3$. The original integral becomes

$$\frac{1}{2}\int_1^3 u^{-3}\,du = \frac{1}{2}\left[-\frac{1}{2}u^{-2}\right]\Big|_1^3$$

$$= -\frac{1}{4}\left[\frac{1}{9} - 1\right]$$

$$= \frac{1}{4} \times \frac{8}{9}$$

$$= \frac{2}{9}$$

$$\approx 0.222\ldots$$

8. **(B)**

Let $x = c = 0$

Then $f(0 + 0) = f(0) \times f(0)$, i.e., $f(0) = [f(0)]^2$

There are two possibilities:

(i) $f(0) = 0$

(ii) $f(0) = 1$

We are given that case (ii) is not allowed. Therefore, $f(0) = 0$.

9. **(C)**

$$y = \frac{x-1}{x+1}$$

$$\Rightarrow \frac{dy}{dx} = \frac{1 \times (x+1) - (x-1) \times 1}{(x+1)^2}$$

$$= \frac{x+1-x+1}{(x+1)^2}$$

$$= \frac{2}{(x+1)^2}.$$

Unlike the product rule, we do not add $(1)(x+1)$ and $(1)(x-1)$. If you add them you will get $\dfrac{2x}{(x+1)^2}$, which is incorrect.

10. **(D)**

Referring to the graph in the problem:

Let slope of $L_1 = m_1$

Let slope of $L_2 = m_2$

We know that $m_1\, m_2 = -1$, since the slopes of two, non-vertical, perpendicular lines are negative reciprocals of each other.

$$\Leftrightarrow m_2 = -\frac{1}{2}$$

Since L_2 is tangent to the graph of f at x_0, we have

$$f'(x_0) = -\frac{1}{2}$$

11. **(E)**

$\dfrac{1}{x-2}$ has no limit only at $x = 2$; see the graph below.

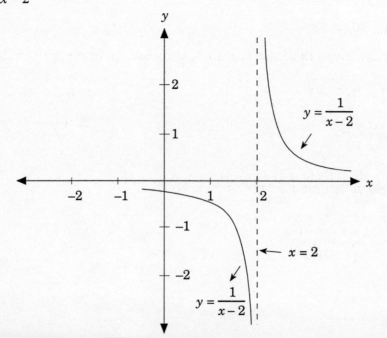

Therefore, $-k + 1 = 2$

$\Leftrightarrow k - 1 = -2$, by multiplying both sides by (-1)

$\Leftrightarrow k = -1$, adding 1 to both sides.

12. **(C)**

The expression $\sqrt{x^2 + 64}$ is defined for all x.

The quotient $\dfrac{1}{10 - \sqrt{x^2 + 64}}$ is not continuous at those values of x for which the denominator vanishes, i.e., where

$10 = \sqrt{x^2 + 64}$.

This occurs when

$x^2 = 36$, that is, when

$x = \pm 6$.

13. **(A)**

$(fg)'(1) = f'(1)g(1) + f(1)g'(1)$
by the product rule(*)

$$f(1) = \frac{1}{1-2} = -1 \qquad\qquad\qquad\text{(i)}$$

$$f'(x) = -\frac{1}{(x-2)^2}$$

Therefore, $f'(1) = -\dfrac{1}{(1-2)^2} = -1$ $\qquad\qquad$ (ii)

$g'(1) = -1$ $\qquad\qquad\qquad\qquad\qquad\qquad$ (iii)

$(fg)'(1) = 6$ $\qquad\qquad\qquad\qquad\qquad\qquad$ (iv)

Now substitute (i) – (iv) in (*) above:

$6 = (-1)g(1) + (-1)(-1)$

$\Leftrightarrow g(1) = -5$

14. **(C)**

From the quotient rule the given expression is the derivative of

$$f(x) = \frac{6x^2 - 1}{x^4 + 5x + 1} + c$$

Since $f(0) = 2$, $c = 3$.

So, $f(x) = \frac{6x^2 - 1}{x^4 + 5x + 1} + 3$.

And $f(1) = \frac{6(1)^2 - 1}{(1)^4 + 5(1) + 1} + 3$

$$= \frac{5}{7} + 3$$

$$= 3\frac{5}{7}$$

$$f(1) = 3\frac{5}{7} \approx 3.714$$

15. **(E)**

By trigonometric identity:

$$\sec^2 x = 1 + \tan^2 x$$

$$\Rightarrow \sec^2 x - \tan^2 x = 1$$

$$\Rightarrow \int_0^1 \left(\sec^2 x - \tan^2 x \right) dx$$

$$= \int_0^1 1 \times dx$$

$$= 1.$$

<u>Remark</u>: Whenever expressions like $\sec^2 x - \tan^2 x$, $\cos^2 x - 1$, $\sin^2 x$, etc. appear in a problem, it is worth trying trigonometric identities first.

16. **(B)**

$\lim_{x \to 1} 2 = 2$, and

$\lim_{x \to 1} (1-x)^2 + 2 = 2$

Therefore, $2 \le \lim_{x \to 1} f(x) \le 2$, from the figure.

$\Leftrightarrow \lim_{x \to 1} f(x) = 2$.

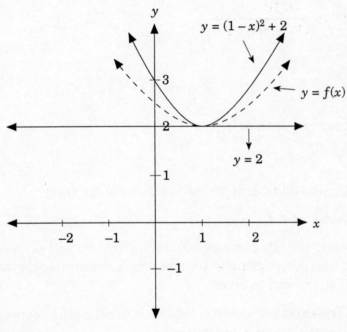

17. **(E)**

$g(x) = [f(x)]^2$

$\Rightarrow g'(x) = 2 \times [f(x)] \times f'(x)$

Therefore, $g'(0) = 2 \times f(0) \times f'(0)$

$= 2 \times (-1)(-1)$

$= 2$

A common arithmetic error is: $2 \, (-1) \, (-1) = -2$.

18. **(D)**

By the method of substitution:

Let $u = 3x^2$

$$\Rightarrow \frac{du}{dx} = 6x$$

$$\Leftrightarrow dx = \frac{du}{6}, \text{ after cross multiplication and division.}$$

Therefore, $\int x\cot(3x^2)\,dx = \frac{1}{6}\int \cot u\,du$

$$= \frac{1}{6}\int \frac{\cos u}{\sin u}\,du$$

$$= \frac{1}{6}\ln|\sin u| + c$$

$$= \frac{1}{6}\ln\left|\sin(3x^2)\right| + c,$$

(substituting u with $3x^2$).

19. **(C)**

$(3x - 2)^3$ is a cubic polynomial, i.e., it is of the form

$ax^3 + bx^2 + cx + d$.

Therefore, after three times differentiating, we will get a non-zero constant. But the derivative of a constant function is zero, so the fourth and higher derivatives will be zero.

Note: To see the answer, you only need to notice the degree. You do not have to do the actual computation.

20. **(E)**

$$\frac{d}{dx}(\arctan(x)) = \frac{d}{dy}\left(\ln(y^2)\right) \times \frac{dy}{dx}$$

$$\frac{1}{1+x^2} = \frac{2y}{y^2} \times \frac{dy}{dx}$$

$$\frac{y}{2(1+x^2)} = \frac{dy}{dx}$$

21. **(E)**

$$\frac{dV}{dt} = -40 + 2(0.2)t$$

$$= -40 + 0.4t$$

Therefore, $\frac{dV}{dt}(40) = -40 + (0.4)(40)$

$$= -24 \text{ in}^2/\text{sec.}$$

You should not change it to positive. It is negative, because V is a decreasing function.

22. **(C)**

Average value of f in

$$[a, b] = \frac{1}{b-a} \int_a^b f(x)\,dx$$

$$\Leftrightarrow 4 = \frac{1}{b-2} \times 8$$

substituting the given values

$$\Leftrightarrow 4(b-2) = 8$$

$$\Leftrightarrow b = 4.$$

23. **(B)**

$$\frac{d}{dx}\int_a^x f(t)\,dt = f(x) \text{ whenever } f \text{ is continuous in } [a, b].$$

Since $\dfrac{d}{dx}\displaystyle\int_x^0 \dfrac{dt}{2+t} = \dfrac{d}{dx}\left(-\displaystyle\int_0^x \dfrac{dt}{2+t}\right)$

$$= -\frac{d}{dx}\left(\int_0^x \frac{dt}{2+t}\right),$$

we get $\dfrac{d}{dx}\displaystyle\int_x^0 \dfrac{dt}{2+t} = -\dfrac{1}{2+x}$, since $\dfrac{1}{2+t}$ is continuous in $[0, 1]$.

24. **(D)**

$$\frac{x+x^2}{x^2-1} = \frac{x(1+x)}{(x-1)(x+1)}$$

$$= \frac{x}{x-1}, \text{ for } x \neq 1.$$

Therefore, $\lim\limits_{x \to -1} \dfrac{x+x^2}{x^2-1} = \lim\limits_{x \to -1} \dfrac{x}{x-1}$

$$= \frac{-1}{-1-1}$$

$$= \frac{1}{2}$$

<u>Remark</u>: The limit at $x = -1$ exists though the function is not defined there.

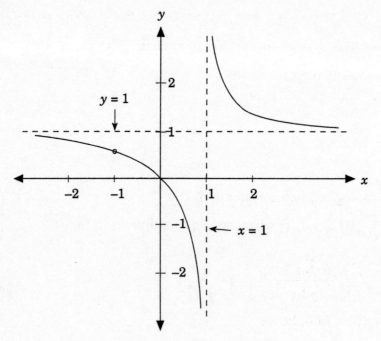

25. **(C)**

$$\frac{1}{h}\left(\frac{1}{x+h}-\frac{1}{x}\right) = \frac{1}{h}\frac{(x-(x+h))}{(x+h)x}, \quad \text{for } x \neq 0.$$

$$= \frac{1}{h}\frac{(-h)}{(x+h)x}$$

$$= -\frac{1}{(x+h)x} \qquad \text{(i)}$$

Thus, $\displaystyle\lim_{h\to 0}\frac{1}{h}\left(\frac{1}{x+h}-\frac{1}{x}\right) = \lim_{h\to 0}\left(\frac{-1}{x+h}\right)\left(\frac{1}{x}\right)$ from (i) above.

$$= -\frac{1}{x}\times\frac{1}{x}$$

$$= -\frac{1}{x^2}$$

Or, simply, if you observe, the limit desired is

$$\frac{d}{dx}\left(\frac{1}{x}\right) = -\frac{1}{x^2}$$

26. **(A)**

Using implicit differentiation

$$6x^2 + 3xy' + 3y + e^y y' = 0, \quad \text{so}$$

$$y' = -\frac{6x^2 + 3y}{3x + e^y}$$

$y(0) = \ln 6$, hence

$$y'(0) = \frac{-3\ln 6}{6} = -\frac{1}{2}\ln 6 = -0.896$$

27. **(C)**

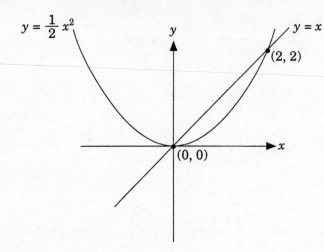

The curve is below the line, so

$$\text{Area} = \int_0^2 \left(x - \frac{1}{2}x^2 \right) dx = \left(\frac{x^2}{2} - \frac{x^3}{6} \right)\Big|_0^2 = 2 - \frac{8}{6} = \frac{2}{3}.$$

28. **(A)**

The area of an ellipse $= \pi ab$, so $\pi ab = 9\pi$, $b = \dfrac{9}{a}$.

Thus, $\dfrac{db}{dt} = \dfrac{-9}{a^2}\dfrac{da}{dt} = -9\left(-\dfrac{1}{2} \right) = 4\dfrac{1}{2}.$

29. **(D)**

Solve

$$2\sqrt{c} = \frac{1}{\sqrt{c}}$$

$$2c = 1$$

$$c = \frac{1}{2}$$

30. **(B)**

$$x(4) - x(0) = \int_0^4 V(t)\, dt$$

$$= \int_0^2 t^2 dt + \int_2^4 (t+2)\, dt$$

$$= \frac{t^3}{3}\Big|_{t=0}^{t=2} + \left(\frac{t^2}{2} + 2t\right)\Big|_{t=2}^{t=4}$$

$$= \left(\frac{8}{3} - 0\right) + \left(\frac{16}{2} + 8\right) - \left(\frac{4}{2} + 4\right)$$

$$= 12\frac{2}{3}$$

Hence, $x(4) = 12\frac{2}{3} + x(0)$

$$= 12\frac{2}{3} + 0$$

since it started at the origin.

31. **(B)**

$$f'(x) = g'(x)$$

$$\Leftrightarrow f'(x) - g'(x) = 0$$

$$\Leftrightarrow \frac{d}{dx}(f(x) - g(x)) = 0$$

$\Leftrightarrow f(x) - g(x)$ is a constant, since the only function whose derivative is zero on an interval is a constant function.

But, $f(0) - g(0) = 2$. Thus, $f(x) - g(x) = 2$ throughout $[-1, 1]$.

Hence, $\int_{-1}^{1} [f(x) - g(x)]\, dx = \int_{-1}^{1} 2\, dx$

$$= 2x\Big|_{-1}^{1}$$

$$= 2 - (-2)$$

$$= 4$$

32. **(D)**

Let $u = 16 + x^2$

$du = 2x\,dx$

then

$$\int \frac{x}{\sqrt{16 + x^2}}\,dx = \int \frac{x}{2x\sqrt{u}}\,du$$

$$= \frac{1}{2}\int \frac{du}{\sqrt{u}}$$

$$= \frac{1}{2}\int u^{\frac{-1}{2}}\,du$$

$$= \frac{1}{2} \times \frac{u^{\frac{1}{2}}}{\frac{1}{2}} + C$$

$$= u^{\frac{1}{2}} + C$$

$$= \sqrt{16 + x^2} + C$$

Letting $C = 0$, we see that $\sqrt{16 + x^2}$ is an antiderivative.

33. **(E)**

$$\lim_{x\to\infty}\frac{(1-2x^2)^3}{(x^2+1)^3}=\left(\lim_{x\to\infty}\frac{(1-2x^2)}{(x^2+1)}\right)^3$$

$$=\left(\lim_{x\to\infty}\frac{-2x^2+1}{x^2+1}\right)^3$$

$$=\left(\lim_{x\to\infty}\frac{-2+\dfrac{1}{x^2}}{1+\dfrac{1}{x^2}}\right)^3$$

$$=(-2)^3$$

$$=-8$$

34. **(D)**

$$f'(x)=1-\frac{1}{x^2} \qquad\qquad (i)$$

$$\Leftrightarrow f'(x)=\frac{x^2-1}{x^2}$$

Therefore, $f'(x)=0 \Leftrightarrow x=\pm1$.

$$f''(x)=\frac{d}{dx}\left(1-x^{-2}\right) \text{ differentiating (i) above.}$$

$$=\frac{2}{x^3}$$

$$\Rightarrow f''(1)=2>0 \text{ and } f''(-1)=-2<0.$$

Hence, f has relative min. at $x=1$.

35. **(B)**

$$8+2x-x^2=0$$

$$\Leftrightarrow -(x^2-2x-8)=0$$

$\Leftrightarrow x = 4$ or $x = -2$

The graph of $y = 8 + 2x - x^2$ from $(-2, 4)$ is

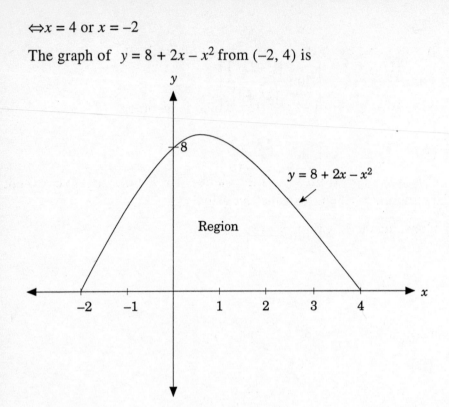

Now, area of region $= \int_{-2}^{4} \left(8 + 2x - x^2 \right) dx$

$$= \left(8x + x^2 - \frac{x^3}{3} \right) \Bigg|_{x=-2}^{x=4}$$

$$= \left(32 + 16 - \frac{64}{3} \right) - \left(-16 + 4 - \frac{(-2)^3}{3} \right)$$

$$= 64 - \frac{84}{3}$$

$$= 36$$

<u>Remark</u>: You have to be careful in handling $\dfrac{-(-2)^3}{3}$ in the second set of parentheses: $(-2)^3 = -8$

$$\Rightarrow \frac{-(-2)^3}{3} = \frac{-(-8)}{3}$$

$$= \frac{8}{3}$$

If you make the error $\dfrac{-(-2)^3}{3} = \dfrac{-8}{3}$, you will get:

$32 + 16 - \dfrac{64}{3} + 16 - 4 + 41\dfrac{1}{3}$, which is incorrect.

36. (A)

When x ranges from -1 to 1 the values of $x^2 - 1$ are negative (except at the endpoints, when this function vanishes).

Consequently, $|x^2 - 1| = -(x^2 - 1)$

$$= 1 - x^2$$

for $-1 \le x \le 1$.

Thus, $\displaystyle\int_{-1}^{1} |(x^2 - 1)| \, dx = \int_{-1}^{1} (1 - x^2) \, dx$

$$= \left(x - \dfrac{x^3}{3} \right)\Big|_{-1}^{1}$$

$$= \dfrac{4}{3}$$

You have to take the same precaution as in problem 35.

37. (C)

Draw the graph of $f(x)$.

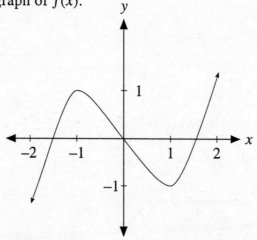

Since $f(x)$ is an odd function of x, the answer must be (C).

38. **(E)**

A function is symmetric with respect to the origin if and only if $f(-x) = -f(x)$ for every real number x. You can also simply answer the question by looking at the graphs. As you will see below, for the first four graphs the reflection through the origin of a point $(x, f(x))$ is the point $(-x, f(-x))$:

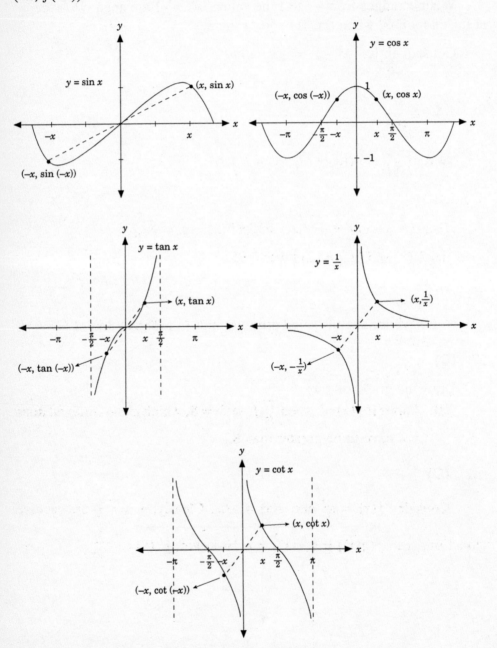

39. **(A)**

We have $y' = \dfrac{-1}{2\sqrt{1-x}}$.

This is clearly a strictly decreasing function as x ranges from 0 to 0.8. Its longest magnitude is then at the endpoint $x = 0.8$ when

$$|y'| = \frac{1}{2\sqrt{0.2}}$$

$$= \frac{1}{\sqrt{0.8}}$$

$$\cong \frac{1}{0.9}$$

$y'(0.8) = -1.118$.

40. **(B)**

Use the calculator directly to find (2). For example,

der 1 $(x^\wedge\ 0.5\ \ln x,\ x,\ 2)$ gives 0.95.

41. **(B)**

I. False: $f(x) = |x|$ is continuous at $x = 0$, but is not differentiable at $x = 0$.

II. True.

III. False: If $f(x) = 2$, then $\int_3^7 f(x)\,dx = 8$, which means integral does not have to be greater than 8.

42. **(D)**

Consider $f(x) = x^2$ and $g(x) = \sqrt{x}$. Clearly, f and g are inverse functions, i.e., $f(g(x)) = g(f(x)) = x$. However, $g'(x) \neq \dfrac{1}{f'(x)}$.

43. **(C)**

period of tan $\left(2 - \dfrac{x}{2}\right) = \pi \div \dfrac{1}{2} = 2\pi$

period of cos $(x - \pi)$ = period of cos $(-x + \pi) = 2\pi$.

$\dfrac{d}{dx}(\cos(-x + \pi)) = (-1)(-\sin(-x + \pi))$, by the chain rule.

$$= \sin(-x + \pi).$$

$\Rightarrow \dfrac{d^2}{dx^2}(\cos(-x + \pi)) = \dfrac{d}{dx}\sin(-x + \pi)$

$$= \cos(-x + \pi), \text{ by the chain rule.}$$

Therefore, $\dfrac{d^2}{dx^2} + y = \cos(-x + \pi) + (-1)\cos(-x + \pi) = 0.$

Moreover, if $f(x) = \cos(-x + \pi)$, then

$$f''(x) = -\cos(-x + \pi).$$

Therefore, $f''\left(-\dfrac{\pi}{2}\right) = -\cos\left(-\left(-\dfrac{\pi}{2}\right) + \pi\right)$

$$= -\cos\dfrac{3\pi}{2}$$

$$= 0$$

Also, $f''\left(\dfrac{\pi}{2}\right) = -\cos\left(-\dfrac{\pi}{2}\right) + \pi$

$$= -\cos\dfrac{3\pi}{2}$$

$$= 0$$

Hence, it will have more than one inflection point.

44. **(C)**

Indeterminate form $\dfrac{0}{0}$, so by L'Hôpital's rule:

$$\lim_{x\to 0}\frac{\sin 2x - 2x}{x^3} = \lim_{x\to 0}\frac{2\cos 2x - 2}{3x^2} = \frac{0}{0}$$

Apply L'Hôpital again:

$$\lim_{x\to 0}\frac{-4\sin 2x}{6x} = \lim_{x\to 0}\frac{-8\cos 2x}{6} = -\frac{4}{3}$$

45. **(D)**

Integrating by parts,

$$\int_0^\infty xe^{ax}\,dx = \lim_{b\to\infty}\left\{\frac{xe^{ax}}{a}\bigg|_0^b - \int_0^b \frac{1}{a}e^{ax}\,dx\right\}$$

$$= \lim_{b\to\infty}\left(\frac{be^{ab}}{a} - \frac{e^{ab}}{a^2} + \frac{1}{a^2}\right).$$

In order to have $e^{ab} \to 0$ as $b \to \infty$ we must have $a < 0$.

SECTION II

1. (A)

Let $g(x) = x - f(x)$. Since $0 \le f(x) \le 1$ for $0 \le x \le 1$ we know that $g(0) \le 0$ and that $g(1) \ge 0$.

Three cases:

1. If $g(0) = 0$ then $f(0) = 0$

2. If $g(1) = 0$ then $f(1) = 1$, ... otherwise:

3. For this case, the continuous function assumes positive and negative values for certain values of its domain. By the I.V. Theorem, they must exist some value c of the domain such that $g(c) = 0$ in which case $c = f(c)$.

Alternatively, the graph of f should take one of the following forms:

If f does not start at the origin, then its graph will be like those in (A), (C) or (F). If f does not touch the point $(1,1)$, then its graph will resemble (B), (C), or (D); otherwise it will be like (E). In either case the graph of $y = f(x)$ will intersect the graph of $y = x$ at some $x = c$.

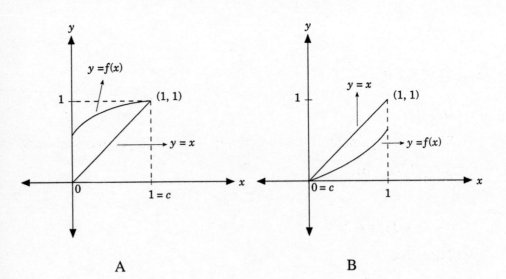

A   B

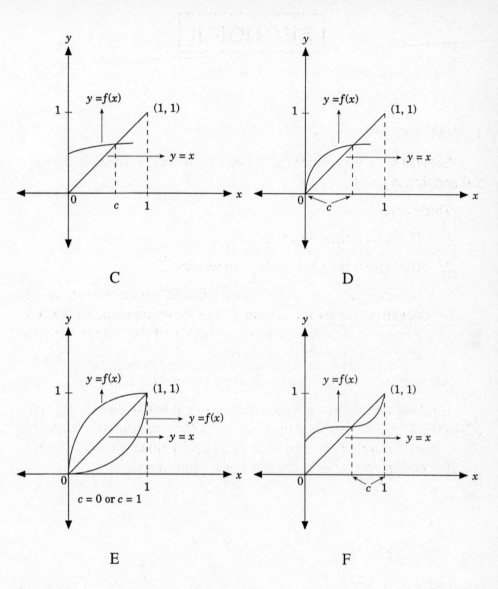

C

D

E

F

2. (A)

    Since the argument of the function ln ( ) must be positive, we have

    $0 < (x^2 - x - 6)$

    or

    $0 < (x - 3)(x + 2)$

    Therefore,

$x < -2$ or $x > 3$.

(B)

Use your calculator to find $f(5) = 2.64$.

(C)

Use your calculator directly and perform

der 1 (ln $x\wedge 2 - x - 6$, x, -3),

which should give -1.17.

3. (A)

Domain $= R$, since $x^2 + 1 \neq 0$, for all real x.

(B)

$$\frac{1-x^2}{x^2+1} = \frac{1-x^2}{x^2} \div \frac{x^2+1}{x^2}$$

dividing both numerator and denominator by x^2

$$= \left(\frac{1}{x^2} - 1\right) \div \left(1 + \frac{1}{x^2}\right)$$

Therefore, $\lim\limits_{x \to \pm\infty} \left(\frac{1-x^2}{x^2+1}\right) = \lim\limits_{x \to \pm\infty} \left[\left(\frac{1}{x^2} - 1\right) \div \left(1 + \frac{1}{x^2}\right)\right]$

$$= -1 \div 1$$

$$= -1$$

(C)

We can tell when the function is increasing or decreasing by investigating the sin of $f'(x)$.

$f'(x) = -\dfrac{4x}{\left(x^2+1\right)^2}$, by the quotient rule   (i)

Also, $(x^2 + 1)^2 > 0$, for any x,

$-4x > 0$, when $x < 0$,

$-4x < 0$, when $x > 0$.

Hence, $\quad -\dfrac{4x}{\left(x^2+1\right)^2} > 0$, when $x < 0$, and

$$-\dfrac{4x}{\left(x^2+1\right)^2} < 0, \text{ when } x > 0.$$

Therefore, $\quad f'(x) > 0$ when $x < 0$, and

$$f'(x) < 0 \text{ when } x > 0.$$

(D)

The tangent line is parallel to the x-axis so its slope is zero. It is seen that $f'(x)$ vanishes for $x = 0$.

Since $f(0) = 1$, the point of tangency is $(0, 1)$ and the equation of the tangent line is $y = 1$.

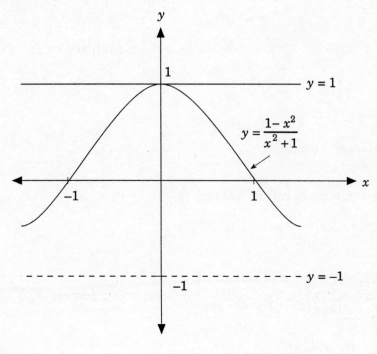

4.   (A)

Since $V = \dfrac{\pi}{3}r^2h$ of $r = \dfrac{h}{3}$, we have $V = \dfrac{\pi}{27}h^3$.

Therefore, $\dfrac{dV}{V} = 3\dfrac{dh}{h}$ and so

$$\frac{dV}{dt} = 3 \times \frac{V}{h} \times \frac{dh}{dt}.$$

When $h = 6$, $V = 8\pi$. Since $\dfrac{dV}{dt} = 2$, we get

$$\frac{dh}{dt} = \frac{1}{2\pi} \text{ inches/min.}$$

(B)

When the cup is full its volume $= \dfrac{1}{3}\pi 4^2 \times 12$

$$= 64 \ \pi \text{ in}^3$$

Therefore, when it is half full $V(t) = 32\pi \text{ in}^3$.   (iv)

Substituting (iv) in (ii) we get:

$$32\pi = \frac{1}{27}\pi h^3$$

$$\Leftrightarrow h = 6\sqrt[3]{4}\,. \tag{v}$$

Finally using (i), (iii) and (v):

$$\frac{dh}{dt} = \frac{18}{\pi\left(6\sqrt[3]{4}\right)^2} \text{ inches/min.}$$

$$= \frac{1}{2\pi\sqrt[3]{4^2}} \text{ inches/min.}$$

$$= \frac{\sqrt[3]{4}}{8\pi} \text{ inches/min.}$$

5. (A)

$$\frac{d^2}{dx^2}(-2f) = -2f''.$$

From the chart, $-2f'' > 0$ in $(-\infty, 0)$, and

$$-2f'' < 0 \quad \text{in} \quad (0, \infty).$$

Therefore, $-2f$ has inflection point at $x = 0$.

(B)

(i) $\dfrac{d}{dx}(-2f) = -2f' < 0$ in $(-\infty, -2)$ from the chart.

$-2f' > 0$ in $(-2, 0)$ from the chart.

$\Rightarrow -2f$ has relative min. at $x = -2$.

(ii) By similar argument as in (i), $-2f$ has relative max at $x = 2$ and equals 0.

(C)

Again from the table, $-2f'' > 0$ in $(-\infty, 0)$, and

$$-2f'' < 0 \quad \text{in} \quad (0, \infty).$$

So, it is concave upward in $(-\infty, 0)$ and concave downward in $(0, \infty)$.

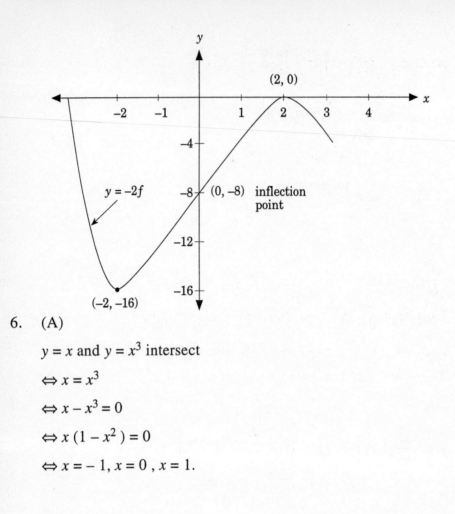

6. (A)

    $y = x$ and $y = x^3$ intersect

    $\Leftrightarrow x = x^3$

    $\Leftrightarrow x - x^3 = 0$

    $\Leftrightarrow x (1 - x^2) = 0$

    $\Leftrightarrow x = -1, x = 0 , x = 1.$

    (B)

    Determine which lies above the other:

x	x		x^3
$-\dfrac{1}{2}$	$-\dfrac{1}{2}$	$<$	$-\dfrac{1}{8}$
$\dfrac{1}{2}$	$\dfrac{1}{2}$	$>$	$\dfrac{1}{8}$

    Therefore, $y = x^3$ lies above $y = x$ in $(-1, 0)$ and $y = x$ lies above $y = x^3$ in $(0, 1)$.

Area $= \int_{-1}^{0} \left(x^3 - x\right) dx + \int_{0}^{1} \left(x - x^3\right) dx$

$= 2 \int_{0}^{1} \left(x - x^3\right) dx$

$= 2 \left(\dfrac{x^2}{2} - \dfrac{x^4}{4} \right) \Big|_{0}^{1}$

$= \dfrac{1}{2}$

(C)

Volume $= \int_{-1}^{0} \pi \left(x^2 - x^6\right) dx + \pi \int_{0}^{1} \left(x^2 - x^6\right) dx$,

since $x^2 > x^6$ in $(-1, 0)$; look at the figure.

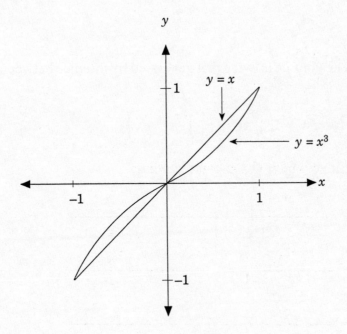

Remark: Do not write $\int_{-1}^{0} \left(x - x^3\right) dx$, since area is non-negative.

Also, do not write $\int_{-1}^{0} \left(x^6 - x^2\right) dx$ since volume is non-negative.

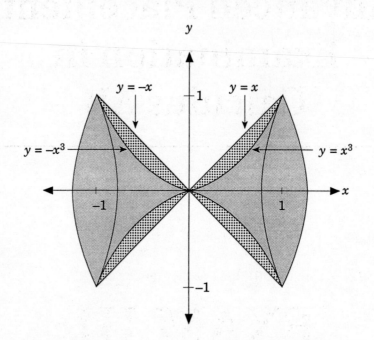

(C) The volume is twice that generated by the slice between 0 and 1.

Therefore, $V = 2\left(\int_{1}^{0} \pi x^2 \, dx - \int_{0}^{1} \pi x^6 \, dx\right)$

$$= 2\pi \int_{0}^{1} \left(x^2 - x^6\right) dx$$

$$= 2\pi \left(\frac{1}{3} - \frac{1}{7}\right)$$

$$= \frac{8\pi}{21}$$

Advanced Placement Examination in Calculus AB

EXAM III

ADVANCED PLACEMENT CALCULUS AB EXAM III

SECTION I

PART A

Time: 55 minutes
28 questions

DIRECTIONS: Each of the following problems is followed by five choices. Solve each problem, select the best choice, and blacken the correct space on your answer sheet. Calculators may not be used for this section of the exam.

NOTE: Unless otherwise specified, the domain of function f is assumed to be the set of all real numbers x for which $f(x)$ is a real number.

---

1. For what value of x will the tangent lines to $y_1 = \ln x$ and $y_2 = 2x^2$ be parallel?

   (A) 0   (D) 1

   (B) $\dfrac{1}{4}$ (E) 2

   (C) $\dfrac{1}{2}$

2. If $f(x) = 2^{x^3+1}$, then $f'(1)$ is approximately

   (A) 2.000   (D) 2.773

   (B) 4.000   (E) 8.318

   (C) 6.000

3. Let $f'(x) = \sin(\pi x)$ and $f(0) = 0$. Then $f(1) = ?$

(A) $-\dfrac{1}{\pi}$

(D) $\dfrac{2}{\pi}$

(B) $\dfrac{1}{\pi}$

(E) None of these

(C) $-\dfrac{2}{\pi}$

4. Let the velocity at a time t of a point moving on a line be defined by $V(t) = 2^t \ln 2$ cm/sec. How many centimeters did the point travel from $t = 0$ sec. to $t = 2.5$ sec.?

(A) 8.882

(D) 8.121

(B) 9.882

(E) 10.003

(C) 4.104

5. Find the slope of the tangent line to the graph of $y = \dfrac{5}{4 + x^3}$ when $x = 1$.

(A) 8.047

(D) 1.000

(B) –0.600

(E) None of the above

(C) –0.200

6. Let $f(x) = e^{bx}$, $g(x) = e^{ax}$ and find the value of b such that

$$D_x\left(\frac{f(x)}{g(x)}\right) = \frac{f'(x)}{g'(x)}$$

(A) $\dfrac{a^2}{a^2 - 1}$

(D) $\dfrac{a-1}{a^2}$

(B) $\dfrac{a^2}{a+1}$

(E) $\dfrac{a^2}{a-1}$

(C) $\dfrac{a+1}{a^2}$

7. Suppose $x^2 - xy + y^2 = 3$. Find $\dfrac{dy}{dx}$ at the point (a, b).

    (A) $\dfrac{a - 2b}{2a - b}$ (D) $\dfrac{b - 2a}{2b + a}$

    (B) $\dfrac{b - 2a}{2b - a}$ (E) $\dfrac{b + 2a}{2b + a}$

    (C) $\dfrac{a - 2b}{2a + b}$

8. $\displaystyle\lim_{h \to 0} \dfrac{e^{x+h} - e^x}{h}$ equals

    (A) 0   (D) $-\infty$

    (B) 1   (E) None of these

    (C) $+\infty$

9. $\displaystyle\int_{-2}^{-1} x^{-4} \, dx = \ ?$

    (A) $\dfrac{7}{2}$ (D) $\dfrac{31}{160}$

    (B) $\dfrac{31}{8}$ (E) None of these

    (C) $\dfrac{7}{24}$

10. If $f'(x) = \dfrac{x^2}{2}$ where $f(0) = 0$ then $3f(4) =$

(A) 0

(D) 24

(B) 3

(E) 32

(C) 12

11. $\displaystyle\lim_{x \to +\infty}\left(\dfrac{1}{x} - \dfrac{x}{x-1}\right) = ?$

(A) –1

(D) 2

(B) 0

(E) None of these

(C) 1

12. Let $R = \displaystyle\int_0^a \cos\!\left(x^2\right)dx$ and $S = \displaystyle\int_0^a \tan x\, dx$.

Find $\displaystyle\int_{-a}^a \left[\cos\!\left(x^2\right) + \tan x\right]dx$.

(A) $2R$

(D) $S + 2R$

(B) $2S$

(E) $2R + 2S$

(C) $R + 2S$

13. If $\sin y = \cos x$, then find $\dfrac{dy}{dx}$ at the point $\left(\dfrac{\pi}{2},\ \pi\right)$.

(A) –1

(D) $\dfrac{\pi}{2}$

(B) 0

(E) None of these

(C) 1

14. For which of the following intervals is the graph of

    $y = x^4 - 2x^3 - 12x^2$ concave down?

    (A) $(-2, 1)$

    (D) $(-\infty, -1)$

    (B) $(-1, 2)$

    (E) $(-1, +\infty)$

    (C) $(-1, -2)$

15. $\int_1^e x \ln x \, dx = ?$

    (A) e

    (D) $\dfrac{e-1}{2}$

    (B) $\dfrac{e^2 - 1}{2}$

    (E) None of these

    (C) $\dfrac{e^2 + 1}{4}$

16. If $f'(x) = 2(3x + 5)^4$, then the fifth derivative of $f(x)$ at

    $x = -\dfrac{5}{3}$ is

    (A) 0

    (D) 3,888

    (B) 144

    (E) None of these

    (C) 1,296

17. Let $f'(x) = \dfrac{x}{\sqrt{x^2 - 8}}$. Which of the following interval notations represents the most inclusive domain for f?

(A) $\left(2\sqrt{2}, -2\sqrt{2}\right)$

(B) $\left[2\sqrt{2}, -2\sqrt{2}\right]$

(C) $(-\infty, +\infty)$

(D) $\left(-\infty, -2\sqrt{2}\,\right] \cup \left[\,2\sqrt{2}, +\infty\right)$

(E) $\left(-\infty, -2\sqrt{2}\right) \cup \left(2\sqrt{2}, +\infty\right)$

18. If $f(x) = \ln x$, then $f\left(\dfrac{3}{2}\right) =$

(A) $\dfrac{\ln 3}{\ln 2}$

(B) $\ln 2 - \ln \dfrac{1}{2}$

(C) $\displaystyle\int_{\ln 2}^{\ln 3} e^t \, dt$

(D) $\displaystyle\int_{2}^{3} \ln t \, dt$

(E) $\displaystyle\int_{2}^{3} \dfrac{1}{t} \, dt$

19. If $y = \dfrac{3}{\sin x + \cos x}$ then $\dfrac{dy}{dx} =$

(A) $3 \sin x - 3 \cos x$

(B) $\dfrac{6\sin x}{1 + 2\sin x \cos x}$

(C) $\dfrac{3}{\cos x - \sin x}$

(D) $\dfrac{-3}{(\sin x + \cos x)^2}$

(E) $\dfrac{3(\sin x - \cos x)}{1 + 2\sin x \cos x}$

20. $\int_{-2}^{-1} |x^{-3}| \, dx =$

(A) $\dfrac{3}{8}$

(D) $\dfrac{15}{64}$

(B) $\dfrac{5}{8}$

(E) None of these

(C) $\dfrac{15}{4}$

21. $\displaystyle\lim_{x\to 0} \dfrac{\dfrac{3}{x^2}}{\dfrac{2}{x^2} + \dfrac{105}{x}} =$

(A) 0

(D) $\dfrac{3}{107}$

(B) 1

(E) None of these

(C) $\dfrac{3}{2}$

22. The graph of f is shown in the figure. Which of the following could be the graph of $\int f(x) \, dx$?

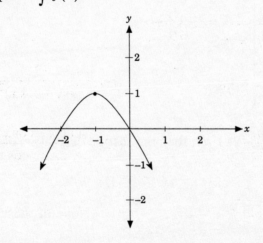

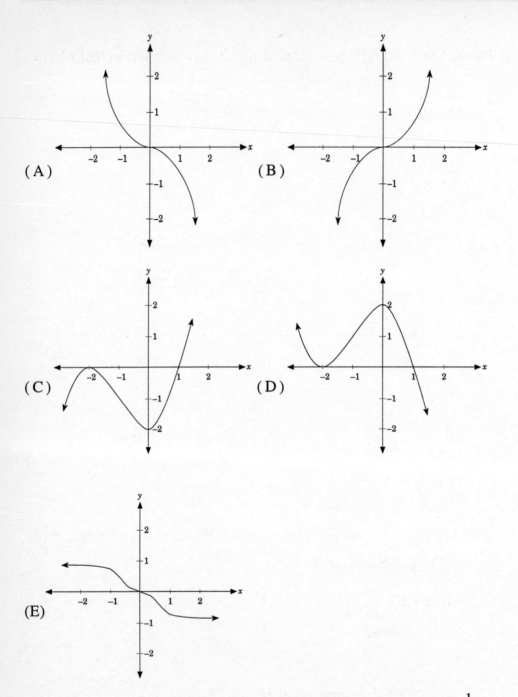

(A)

(B)

(C)

(D)

(E)

23. If $f(x) = \int (1-2x)^3 dx$, then the second derivative of $f(x)$ at $x = \dfrac{1}{2}$ is

(A) –48

(D) 96

(B) –12

(E) None of these

(C) 0

24. Let $F(x) = \int_1^x f(t)\, dt$, and use the graph given of $f(t)$ to find $F'(1) =$

(A) 0

(D) $\dfrac{1}{2}$

(B) 1

(E) None of these

(C) 2

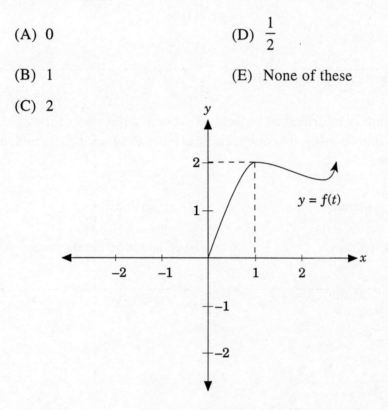

25. $\int x^{-1}\, dx =$

(A) $\dfrac{x^{-2}}{-2} + C$

(D) $-x + c$

(B) $x + C$

(E) None of these

(C) Undefined

26. $\int_0^4 \dfrac{dx}{(x-1)^{2/3}} =$ approximately

(A) 1.327

(D) 4.326

(B) 7.326

(E) None of the above

(C) 3

27. How many relative or absolute maxima does $x - \cos x$ have on the interval $(-2\pi, 2\pi)$?

(A) 1

(D) 4

(B) 2

(E) 5

(C) 3

28. A square is inscribed in a circle. How fast is the area of the square changing when the area of the circle is increasing one square inch per minute?

(A) $\dfrac{1}{2}$ in²min

(D) $\dfrac{\pi}{2}$ in²/min

(B) 1 in²/min

(E) Cannot be determined

(C) $\dfrac{2}{\pi}$ in²min

PART B

Time: 50 minutes
17 questions

DIRECTIONS: Calculators may be used for this section of the test. Each of the following problems is followed by five choices. Solve each problem, select the best choice, and blacken the correct space on your answer sheet.

NOTES:
1. Unless otherwise specified, answers can be given in unsimplified form.

2. The domain of function f is assumed to be the set of all real numbers x for which $f(x)$ is a real number.

---

29. The area that is enclosed by $y = x^3 + x^2$ and $y = 6x$ for $x \geq 0$ is

(A) $\dfrac{29}{12}$　　　　　　　　(D) 6

(B) 3　　　　　　　　　　　(E) $\dfrac{32}{3}$

(C) $\dfrac{16}{3}$

30. $\displaystyle\lim_{x \to 0} \dfrac{\arctan x}{\tan x}$ equals

(A) 0　　　　　　　　　　(D) $-\infty$

(B) 1　　　　　　　　　　(E) None of these

(C) $+\infty$

31. Find the area in the first quadrant that is enclosed by $y = \sin 3x$ and the x–axis from $x = 0$ to the first x–intercept on the positive x–axis.

(A) $\dfrac{1}{3}$ (D) 2

(B) $\dfrac{2}{3}$ (E) 6

(C) 1

32. A particle moves along a straight line. Its velocity is

$$V(t) = \begin{cases} t^2 & \text{for } 0 \le t \le 2 \\ t+2 & \text{for } t \ge 2 \end{cases}$$

The distance travelled by the particle in the interval $1 \le t \le 3$ is

(A) 3   (D) 5

(B) 7.1   (E) 6.8

(C) 4.3

33. Let $f(x) = x + \dfrac{1}{x^{1.6}}$. Then, $\int_{0.1}^{2} f(x)$ equals

(A) 3.64   (D) 5.1

(B) 4.99   (E) 11.2

(C) 7.53

34. $\displaystyle \lim_{x \to -4^+} \dfrac{4x - 6}{2x^2 + 5x - 12}$ equals

(A) 0   (D) $-\infty$

(B) 1   (E) None of these

(C) $+\text{-}\infty$

35. Let $g(x) = e^{-x^2}$ and determine which one of the following statements is true.

    (A) g is a decreasing function.

    (B) g is an odd function.

    (C) g is symmetric with respect to the x–axis.

    (D) $(0.5, e^{-0.25})$ is a point of inflection.

    (E) None of these.

36. The graph shown represents $y = f(x)$. Which one of the following is NOT true?

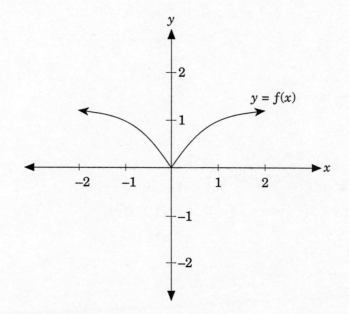

    (A) f is continuous on $(-2, 2)$.

    (B) $\lim\limits_{x \to 0} f(x) = f(0)$.

    (C) f is differentiable on $(-2, 2)$.

    (D) $\lim\limits_{x \to 0^-} f(x) = f(0)$.

    (E) $f'(x) < 0$ for $x < 0$

37. Which one of the following is NOT an antiderivative of sec x?

   (A) $\ln|\sec x + \tan x| + C$

   (B) $-\ln|\sec x - \tan x| + C$

   (C) $\ln\left|\dfrac{1-\sin x}{\cos x}\right| + C$

   (D) $\ln\left|\dfrac{1+\sin x}{\cos x}\right|$

   (E) $\ln\left|\dfrac{\cos x}{1-\sin x}\right|$

38. If $8 + 2x - x^2 = 6x^3$, one solution for x is

   (A) 1.143

   (B) 2.25

   (C) −17.2

   (D) 5.78

   (E) 12.3

39. Let $f(x) = \dfrac{\sin x \cos x}{\cos 9x \tan 2x}$. $f'(0.5)$ equals

   (A) 3.8

   (B) −2.5

   (C) −49.5

   (D) 70.1

   (E) −5

40. Let $f(x) = \dfrac{x}{\sqrt{4-x^2}}$. The minimum of $f'(x)$ is

   (A) 0.5

   (B) 1

   (C) −1

   (D) −0.5

   (E) 2

41. Suppose $f(x)$ is a continuous function on $[1, 2]$ and $f(1) = 2$, $f(1.5) = 0.5$, and $f(2) = -3$. Which of the following is FALSE?

    (A) The maximum value of f in $[1, 2]$ is 2.

    (B) $f(c) = 0$ for some real value of c.

    (C) $\lim\limits_{x \to 2^-} f(x) = -3$

    (D) $|f(2)| - |f(1)| \le |f(2) - f(1)|$

    (E) $\lim\limits_{x \to \frac{5}{4}} f(x) = f\left(\frac{5}{4}\right)$

42. Find the value of c such that the area between the line $y = c$ and the parabola $y = x^2$ is $\dfrac{1}{48}$.

    (A) $\dfrac{1}{512}$

    (D) $\dfrac{1}{16}$

    (B) $\dfrac{1}{64}$

    (E) None of these

    (C) $\dfrac{1}{32}$

43. Let f', g' be differentiable functions that are derivatives of f and g, respectively. If $f'(x) \le g'(x)$ for all real x, which of the following must be true (if $b > a$)?

    I. $\lim\limits_{x \to a} f'(x) \le \lim\limits_{x \to a} g'(x)$

    II. $\int_a^b f'(x)\, dx \le \int_a^b g'(x)\, dx$

    III. $f(x) \le g(x)$, for all real x

    IV. $\int_a^b f(x)\, dx \le \int_a^b g(x)\, dx$

(A) I only

(D) I, II, and III

(B) II only

(E) I, II, III, and IV

(C) I and II only

44. The volume generated by revolving $y = x^3 (-1 \le x \le 1)$ around the y-axis is

(A) π

(D) $\dfrac{2\pi}{5}$

(B) 2π

(E) $\dfrac{4\pi}{5}$

(C) $\dfrac{6\pi}{5}$

45. The curves $y = \dfrac{x^2}{2}$ and $y = 1 - \dfrac{x^2}{2}$ intersect in the first quadrant. The angle at which they intersect is

(A) $30°$

(D) $90°$

(B) $45°$

(E) $0°$

(C) $60°$

SECTION II

Time: 1 hour and 30 minutes
6 problems*

DIRECTIONS: Show all your work. Grading is based on the methods used to solve the problems as well as the accuracy of your final answers. Please make sure all procedures are clearly shown. For some problems or parts of problems it will be necessary to use a calculator.

NOTES:

1. Unless otherwise specified, answers can be given in unsimplified form.

2. The domain of function f is assumed to be the set of all real numbers x for which $f(x)$ is a real number.

---

1. Let f be the function defined by $f(x) = \dfrac{x}{(x-1)^2}$

   (A) Sketch the graph of $y = f(x)$. Be sure to label all relative extrema, points of inflection, and asymptotes.

   (B) Use interval notation to indicate where the function is increasing, decreasing, concave up, and concave down.

   (C) State the domain and range of the function and indicate why the function does not have an inverse over its domain.

---

*The practice tests in this book incorporate Section II free-response solutions that approximate the content breakdown you will encounter on the AP exam. The overall timing and formatting of the practice tests in this book mirror the actual test; examinees should note, however, that this section is split into two parts on the AP exam. Furthermore, prospective examinees should pay attention to restrictions on calculator use. For details, consult current official College Board materials in print or on the Web.

(D) Write the equation (in standard form) for the tangent line to $y = f(x)$ that passes through a point of inflection.

2. Let $f(x) = \dfrac{3}{2 + 105x}$

   (A) Find $f'(0)$

   (B) What happens to the graph of $f(x)$ versus x near $x = -0.019$? Explain.

   (C) Find $\displaystyle\int_0^2 f(x)\, dx$.

3. Let the growth rate (in grams/sec) of a plant culture be directly proportional to the weight (in grams) of the plant culture present at the same instant.

   (A) Write a formula for the rate of growth of the plant culture in terms of the current weight of the plant culture.

   (B) Solve the differential equation in part (A) to find the weight of the plant culture X as a function of time.

   (C) If the weight of the culture at the beginning of the experiment $(t = 0)$ is 10 grams, and the weight after one second $(t = 1)$ is 100 grams, find the weight of the culture after 0.5 seconds.

   (D) Find the difference between the instantaneous rate of growth when t is one second and the average rate of growth for the first second.

4. Let $y = \cos(2x^2)$ for x in the interval $[0, c]$ where c is the first positive x-intercept.

   (A) Find the volume of the region between $y = f(x)$ and $y = 0$ in the interval $[0, c]$, rotating about the y-axis.

   (B) Find the average value of $y = f'(x)$ over the given interval.

(C) Write (DO NOT EVALUATE) the definite integral expression for the volume of the region between $y = 1$ and $y = f(x)$ on the given interval, rotating about the x–axis.

5. Assume the volume V of a cube is increasing at a constant rate of 3 cm^3 per second. Let t_0 be the instant when the rate of change of the volume (cm^3/sec) is numerically equal to the rate of change of the surface area (cm^2/sec) for the cube. Assume $V = 0$ when $t = 0$.

(A) Find the value(s) of t_0.

(B) Find the rate of change of the length of a side when $t = t_0$.

(C) Find the rate of change of the surface area when $t = t_0$.

6. The vertical speed of a glider (ft/min) is indicated by the following graph.

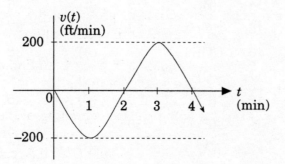

(A) Let $t \in [0,4]$ and sketch the graph of $y(t)$, where y is the altitude in feet and t is the time in minutes. Assume $y(0) = 627$ ft $\approx$ $\left(500 + \dfrac{400}{\pi} \right)$ ft.

(B) For what value(s) of t will the glider be at a minimum altitude for Let $t \in [0,4]$?

(C) For what value(s) of t will the glider be at a maximum altitude for Let $t \in [0, 4]$?

(D) For what value(s) of t is the graph of $y = f(t)$ concave up?

ADVANCED PLACEMENT CALCULUS AB EXAM III

ANSWER KEY

Section I

1.	(C)	12.	(A)	23.	(C)	34.	(C)
2.	(E)	13.	(C)	24.	(C)	35.	(E)
3.	(D)	14.	(B)	25.	(E)	36.	(C)
4.	(A)	15.	(C)	26.	(B)	37.	(C)
5.	(B)	16.	(D)	27.	(A)	38.	(A)
6.	(E)	17.	(D)	28.	(C)	39.	(C)
7.	(B)	18.	(E)	29.	(C)	40.	(A)
8.	(E)	19.	(E)	30.	(B)	41.	(A)
9.	(C)	20.	(A)	31.	(B)	42.	(D)
10.	(E)	21.	(C)	32.	(E)	43.	(C)
11.	(A)	22.	(D)	33.	(C)	44.	(C)
						45.	(D)

Section II

See Detailed Explanations of Answers.

ADVANCED PLACEMENT
CALCULUS AB
EXAM III

DETAILED EXPLANATIONS
OF ANSWERS

$$\boxed{\textbf{SECTION I}}$$

1. **(C)**

$y_1 = \ln x$ and $y_2 = 2x^2$, with $y_1' = \dfrac{1}{x}$ and $y_2' = 4x$

Set the derivatives equal and get

$\dfrac{1}{4} = 4x$, or

$\dfrac{1}{4} = x^2$. This has the solutions $x = \pm\dfrac{1}{2}$

Since $y = \ln x$ is not defined for $x = -\dfrac{1}{2}$, the solution is $x = \dfrac{1}{2}$.

2. **(E)**

$$f(x) = 2^{x^3+1} \text{ then } f'(x) = 2^{x^3+1}(\ln 2)\, D\left(x^3 + 1\right)$$

If

$$= 2^{x^3+1}(\ln 2)\left(3x^2\right)$$

So $f'(1) = 2^2(\ln 2)(3)$

$$= 12 \ln 2$$

$$\approx 8.318$$

3. **(D)**

$$y = f(x) = \int \sin(\pi x)\, dx$$

$$= -\frac{1}{\pi}\cos(\pi x) + C$$

Since $y = 0$ when $x = 0$:

$$0 = -\frac{1}{\pi}\cos 0 + C, \quad \text{so} \quad C = \frac{1}{\pi} \quad \text{and}$$

$$f(x) = -\frac{1}{\pi}\cos(\pi x) + \frac{1}{\pi}.$$

Therefore, $f(1) = -\frac{1}{\pi}\cos\pi + \frac{1}{\pi}$

$$= -\frac{1}{\pi}(-1) + \frac{1}{\pi}$$

$$= \frac{2}{\pi}$$

4. **(A)**

$V(t) = 2^t \ln 2, \quad \text{so} \quad s(t) = 2^t + c.$

We can set $c = 0$ since it is subtracted out.

$s(0) = 2^0 = 1$

$s(2.5) = 2^{2.5}$

$$\cong 5.657$$

Distance $= s(2.5) - s(0)$

$$= (9.882 + c) - (1 + c)$$

= 8.882 cm.

Distance traveled = 4.657 cm.

5. **(B)**

$y' = 5 \times (-1)(4 + x^3)^{-2}(3x^2)$. When $x = 1$ this becomes

$= -5(5)^{-2}(3)$

$= -\dfrac{15}{25}$

$= -\dfrac{3}{5}$

Therefore, $y'(1) = -0.600$

6. **(E)**

$D_x\left(\dfrac{f(x)}{g(x)}\right) = \dfrac{e^{ax}be^{bx} - e^{bx}ae^{ax}}{e^{2ax}}$

$= \dfrac{(b-a)e^{bx}}{e^{ax}}$

$\dfrac{f'(x)}{g'(x)} = \dfrac{be^{bx}}{ae^{ax}}$

Now equate the two to get

$\dfrac{b}{a} = b - a$ or $b = ab - a^2 \Rightarrow$

$a^2 = ab - b \Rightarrow a^2 = b(a - 1)$

Therefore, $\dfrac{a^2}{a-1} = b$

7. **(B)**

Differentiate $x^2 - xy + y^2 = 3$ implicitly to get

$2x - (xy' + y) + 2yy' = 0.$

Now solve for y':

$2x - xy' - y + 2yy' = 0$

$y'(2y - x) = y - 2x$

$y' = \dfrac{y - 2x}{2y - x}.$

Let $x = a$, $y = b$ to get $y' = \dfrac{b - 2a}{2b - a}.$

8. **(E)**

$\displaystyle\lim_{h \to 0} \dfrac{e^{x+h} - e^x}{h}$ equals the derivative of e^x by using the definition of the derivative

$f'(x) = \displaystyle\lim_{h \to 0} \dfrac{f(x+h) - f(x)}{h}$

$\qquad = e^x \quad \text{for} \quad f(x) = e^x$

9. **(C)**

$\displaystyle\int_{-2}^{-1} x^{-4}\,dx = \dfrac{x^{-3}}{-3}\Big|_{-2}^{-1}$

$\qquad = -\dfrac{1}{3}\left(\dfrac{1}{-1} - \dfrac{1}{-8}\right)$

$\qquad = -\dfrac{1}{3}\left(-\dfrac{7}{8}\right)$

$\qquad = \dfrac{7}{24}$

10. **(E)**

$$f(x) = \int \frac{x^2}{2} dx$$

$$= \frac{x^3}{6} + C$$

Let $x = 0$; $\quad f(0) = \frac{1}{6}(0)^3 + C \qquad\qquad 0 = C$

$$f(x) = \frac{1}{6}x^3$$

$$3f(4) = 3 \times \frac{1}{6} \times (4)^3$$

$$= 32$$

11. **(A)**

$$\lim_{x \to +\infty} \left(\frac{1}{x} - \frac{x}{x-1} \right) = \lim_{x \to +\infty} \frac{x-1-x^2}{x(x-1)}$$

$$= \lim_{x \to +\infty} \frac{-x^2 + x - 1}{x^2 - x}$$

$$= \lim_{x \to +\infty} \frac{-1 + \dfrac{1}{x} - \dfrac{1}{x^2}}{1 - \dfrac{1}{x}}$$

$$= -1$$

12. **(A)**

$\cos (x^2)$ is an even function and $\tan x$ is an odd function so

$$\int_{-a}^{a} \cos(x^2)\, dx = 2R; \quad \int_{-a}^{0} \tan x\, dx = -\int_{0}^{a} \tan x\, dx$$

Then $\displaystyle\int_{-a}^{a}\left[\cos\left(x^2\right)+\tan x\right]dx = 2R+0$

$$= 2R$$

13. **(C)**

Differentiate $\sin y = \cos x$ implicitly.

$$\frac{dy}{dx}\cos y = -\sin x, \quad \frac{dy}{dx} = -\frac{\sin x}{\cos y}.$$

At $\left(\dfrac{\pi}{2},\ \pi\right)$, $\dfrac{dy}{dx} = -\dfrac{\sin\left(\dfrac{\pi}{2}\right)}{\cos(\pi)}$

$$= \frac{-1}{-1}$$

$$= 1$$

14. **(B)**

$$y = x^4 - 2x^3 - 12x^2$$

$$y' = 4x^3 - 6x^2 - 24x$$

$$y'' = 12x^2 - 12x - 24$$

$$= 12(x-2)(x+1)$$

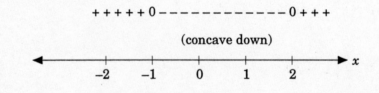

15. **(C)**

Use integration by parts with

$$
\begin{array}{c|c}
u = \ln x & du = \dfrac{1}{x}\,dx \\
\hline
dv = x & v = \dfrac{x^2}{2}
\end{array}
$$

$$
\int_1^e x \ln x\, dx = \frac{x^2}{2}\ln x - \int_1^e \frac{x}{2}\,dx
$$

$$
= \left(\frac{x^2}{2}\ln x - \frac{x^2}{4} \right)\bigg|_1^e
$$

$$
= \frac{e^2 + 1}{4}
$$

16. **(D)**

If $f'(x) = 2\,(3x + 5)^4$; $\qquad f''(x) = 24\,(3x + 5)^3$

$f'''(x) = 216\,(3x + 5)^2$; $\qquad f^{(4)}(x) = 1{,}296\,(3x + 5)$

$f^{(5)}(x) = 3{,}888$ so $f\!\left(-\dfrac{5}{3}\right) = 3{,}888$

17. **(D)**

$$
f'(x) = \frac{x}{\sqrt{x^2 - 8}} \quad \text{then} \quad f(x) = \int x\left(x^2 - 8\right)^{-\frac{1}{2}}\,dx
$$

Let $u = x^2 - 8$ and $du = 2x\,dx$, so

$$
f(x) = \frac{1}{2}\int u^{-\frac{1}{2}}\,du
$$

$$
= \frac{1}{2} \times 2u^{\frac{1}{2}} + C
$$

$$
= \sqrt{x^2 - 8} + C.
$$

We must have $|x^2 - 8| \geq 0$ in order for f to be real-valued so

$$(x + 2\sqrt{2})(x - 2\sqrt{2}) \geq 1$$

$$+ + + + + 0 - - - - - - - - 0 + + + + +$$

$$x \leq -2 \cap \sqrt{2} \quad \text{or} \quad x \geq 2\sqrt{2}x$$

which is written in interval notation as

$$\left(-\infty, \ -2\sqrt{2}\,\right] \cup \left[\, 2\sqrt{2}\,, \ +\infty\right)$$

18. **(E)**

Recall that $\ln x = \int_1^x \frac{1}{t}\,dt$, and that $\ln \dfrac{a}{b} = \ln a - \ln b$

We have: $\ln \dfrac{3}{2} = \ln 3 - \ln 2$

$$= \int_1^3 \frac{1}{t}\,dt - \int_1^2 \frac{1}{t}\,dt$$

$$= \int_2^3 \frac{1}{t}\,dt$$

19. **(E)**

$$y = \frac{3}{\sin x + \cos x} = \frac{3}{u} \quad \text{where } u = \sin x + \cos x$$

So $\dfrac{dy}{dx} = 3(-1)u^{-1-1}\dfrac{du}{dx}$ using the derivative of a power and chain rule theorems.

Thus, $\dfrac{dy}{dx} = \dfrac{-3}{(\sin x + \cos x)^2}(\cos x - \sin x)$

$$= \dfrac{3(\sin x - \cos x)}{\sin^2 x + 2\sin x \cos x + \cos^2 x}$$

$$\dfrac{dy}{dx} = \dfrac{3(\sin x - \cos x)}{1 + 2\sin x \cos x},$$

using the identity $\sin^2 x + \cos^2 x = 1$

20. **(A)**

Note $|n| = \begin{cases} n & \text{if } n \geq 0 \\ -n & \text{if } n < 0 \end{cases}$

so $|x^{-3}| = -x^{-3}$ for x in $[-2, -1]$

Now $\displaystyle\int_{-2}^{-1} |x^{-3}| \, dx = \int_{-2}^{-1} -x^{-3} \, dx$

$$= -\left(\dfrac{x^{-3+1}}{-3+1}\right)\Bigg|_{-2}^{-1}$$

$$= \dfrac{x^{-2}}{2}\Bigg|_{-2}^{-1}$$

$$= \dfrac{1}{2}\left[\dfrac{1}{(-1)^2} - \dfrac{1}{(-2)^2}\right]$$

$$= \dfrac{1}{2}\left[1 - \dfrac{1}{4}\right]$$

$$= \dfrac{1}{2}\left(\dfrac{3}{4}\right)$$

$$= \dfrac{3}{8}$$

21. **(C)**

$$\lim_{x \to 0} \frac{\dfrac{3}{x^2}}{\dfrac{2}{x^2} + \dfrac{105}{x}} \boxed{\dfrac{x^2}{x^2}} = \lim_{x \to 0} \frac{3}{2 + 105x}$$

$$= \frac{3}{2 + 0}$$

$$= \frac{3}{2}$$

22. **(D)**

Consider $\dfrac{d}{dx} \displaystyle\int f(x)\, dx = f(x)$. So the following graph is the graph of

the derivative of $\displaystyle\int f(x)\, dx$. Note the graph of the derivative indicates:

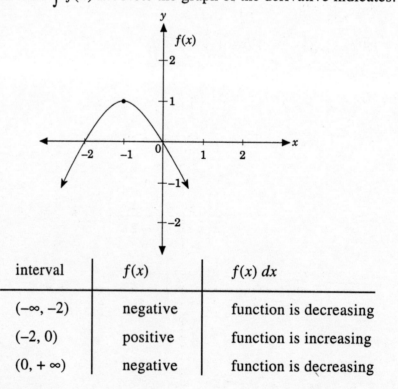

interval	$f(x)$	$f(x)\, dx$
$(-\infty, -2)$	negative	function is decreasing
$(-2, 0)$	positive	function is increasing
$(0, +\infty)$	negative	function is decreasing

Therefore the graph of the function has a relative minimum when $x = -2$ and a relative maximum when $x = 0$. Choice (D) is the only choice with correct locations of the relative minimum and relative maximum. Since $\int f(x)\,dx = F(x)+C$ for any real number C, the graph would be adjusted up if $C > 0$ and down if $C < 0$.

23. **(C)**

If $\quad f(x) = \int (1-2x)^3\,dx$

then $\qquad f'(x) = (1-2x)^3$

since $\qquad \dfrac{d}{dx}\int f(x)\,dx = f(x)$ by definition.

$$f''(x) = 3(1-2x)^2(-2)$$

$$= -6(1-2x)^2$$

$$f''\!\left(\frac{1}{2}\right) = -6\!\left(1-2\!\left(\frac{1}{2}\right)\right)^2$$

$$= 0$$

24. **(C)**

$F(x) = \int_1^x f(t)\,dt$; the graph of $f(t)$ is as shown.

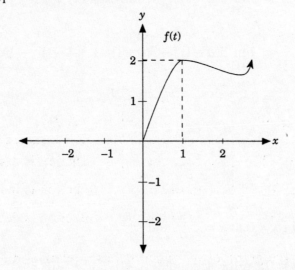

Now $F'(x) = f(x)$ using the Fundamental Theorem of Calculus.

So, $F'(1) = f(1) = 2$, using the graph of f.

25. **(E)**

$$\int x^{-1}\, dx = \int \frac{1}{x}\, dx$$

$$= \ln x + C \quad \text{since} \quad \frac{d}{dx}(\ln x + C)$$

$$= \frac{1}{x}$$

26. **(B)**

Since the function $f(x) = \dfrac{1}{(x-1)^{2/3}}$ becomes infinite at $x = 1$, which lies between the limits of integration, we must split the integral into two parts and take limits.

$$\int_0^4 \frac{dx}{(x-1)^{2/3}} = \lim_{a \to 1^-} \int_0^a \frac{dx}{(x-1)^{2/3}} + \lim_{b \to 1^+} \int_b^4 \frac{dx}{(x-1)^{2/3}}$$

$$= \lim_{a \to 1^-} 3(x-1)^{\frac{1}{3}}\Big|_0^a + \lim_{b \to 1^+} 3(x-1)^{\frac{1}{3}}\Big|_b^4$$

$$= \lim_{a \to 1^-} 3(a-1)^{\frac{1}{3}} - 3(0-1)^{\frac{1}{3}} + 3(4-1)^{\frac{1}{3}} - \lim_{b \to 1^+} 3(b-1)^{\frac{1}{3}}$$

$$= 0 - 3(-1) + 3\sqrt[3]{3} - 0 = 3\sqrt[3]{3} + 3$$

$$= 7.326$$

27. **(A)**

$$y' = 1 + \sin x = 0 \text{ at } x = -\frac{\pi}{2} \text{ and } \frac{3\pi}{2}.$$

$y'' = \cos x = 0$, so the second derivative test fails.

However, notice that $y'(x) \geq 0$ for all x, so y is monotone increasing. Thus, the only max is at 2π.

28. **(C)**

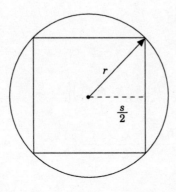

The side of the square, s, is $\sqrt{2}r$. The areas are $A = \pi r^2$ and $A_s = 2r^2$.

Thus, $\dfrac{d}{dt}(A_s) = 4r\dfrac{dr}{dt}$. Since

$$\frac{d}{dt}(A_0) = 1 = 2\pi r\frac{dr}{dt}, \quad \frac{dr}{dt} = \frac{1}{2\pi r}.$$

So, $\dfrac{d}{dt}(A_s) = 4r; \quad \dfrac{1}{2\pi r} = \dfrac{2}{\pi}.$

29. **(C)**

Solve the equations simultaneously to find the points of intersection.

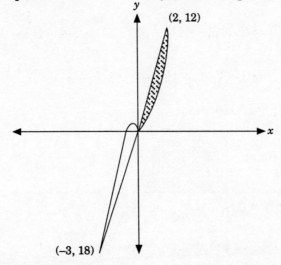

$$x^3 + x^2 = 6x$$

$$x^3 + x^2 - 6x = 0$$

$$x(x+3)(x-2) = 0$$

$$x = 0 \quad \text{or} \quad x = -3 \quad \text{or} \quad x = 2$$

$$A = \int_0^2 \left[6x - \left(x^3 + x^2 \right) \right] dx$$

$$= \left(\frac{6x^2}{2} - \frac{x^4}{4} - \frac{x^3}{3} \right) \Big|_0^2$$

$$= \frac{16}{3}$$

30. **(B)**

$$\lim_{x \to 0} \frac{\arctan x}{\tan x} = \lim_{x \to 0} \frac{\dfrac{1}{1+x^2}}{\sec^2 x} \text{ , using L'Hôpital's Rule,}$$

$$= \frac{1}{1}$$

$$= 1$$

31. **(B)**

The period of $y = \sin(ax)$ is $\dfrac{2\pi}{a}$.

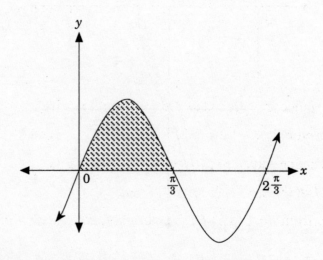

$$\int_0^{\frac{\pi}{3}} \sin(3x)\, dx = \frac{1}{3}\int_0^{\pi} \sin u\, du \text{ where } u = 3x$$

$$A = \frac{1}{3}\left(-\cos u\right)\Big|_0^{\pi}$$

$$= \frac{1}{3}[-(-1) - (-1)]$$

$$= \frac{2}{3}$$

32. **(E)**

The graph of $V(t)$ is

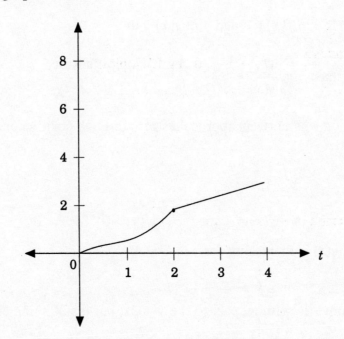

The distance travelled between $t = 1$ and $t = 2$ is

$fnInt(x{\wedge}2, x, 1, 2) = 2.3$.

The distance travelled between $t = 2$ and $t = 3$ is

$fnInt(x + 2, x, 2, 3) = 4.5$.

Hence, from $t = 1$ to $t = 3$, the particle travelled $2.3 + 4.5 = 6.8$.

33. **(C)**

Use your calculator to solve this problem:

$fnInt\left(x+\dfrac{1}{x^\wedge 1.6}, \; x, \; 0.1, \; 2\right)$, which should give 7.53.

34. **(C)**

$$\lim_{x\to-4^+}\frac{4x-6}{2x^2+5x-12}=\lim_{x\to-4^+}\frac{2(2x-3)}{(2x-3)(x+4)}$$

$$=\lim_{x\to-4^+}\frac{2}{x+4}$$

$$=+\infty$$

Note: If $\lim_{x\to a} f(x)=c$ and $\lim_{x\to a} g(x)=0$,

then $\lim_{x\to a}\dfrac{f(x)}{g(x)}=\pm\infty$

depending on whether $g(x)$ approaches zero through positive or negative values of x.

35. **(E)**

$g(x)=e^{-x^2}$ so $g'(x)=-2xe^{-x^2}\Rightarrow g'(x)>0$ for $x<0$

Thus, $g(x)$ is increasing for x in $(-\infty,0)$

$g(-x)=e^{-(-x)^2}=e^{-x^2}\Rightarrow g(x)$ is even.

$g(x)$ is symmetric with respect to the y–axis, but is not symmetric with respect to the x–axis because $y=e^{-x^2}$ is not the same graph as $-y=e^{-x^2}$. $g''(x)=2e^{-x^2}(2x^2-1)$ so points of inflection occur when $2x^2-1=0\Rightarrow x=\pm\sqrt{\dfrac{1}{2}}$. Therefore, answers (A)–(D) are not true.

36. **(C)**

The left-hand derivative at $x = 0$ is negative and the right-hand derivative at $x = 0$ is positive, so the function is not differentiable at $x = 0$. Therefore, f is not differentiable on the entire interval $(-2, 2)$.

37. **(C)**

Let $u = \sec x + \tan x$ and $du = (\sec x \tan x + \sec^2 x)\, dx$

So, $\displaystyle \int \frac{1}{u}\, du = \int \frac{(\sec x + \tan x)\sec x}{(\tan x + \sec x)}\, dx$

$$= \int \sec x\, dx$$

But $\displaystyle \int \frac{1}{u}\, du = \ln|u| + C$

$$= \ln|\sec x + \tan x| + C$$

which is (A)

(B) follows since

$$-\ln|\sec x - \tan x| = \ln\left|\frac{1}{\sec x - \tan x}\right|$$

$$= \ln|\sec x + \tan x|$$

(D) is correct because

$$\sec x + \tan x = \frac{1}{\cos x} + \frac{\sin x}{\cos x}$$

$$= \frac{1 + \sin x}{\cos x}$$

(E) is correct because

$$\frac{1 + \sin x}{\cos x} = \frac{\cos x}{1 - \sin x}$$

38. **(A)**

Let $f(x) = 8 + 2x - x^2$ and $g(x) = 6x^3$. Draw the graph of $f(x)$ and $g(x)$.

$(6x^3 + x^2 - 2x - 8)$ changes sign between $x = 1$ and $x = 2$; one of the roots lies there.

Let $x = 1 + \varepsilon$ (with $x^2 \cong 1 + 2\varepsilon$, $x^3 \cong 1 + 3\varepsilon$). We find that $\varepsilon \approx \dfrac{1}{6}$.

Therefore, the root lies near $x = 1.16$.

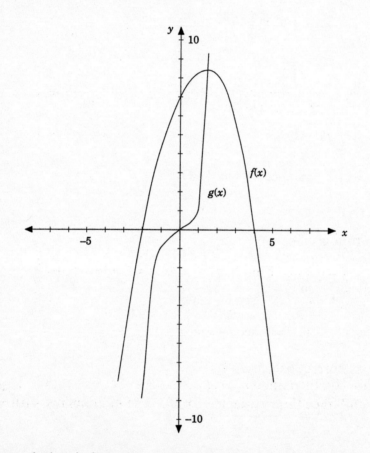

One solution is between 1 and 2 on the x–axis. Reset window to $[1, 2] \times [8, 10]$. This solution can be found to be 1.143.

39. **(C)**

Use your calculator to solve this problem. For example,

$$\text{der } 1\left(\frac{\sin x \cos x}{\cos 9x \, \tan 2x}, \ x, \ 0.5 \right) . -49.5 \text{ will be given as the answer.}$$

40. **(A)**

Draw the graphs of $f(x)$ and $f'(x)$.

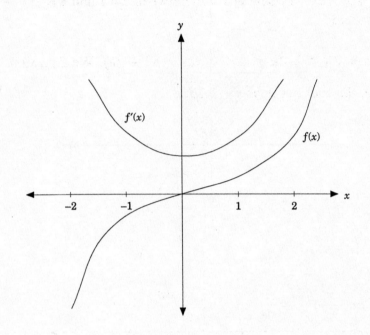

$f'(x) = \dfrac{4}{\left(4-x^2\right)^{\frac{3}{2}}}$. Minimum of f' at $x = 0$ when $f' = \dfrac{4}{4^{\frac{3}{2}}}$

$= \dfrac{1}{2}.$

Obviously, the minimum occurs at $x = 0$. Set the window to $[-2, 2]$ $\times [-1, 1]$ and trace the x variable to $x = 0$. The minimum is $f'(0) = 0.5$.

41. **(A)**

(A) is false. There is not enough information to tell where the maximum is.

(B) is true because of the intermediate value theorem.

(C) is true because of the definition of continuity on $[a, b]$.

(D) is true for any a, b as a consequence of the triangle inequality, i.e., $|a| - |b| \le |a - b|$.

(E) is true because of the definition of continuity.

42. **(D)**

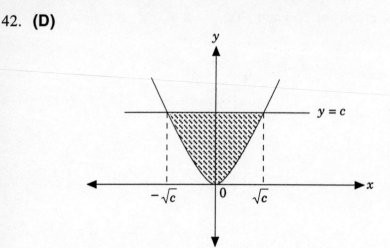

$$2\int_0^{\sqrt{c}} \left(c - x^2\right) dx = \frac{1}{48}$$

$$cx - \frac{x^3}{3}\Big|_0^{\sqrt{c}} = \frac{1}{96}$$

$$\Rightarrow \frac{2}{3}c^{\frac{3}{2}} = \frac{1}{96}$$

$$\Rightarrow \left(c^{\frac{3}{2}}\right)^{\frac{2}{3}} = \left(\frac{1}{64}\right)^{\frac{2}{3}}$$

So, $c = \frac{1}{16}$.

43. **(C)**

III and IV can be shown false by taking

$$f(x) = x^2 + 1$$

$$g(x) = x^2.$$

(I) is true because differentiable functions (in case f' and g') are necessarily continuous; the limit follows from this property. (II) is one of the elementary properties of integrals.

44. **(C)**

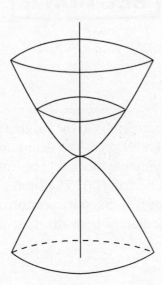

$V = 2 \times$ top half

$$= 2\int_0^1 \pi x^2 dy = 2\pi \int_0^1 y^{\frac{2}{3}} dy = \frac{6\pi}{5} y^{\frac{5}{3}} \Big|_0^1$$

$$= \frac{6\pi}{5}$$

45. **(D)**

Setting $\dfrac{x^2}{2} = 1 - \dfrac{x^2}{2}$, $x = 1$ so $y = \dfrac{1}{2}$

$y_1' = x = 1$, $y_2' = -x = -1$

so $\theta = 45° - (-45°) = 90°$.

SECTION II

1. (A)

   Note that the only intercept is at the origin (0, 0) since 0 is the only number to make the numerator zero. The denominator is zero when $x = 1$, so sketch in a vertical asymptote at $x = 1$. The limit of $f(x)$ as $x \rightarrow + \infty$ is zero through positive values of $f(x)$. The limit $f(x)$ as $x \rightarrow + \infty$ is zero through negative values of $f(x)$. Sketch a portion of the graph as indicated in figure (1a). Next calculate where the first and second derivatives change sign.

$$f'(x) = \frac{\left[(x-1)^2 \times 1\right] - \left[x(2)(x-1)\right]}{(x-1)^2}$$

$$= \frac{-x-1}{(x-1)^3}$$

$$= \frac{1+x}{(1-x)^3}$$

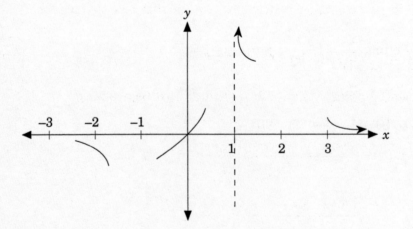

(using the quotient rule for derivatives)

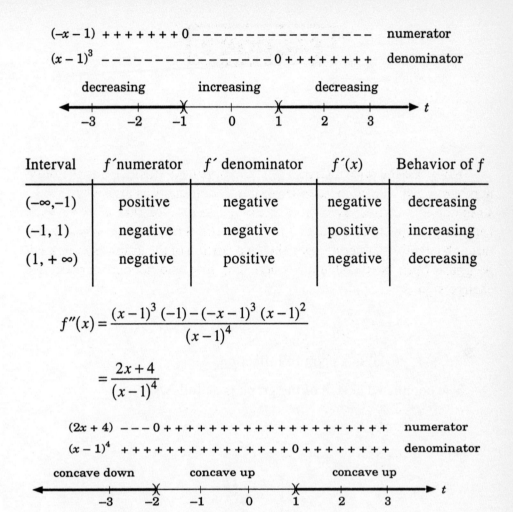

Using the first derivative test, we see that $f'(x) = 0$ when

$$0 = \frac{-x-1}{(x-1)^3} \Rightarrow 0 = -x - 1 \Rightarrow x = -1$$

is a critical point. Taking the second derivative, we have

$$f''(x) = \frac{-(x-1)^3 - (-x-1)^3 (x-1)^2}{(x-1)^6}$$

$$= \frac{(x-1)^2 (-x+1+3x+2)}{(x-1)^6}$$

$$= \frac{2x+4}{(x-1)^4}.$$

At $x = -1$,

$$f''(x) = \frac{2(-1)+4}{(-2)^4}$$

$$= \frac{2}{16} > 0.$$

So, $(-1, f(-1))$ is a relative minimum. To find inflection points, we set $f''(x) = 0$.

$$0 = \frac{2x+4}{(x-1)^4}$$

$$\Rightarrow 2x + 4 = 0$$

$$\Rightarrow x = -2.$$

So, $(-1, f(-1))$ is a point of inflection.

The completed sketch of the graph is as follows:

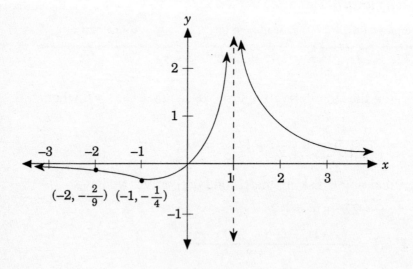

(B)

f is increasing on $(-1, 1)$ and decreasing on $(-\infty, -1)$ and $(1, \infty)$. f is concave down on $(-\infty, -2)$ and concave up on the intervals $(-2, 1)$ and $(1, +\infty)$. See part (A) for appropriate work.

(C)

The domain of f is all reals except $x = 1$. The range of f is all reals greater than or equal to $-\dfrac{1}{4}$. The function f does not have an inverse over the domain of f because f is not a one-to-one function. For example, $f\left(-\dfrac{1}{2}\right) = f(-2) = -\dfrac{2}{9}$, so two different values of x can go to the same value of $y = f(x)$.

(D)

Use the point-slope form for the equation of a line:

$$y - y_1 = m(x - x_1), \quad \text{where} \quad x_1 = -2 \quad \text{and} \quad x_2 = -\frac{2}{9}$$

and $\qquad m = f'(-2)$

$$= \frac{2-1}{(-3)^3}$$

$$y = -\left(-\frac{2}{9}\right)$$

$$= -\frac{1}{27}(x - (-2))$$

or $\qquad x + 27y + 8 = 0$

2. (A)

Using the first derivative formation,

$$\text{der } 1\left(\frac{3}{2 + 105x}, \; x, \; 0\right)$$

$f(0) = -78.75$ can be found.

(B)

Draw the graph of $f(x)$ for $-1 < x < 1$.

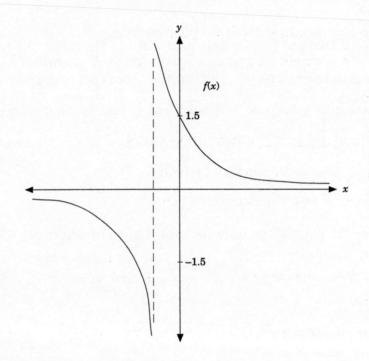

$$f(x) \text{ is defined for } x_o = \frac{-2}{105} \approx -0.019$$

As x approaches x_0 from the left, $f(x) \to -\infty$

As x approaches x_0 from the right, $f(x) \to +\infty$

(C)

Using the calculator to $\int_0^2 f(x)$ by

$$fnInt\left(\frac{3}{2+105x}, \ x, \ 0, \ 2\right)$$

you get

$$\int_0^2 f(x)\, dx = 0.1332$$

3. (A)

Let t = time in seconds for plant growth.

x = weight (in grams) of plant culture X at time t.

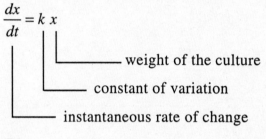

$$\frac{dx}{dt} = k\, x$$

weight of the culture

constant of variation

instantaneous rate of change

(B)

The solution for the differential equation $f'(t) = k\, f(t)$ is $f(t) = A\, e^{kt}$, so let $x = f(t)$ and then $x = A\, e^{kt}$ where $A = x_0$ is the initial value of x.

(C)

For $x = f(t) = A\, e^{kt}$, let $t = 0$ and then $10 = f(0) = A\, e^0$; so $A = 10$. Let $t = 1$ and then $100 = f(1) = 10e^k$.

Dividing by 10 gives $10 = e^{\,k}$, so $k = \ln 10$. This means $x = f(t) = 10\, e^{\,t\,\ln 10} = 10\, e^{\ln 10t} = 10(10^t) = 10^{t+1}$.

If $x = 0.5$ then $f(.5) = 10^{1.5} = 10\sqrt{10}$ grams.

$x = x_0 e^{kt}$ with $x_0 = 10$.

Since $100 = 10 \times e^k$ we have $e^k = 10$.

Therefore, $x\left(\dfrac{1}{2}\right) = 10e^{k\frac{1}{2}}$

$$= 10(10)^{\frac{1}{2}}$$

$$= 10\sqrt{10}$$

(D)

The instantaneous rate of growth is $f'(t) = D_t (10^{t+1})$.

Now $f'(t) = 10^{t+1} \ln 10$, so $f'(1) = 100 \ln 10$ gm/sec.

Average rate of growth $\qquad \dfrac{f(1) - f(0)}{1 - 0} = 100 - 10 = 90$ gm/sec.

Therefore, $f'(1) -$ Ave. rate $= (100 \ln 10 - 90)$ gm/sec.

4. (A)

c is such that $2c^2 = \dfrac{\pi}{2}$, i.e., $c = \dfrac{\sqrt{\pi}}{2}$

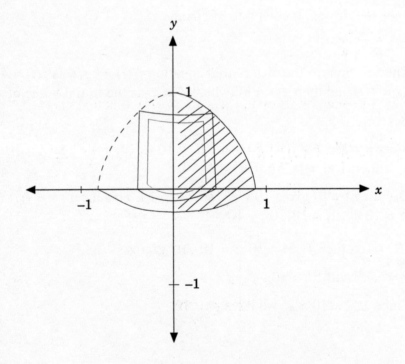

Using the method of shells, the volume $= 2\pi \displaystyle\int_a^b x \, f(x) \, dx$.

Volume $= 2\pi \displaystyle\int_0^{\sqrt{\frac{\pi}{4}}} x \cos(2x^2) \, dx = 2\pi \displaystyle\int_0^{\frac{\pi}{2}} \frac{1}{4} \cos(u) \, du$

where we have set $u = 2x^2$ so, $du = 4x \, dx$

$$\text{Volume} = \frac{\pi}{2} \sin u \Big|_0^{\frac{\pi}{2}}$$

$$= \frac{\pi}{2}$$

(B)

$$\langle f' \rangle = \frac{1}{c-0} \int_0^c \frac{dy}{dx} \, dx$$

$$= \frac{1}{c} u \Big|_0^c$$

$$= -\frac{1}{c} \times 1$$

$$= -\frac{2}{\sqrt{\pi}}$$

(C)

Using the method of cylindrical washers, the volume is

$$\pi \int_a^b \left\{ [f(x)]^2 - [g(x)]^2 \right\} dx \Rightarrow \pi \int_0^{\sqrt{\frac{\pi}{4}}} \left[1^2 - \left(\cos(2x^2) \right)^2 \right] dx$$

$$= \pi \int_0^{\sqrt{\frac{\pi}{4}}} \sin^2(2x^2) \, dx$$

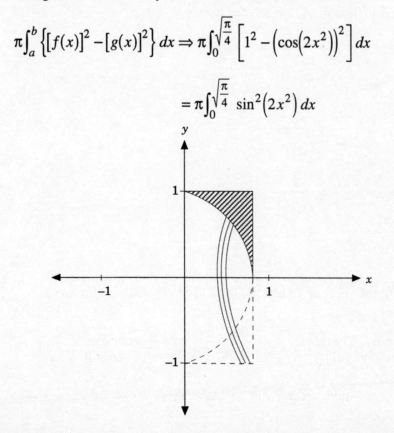

5. **(A)**

$$V'(t) = V(t)$$

$$= \int V'(t)\, dt$$

$$= \int 3\, dt$$

$$= 3t + C$$

Since $\dfrac{dV}{dt} = k$, a constant, and $V(0) = 0$, we must have $V = kt$. Here, $k = 3$ cc/sec.

Length of a side: $L(t) = V^{\frac{1}{3}} = (kt)^{\frac{1}{3}}$

Surface area: $S(t) = 6 \times L^2 = 6(kt)^{\frac{2}{3}}$

Since $V(0) = 0$, $V(t) = 3t$ so $t_0 = \dfrac{1}{3} V(t_0)$.

Therefore, $\qquad \dfrac{dV}{dt} = k$

$$\dfrac{ds}{dt} = \dfrac{4k}{(kt)^{\frac{1}{3}}}$$

$$\dfrac{dL}{dt} = \dfrac{k}{3(kt)^{\frac{2}{3}}}$$

At t_0, we have $k = \dfrac{4k}{(kt_0)^{\frac{1}{3}}}$

or, $kt_0 = 64$. Therefore, $t_0 = \dfrac{64}{k} = \dfrac{64}{3} = 21\dfrac{1}{3}$ seconds.

(B)

$$\frac{dL}{dt} = \frac{k}{3(kt)^{\frac{2}{3}}} \quad \text{at } t = t_0; \ kt_0 = 64. \text{ Therefore,}$$

$$\frac{dL}{dt} = \frac{3}{3(64)^{\frac{2}{3}}}$$

$$= \frac{1}{16} \ \text{cm/se}$$

(C)

$$\frac{ds}{dt} = \frac{4k}{(kt)^{\frac{1}{3}}} \quad \text{at } t_0; \ kt_0 = 64. \text{ Therefore,}$$

$$\frac{ds}{dt} = 3\text{cm}^2/\text{sec}.$$

6. (A)

Integration of the speed with respect to the time shows that $y(t) =$ constant $+ \dfrac{400}{\pi}\cos\left(\dfrac{2\pi t}{4}\right)$. The initial condition $y(0) \approx 500 + \dfrac{400}{\pi}$ leads to $y(t)$

$$= 500 + \frac{400}{\pi}\cos\left(\frac{2\pi t}{4}\right).$$

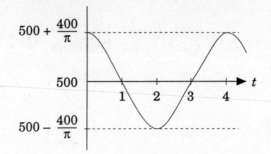

(B)

Minimum altitude when $\dfrac{2\pi t}{4} = \pi \Rightarrow t = 2$ min.

(C)

Maximum altitude when $\dfrac{2\pi t}{4} = 0$ or $2\pi \Rightarrow t = 0$ or 4 min.

(D)

$y(t)$ is concave up for $\dfrac{\pi}{2} < \dfrac{2\pi t}{4} < \dfrac{3\pi}{2} \Rightarrow 1 < t < 3$

Advanced Placement Examination in Calculus AB

EXAM IV

ADVANCED PLACEMENT CALCULUS AB EXAM IV

SECTION I

PART A

Time: 55 minutes
28 questions

> **DIRECTIONS:** Each of the following problems is followed by five choices. Solve each problem, select the best choice, and blacken the correct space on your answer sheet. Calculators may not be used for this section of the exam.
>
> **NOTE:** Unless otherwise specified, the domain of function f is assumed to be the set of all real numbers x for which $f(x)$ is a real number.

1. Which of the following represents a function?

   (A) $x^2 + y^2 = 1$ (C) $x^2 - y = 0$

   (B) $y^2 = x$ (D) $y = \pm\sqrt{1 - x^2}$

   (E)

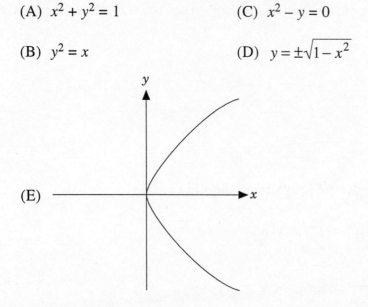

2. If $f(x) = x - 2$ and $g(x) = |x|$, then

    (A) $(g \circ f)(3) + f(3) = 0$

    (B) $(g \circ f)(1) - f(1) = 0$

    (C) $\dfrac{(g \circ f)(0)}{f(0)} = -1$

    (D) $\dfrac{(g \circ f)(0)}{f(0)} = 1$

    (E) $2(g \circ f)(x) \neq f(x)$ for every x

3. If $\dfrac{x^2}{1 - x^2}$, then

    (A) Domain of $f = R\backslash\{1\}$

    (B) f is an odd function

    (C) The line $y = -1$ is a horizontal asymptote

    (D) $x = -1$ is the only vertical asymptote

    (E) f is never zero

4. If $f(x) = a \sin (bx + c)$ and $f'(x) = 2a \cos (bx + c)$, then the period of f is

    (A) π (D) $\dfrac{\pi}{2}$

    (B) 4π (E) 3π

    (C) 2π

5. If the graph of f is as shown as follows, then

    $$\lim_{x \to 3}\left([f(x)]^2 + 2f(x) + 1\right) =$$

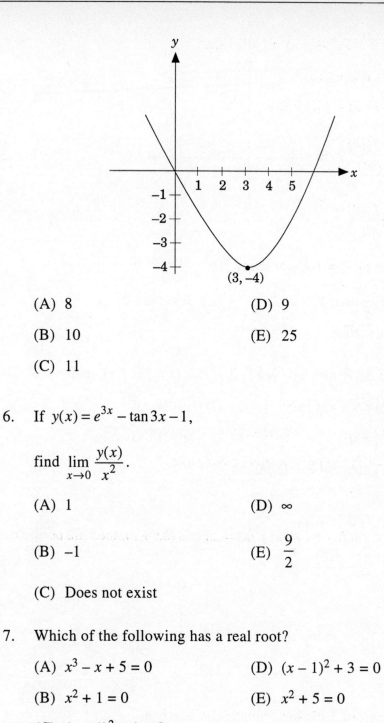

(3, −4)

(A) 8   (D) 9

(B) 10   (E) 25

(C) 11

6. If $y(x) = e^{3x} - \tan 3x - 1$,

   find $\lim\limits_{x \to 0} \dfrac{y(x)}{x^2}$.

   (A) 1   (D) ∞

   (B) −1   (E) $\dfrac{9}{2}$

   (C) Does not exist

7. Which of the following has a real root?

   (A) $x^3 - x + 5 = 0$ (D) $(x - 1)^2 + 3 = 0$

   (B) $x^2 + 1 = 0$ (E) $x^2 + 5 = 0$

   (C) $(x + 1)^2 + 1 = 0$

8. The graph of $f(x)$ is as shown below. If the graph of $-f(x) + c$, c a constant, does not intersect the x-axis, then c must be

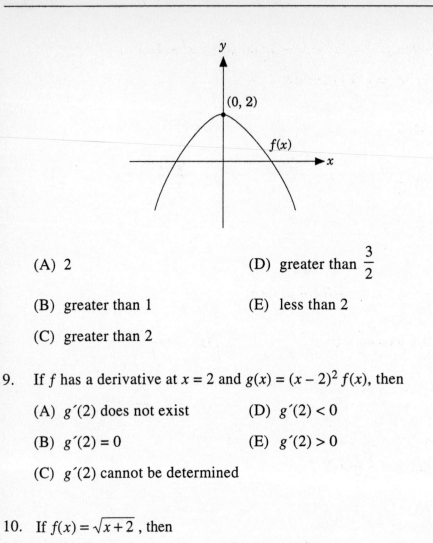

(A) 2

(B) greater than 1

(C) greater than 2

(D) greater than $\dfrac{3}{2}$

(E) less than 2

9. If f has a derivative at $x = 2$ and $g(x) = (x - 2)^2 f(x)$, then

(A) $g'(2)$ does not exist

(B) $g'(2) = 0$

(C) $g'(2)$ cannot be determined

(D) $g'(2) < 0$

(E) $g'(2) > 0$

10. If $f(x) = \sqrt{x + 2}$, then

$$\lim_{h \to 0} \frac{f(2 + h) - f(2)}{h} =$$

(A) 4

(B) 0

(C) $\dfrac{1}{2}$

(D) $\dfrac{1}{4}$

(E) 1

11. Given $f(x) = 2x^2 - 3x + 5$ and $g(x) = x^2 + 2x + 4$,

   if $f'(a) = g'(a)$ then $a =$

   (A) 2

   (D) $\dfrac{2}{5}$

   (B) $\dfrac{5}{6}$

   (E) $\dfrac{5}{2}$

   (C) $-\dfrac{2}{5}$

12. If $y = A \sin x + B \cos x$, then

   (A) $y + \dfrac{d^2 y}{dx^2} = 0$

   (D) $y + \dfrac{d^2 y}{dx^2} < 0$

   (B) $y + \dfrac{d^2 y}{dx^2} \neq 0$

   (E) $-y + \dfrac{d^2 y}{dx^2} = 0$

   (C) $y + \dfrac{d^2 y}{dx^2} > 0$

13. Let $f(x) = \dfrac{2}{3}x^{\frac{3}{2}}$ and suppose that the line $y = 2.5x$ is parallel to the tangent of $f(x)$ at x_0. x_0 must approximately equal

   (A) –6.25

   (D) 0.71

   (B) 4.00

   (E) 12.50

   (C) 6.25

14. The value of $\dfrac{dy}{dx}$ when $x = 1$ and $y = -1$ given that

$4x^2 + 2xy - xy^3 = 0$ is

(A) 7

(B) 5

(C) 9

(D) 11

(E) 6

15. The domain of $y = \sqrt{(x-1)(x-2)}$ is

(A) $|x| < 2$

(B) $(1, 2)$

(C) $|x| > 1$

(D) $(-\infty, 1] \cup [2, \infty)$

(E) $[1, 2]$

16. If the graph of $f(x)$ is as shown below, then

(A) Domain of $\dfrac{1}{f'(x)} = (1, 4)$

(B) Domain of $\dfrac{1}{f'(x)} = [1, 4]$

(C) $f'(x) > 0$ on $(1, 4)$

(D) $f'(x) < 0$ on $(1, 4)$

(E) $f'(x_0) = 0$ at some point in $(1, 4)$

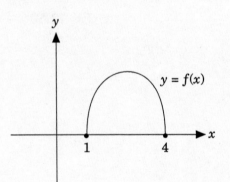

17. If $\dfrac{dy}{dx} = 3\cos^2 x - 3\sin^2 x$, then $y =$

(A) $\sin(2x) + C$

(D) $\dfrac{3}{2}\cos(2x) + C$

(B) $3\sin(2x) + C$

(E) $\dfrac{2}{3}\sin(2x) + C$

(C) $\dfrac{3}{2}\sin(2x) + C$

18. $\lim\limits_{x \to 0} \dfrac{x - \tan x}{x - \sin x} =$

(A) -2

(D) $-\dfrac{1}{2}$

(B) 2

(E) Does not exist

(C) 0

19. If $\lim\limits_{n \to \infty} \dfrac{6n^2}{200 - 4n + kn^2} = \dfrac{1}{2}$, then $k =$

(A) 3

(D) 8

(B) 6

(E) 2

(C) 12

20. If $\lim\limits_{n \to \infty}\left(1 + \dfrac{1}{n}\right)^{kn} = \dfrac{1}{e^2}$, then $k =$

(A) 1

(D) $-\dfrac{1}{e}$

(B) -2

(E) $\dfrac{1}{e}$

(C) $\dfrac{1}{2}$

21. If $y = -\dfrac{1}{\sqrt{x^2+1}}$, then $\dfrac{dy}{dx} =$

(A) $\dfrac{x}{\left(x^2+1\right)^{\frac{1}{2}}}$

(D) $\dfrac{x}{\left(x^2+1\right)^{\frac{3}{2}}}$

(B) $-\dfrac{x}{\left(x^2+1\right)^{\frac{1}{2}}}$

(E) $\dfrac{x}{x^2+1}$

(C) $-\dfrac{x}{\left(x^2+1\right)^{\frac{3}{2}}}$

22. If $y = \ln\,[(x+1)\,(x+2)]$, then $\dfrac{dy}{dx} =$

(A) $\dfrac{1}{x+1}+(x+2)$

(D) $\dfrac{x+1}{x+2}$

(B) $\dfrac{1}{(x+2)}+(x+1)$

(E) $\dfrac{1}{x+1}+\dfrac{1}{x+2}$

(C) $\dfrac{1}{(x+1)(x+2)}$

23. If $f(x) = ae^{kx}$ and $\dfrac{f'(x)}{f(x)} = -\dfrac{5}{2}$ then $k =$

(A) -5

(D) $\dfrac{5}{2}$

(B) $-\dfrac{5}{2}$

(E) $\dfrac{2}{5}$

(C) $-\dfrac{2}{5}$

24. The rate of change of the area of an equilateral triangle with respect to its side S at $S = 2$ is

(A) 0.43

(D) 7.00

(B) 1.73

(E) 0.50

(C) 0.87

25. If $f(x) = e^{\frac{x^3}{3} - x}$, then $f(x)$

(A) increases in the interval $(-1, 1)$

(B) decreases for $|x| > 1$

(C) increases in the interval $(-1, 1)$ and decreases in the intervals $(-\infty, -1) \cup (1, \infty)$

(D) increases in the intervals $(-\infty, -1) \cup (1, \infty)$ and decreases in the interval $(-1, 1)$

(E) increases in the interval $(-\infty, \infty)$

26. $\int_1^2 \frac{x^2 + 1}{x^3 + 3x + 1} dx =$

(A) 0.231

(D) 0.535

(B) 0.406

(E) 1.609

(C) 0.366

27.

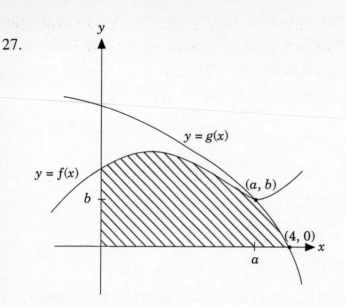

The curves $y = f(x)$ and $y = g(x)$ shown in the figure above intersect at the point (a, b). The area of the shaded region, bounded by these curves and the coordinate axes, is given by

(A) $\int_0^a (f(x) - g(x))\, dx$

(B) $\int_0^a (g(x) - f(x))\, dx$

(C) $\int_0^a f(x)\, dx - \int_a^4 g(x)\, dx$

(D) $\int_0^a f(x)\, dx + \int_a^4 g(x)\, dx$

(E) $\int_0^4 g(x)\, dx - \int_0^a f(x)\, dx$

28. Let $f(x) = \sqrt{x-1}$ for $x \geq 1$. What are the possible x-values, usually denoted by c in the statement of the Mean Value Theorem, at which f' attains its mean value over the interval $1 \leq x \leq 5$?

(A) 1   (D) 1 and 2

(B) 2   (E) 1 and 4

(C) 4

PART B

Time: 50 minutes
17 questions

DIRECTIONS: Calculators may be used for this section of the test. Each of the following problems is followed by five choices. Solve each problem, select the best choice, and blacken the correct space on your answer sheet.

NOTES:
1. Unless otherwise specified, answers can be given in unsimplified form.

2. The domain of function f is assumed to be the set of all real numbers x for which $f(x)$ is a real number.

29. If $f(x) = x - \dfrac{1}{x}$, which of the following is <u>NOT</u> true?

(A) $f\left(\dfrac{1}{x}\right) = -f(x)$

(B) $f\left(\dfrac{1}{x}\right) = f(-x)$

(C) $f(x) = f(-x)$

(D) $f(-x) = -f(x)$

(E) None of these

30. If x and y are two positive numbers such that $x + y = 20$ and xy is as large as possible then

(A) $x = 12$ and $y = 8$

(B) $x = 10$ and $y = 10$

(C) $x = 5$ and $y = 15$

(D) $x = 20$ and $y = 0$

(E) $x = 8$ and $y = 12$

31. If the rate of change of $f(x)$ at $x = x_0$ is twice the rate of change of $f(x)$ at $x = 4$, and $f(x) = 2\sqrt{x}$ then x_0 is

(A) 8

(D) 16

(B) 1

(E) 4

(C) 2

32. The area enclosed by $f(x) = x^3 + x^2$ and $g(x) = \ln(x + 1)$ for $x > 0$ is

(A) 0.0513

(D) 2.89

(B) 0.01

(E) 7.8

(C) 2.5

33. The area in the first quadrant that is enclosed by $y = \sin 3x \cos x$ and the x-axis from $x = 0$ to the first x-intercept on the positive side is

(A) 1

(D) 2.5

(B) 0.56

(E) 1.5

(C) 0.78

34. If the graph of f is as shown below, then the graph of

$y = 2 + f(x)$

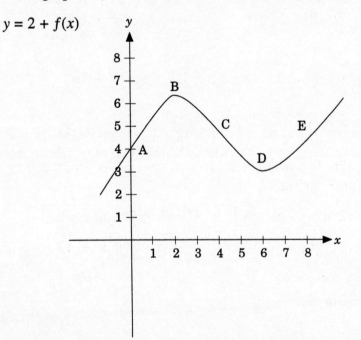

(A) is concave downward in the interval (2, 6)

(B) is concave upward in the interval (0, 8)

(C) has an inflection point at $x = 5$

(D) is concave downward in the interval (0, 3)

(E) is concave downward in the interval (0, 8)

35. If $f(x) = g(x) - \dfrac{1}{g(x)}$, $g(0) = 3$ and $g'(0) = 2$, then $f'(0)$ is approximately

(A) 1.778

(D) 2.222

(B) 2.333

(E) 1.222

(C) 3.222

36. If the acceleration (ft/sec^2) of a moving body is $\sqrt{4t+1}$ and the velocity at $t = 0$, $v(0) = -4\dfrac{1}{3}$, then the distance travelled between time $t = 0$ and $t = 2$ is

(A) $\dfrac{119}{30}$

(D) $\dfrac{149}{30}$

(B) $-\dfrac{119}{30}$

(E) -4

(C) $-\dfrac{149}{30}$

37. If the volume of a cube is increasing at a rate of 300 in^3/min at the instant when the edge is 20 inches, then the rate at which the edge is changing is

(A) $\dfrac{1}{4}$ in/min

(D) 1 in/min

(B) $\dfrac{1}{2}$ in/min

(E) $\dfrac{3}{4}$ in/min

(C) $\dfrac{1}{3}$ in/min

38. $6\displaystyle\int_{-1}^{1}\frac{x^3+1}{x+1}\,dx =$

    (A) 4   (D) 8

    (B) 2   (E) 16

    (C) 12

39. If $f(x) = x^3 - 2x$, then f has

    (A) a relative Max. at $x = \sqrt{\dfrac{2}{3}}$ and a relative Min. at $x = -\sqrt{\dfrac{2}{3}}$

    (B) an absolute Max. at $x = -\sqrt{\dfrac{2}{3}}$

    (C) a relative Min. at $x = \sqrt{\dfrac{2}{3}}$ and a relative Max. at $x = -\sqrt{\dfrac{2}{3}}$

    (D) an absolute Min. at $x = \sqrt{\dfrac{2}{3}}$

    (E) a relative Min. at $x = -\sqrt{\dfrac{2}{3}}$ and a relative Max. at $x = \sqrt{\dfrac{2}{3}}$

40. If $f(x) = 256x^{-\frac{1}{2}} + 64x^{\frac{1}{2}} + 3x^{\frac{2}{3}}$, then $f'(64)$ equals

    (A) 4.25   (D) 10.25

    (B) 8.75   (E) 5.78

    (C) 0.75

41. The smallest value of $y = x^2(1 - x^{-1})$ is

    (A) 0   (D) –1

    (B) –0.25   (E) 1

    (C) 0.25

42. Given the following graph of the continuous function $f(x)$,

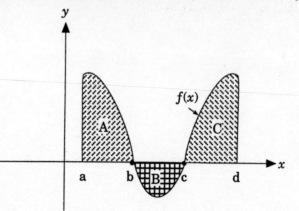

with: area of region $A = 3$

area of region $B = 1\dfrac{1}{2}$

area of region $C = 2$, then $\displaystyle\int_a^d f(x)\, dx =$

(A) $\dfrac{5}{2}$

(D) 5

(B) $\dfrac{7}{2}$

(E) $\dfrac{2}{5}$

(C) $\dfrac{13}{2}$

43. $\displaystyle\int x\cos(4x)\, dx =$

(A) $\dfrac{1}{4}\sin(4x) + C$

(B) $\dfrac{x}{4}\sin(4x) + C$

(C) $\dfrac{x}{4}\sin(4x) + \dfrac{1}{16}\cos(4x) + C$

(D) $\dfrac{x}{4}\sin(4x)-\dfrac{1}{16}\cos(4x)+C$

(E) $\dfrac{x}{4}-\dfrac{1}{16}\cos(4x)+C$

44. If $x=t^3-3t$ and $y=\left(t^2+1\right)^2$, then at $t=2$, $\dfrac{dy}{dx}$ is

(A) 40

(D) $\dfrac{9}{40}$

(B) 9

(E) 0

(C) $\dfrac{40}{9}$

45. An equation of the line normal to the graph of $y=x^4-3x^2+1$ at the point where $x=1$ is

(A) $2x-y+3=0$

(D) $x-2y-3=0$

(B) $x-2y+3=0$

(E) $x-2y=0$

(C) $2x-y-3=0$

SECTION II

Time: 1 hour and 30 minutes
6 problems*

DIRECTIONS: Show all your work. Grading is based on the methods used to solve the problems as well as the accuracy of your final answers. Please make sure all procedures are clearly shown. For some problems or parts of problems it will be necessary to use a calculator.

NOTES:
1. Unless otherwise specified, answers can be given in unsimplified form.

2. The domain of function f is assumed to be the set of all real numbers x for which $f(x)$ is a real number.

---

1. If $f(x) = \dfrac{1}{2} + \dfrac{1}{2} \cos(2x)$, $0 \le x \le \pi$, then

    (A) find $\lim\limits_{x \to \frac{\pi}{4}} f(x)$

    (B) find the average value of f on $[0, \pi]$.

    (C) show that $|f(b) - f(a)| \le |b - a|$ for any $a < b$.

* The practice tests in this book incorporate Section II free-response solutions that approximate the content breakdown you will encounter on the AP exam. The overall timing and formatting of the practice tests in this book mirror the actual test; examinees should note, however, that this section is split into two parts on the AP exam. Furthermore, prospective examinees should pay attention to restrictions on calculator use. For details, consult current official College Board materials in print or on the Web.

2. Given $f(x) = 2x^2 - 2x + 5$ and $g(x) = x^2 + 2x + 4$

   (A) Find the values of x where $f(x) = g(x)$.

   (B) If $f'(a) = g'(a)$, find a.

   (C) Use the results from (A) to find $\int_a^b (g(x) - f(x))$, where a and b are where $f(x) = g(x)$.

3. Let f be an even function which has a derivative at every value of x in its domain. If $f(2) = 1$ and $f'(2) = 5$, then

   (A) Find $f'(-2)$ and $f'(0)$.

   (B) Let L_1 and L_2 be the tangents to the graph of f at $x = 2$ and $x = -2$, respectively. Find the coordinates of the point p at which L_1 and L_2 intersect.

4. The graphs of f, g, and h are as given below:

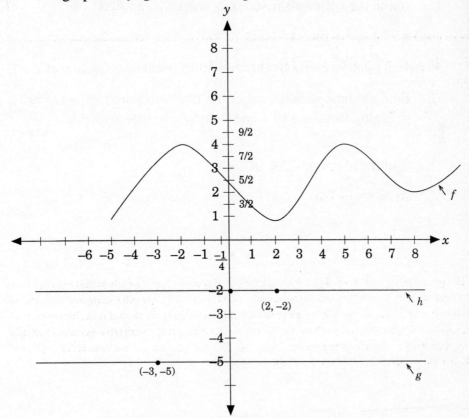

(A) Where is $(h - g)f$ concave upward and where is it concave downward?

(B) Sketch $(h - g)f$.

5. (A) At which point(s), if any, do $y = \sin x$ and $y = \cos x$ intersect in the interval $\left[0, \dfrac{\pi}{2}\right]$.

    (B) Find the area of the region between $y = \sin x$, and

    $$y = \cos x, \text{ from } x = 0 \text{ to } x = \frac{\pi}{2}.$$

    (C) Set up an integral for the volume obtained by rotating the region in (b) about the x-axis.

6. (A)

    Determine the constants a and b in order for the function

    $f(x) = x^3 + ax^2 + bx + c$

    to have a relative minimum at $x = 4$ and a point of inflection at $x = 1$.

    (B) Find a relative maximum of the function found in (A) after plugging in values of a and b, provided that $f(0) = 1$.

ADVANCED PLACEMENT CALCULUS AB EXAM IV

ANSWER KEY

Section I

1.	(C)	12.	(A)	23.	(B)	34.	(D)
2.	(C)	13.	(C)	24.	(B)	35.	(D)
3.	(C)	14.	(A)	25.	(D)	36.	(C)
4.	(A)	15.	(D)	26.	(C)	37.	(A)
5.	(D)	16.	(E)	27.	(D)	38.	(E)
6.	(E)	17.	(C)	28.	(B)	39.	(C)
7.	(A)	18.	(A)	29.	(C)	40.	(A)
8.	(C)	19.	(C)	30.	(B)	41.	(B)
9.	(B)	20.	(B)	31.	(B)	42.	(B)
10.	(D)	21.	(D)	32.	(A)	43.	(C)
11.	(E)	22.	(E)	33.	(B)	44.	(C)
						45.	(D)

Section II

See Detailed Explanations of Answers.

DETAILED EXPLANATIONS OF ANSWERS

SECTION I

1. **(C)**

$$x^2 - y = 0 \Leftrightarrow y = x^2$$

is represented by the parabola shown below, and no vertical line intersects the graph in more than one point, so $y = x^2$ is a function.

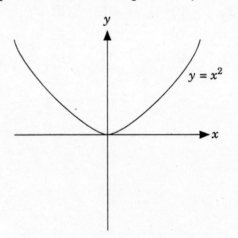

The graph of $y = y = \pm\sqrt{1 - x^2}$ is also the circle as shown above.

The graph of $y^2 = x$ is the one shown in choice (E).

In (A), (B), (D), and (E) there is a line parallel to the y-axis (a vertical line) that cuts the graph of the given relations more than once. Hence they do not represent functions.

The graph of $x^2 + y^2 = 1$ is the circle:

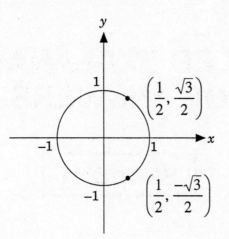

2. **(C)**

$$(g \circ f)(x) = g(f(x))$$
$$= g(x - 2)$$
$$= |x - 2|$$

Therefore,

(i) $(g \circ f)(3) + f(3) = |3 - 2| + (3 - 2)$
$$= 1 + 1$$
$$= 2$$
$$\neq 0.$$

(ii) $(g \circ f)(1) - f(1) = |1 - 2| - (1 - 2)$
$$= |-1| - (-1)$$
$$= 1 + 1$$
$$= 2$$
$$\neq 0$$

(iii) $\dfrac{(g \circ f)(0)}{f(0)} = \dfrac{|0-2|}{0-2}$

$$= \dfrac{|-2|}{-2}$$

$$= -\dfrac{2}{2}$$

$$= -1$$

$$\neq 1$$

(iv) $2(g \circ f)(x) = 2|x-2|$

$$f(x) = x-2$$

$$\Rightarrow 2(g \circ f)(x)$$

$$= f(x)$$

for $x = 2$, since both are zero at $x = 2$.

Hence, only (C) is true.

3. **(C)**

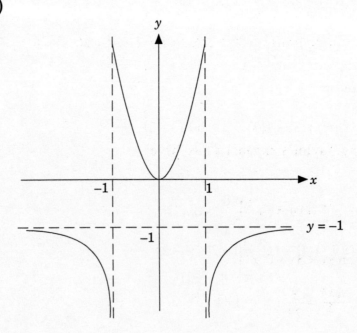

$$f(x) = \frac{x^2}{1-x^2} = -1 + \frac{1}{1-x^2}.$$

The graph of f shows that (D) and (E) are false and (C) is true. Also, since the graph is symmetric with respect to the y-axis, it shows that f is an even function, so (B) is false. Domain $f = R \setminus \{-1, 1\}$, so (A) is false.

4.   **(A)**

$f(x) = a \sin (bx + c)$

$\Rightarrow f'(x) = ab \cos (bx + c)$ by the chain rule, and

$f'(x) = 2a \cos (bx + c)$ from what is given,

$\Rightarrow b = 2.$

Hence, $f(x) = a \sin (2x + c)$ and the period $= \dfrac{2\pi}{2} = \pi.$

5.   **(D)**

From the graph,

$\lim\limits_{x \to 3} f(x) = -4$

Therefore, $\lim\limits_{x \to 3}\left([f(x)]^2 + 2f(x) + 1\right) = (-4)^2 + 2(-4) + 1$

$$= 9$$

6.   **(E)**

Using Taylor's expansion, we have:

$$e^{3x} \approx 1 + 3x + \frac{(3x)^2}{2!} + 0(x^3)$$

$$\tan 3x \approx 3x + 0(x^3)$$

$$\lim\limits_{x \to 0} \frac{y(x)}{x^2} = \frac{9}{2!}$$

$$= \frac{9}{2}.$$

Note: The sine or cosine of any angle is always between −1 and 1. Therefore, even though $\dfrac{1}{x}$ gets larger and larger as $x \to 0$ $\sin\left(\dfrac{1}{x}\right)$ and $\cos\left(\dfrac{1}{x}\right)$ are confined to lie between −1 and 1.

7. **(A)**

Let $f(x) = x^3 - x + 5$

It is possible to find two values of x at which f has different signs, say at $x = -2$ and $x = 0$:

$$f(-2) = (-2)^3 - (-2) + 5$$
$$= -8 + 2 + 5$$
$$= -1 < 0 \qquad \text{and}$$
$$f(0) = 5 > 0$$

Therefore, by the Intermediate Value Theorem, $x^3 - x + 5 = 0$ has a real root between $x = -2$ and $x = 0$.

All of the other choices have imaginary roots only, as they are of the form $= y^2 = -c, c > 0$

For example, in (D) $(x - 1)^2 + 3 = 0 \Rightarrow (x - 1)^2 = -3$

and only an imaginary number can have a square which is a negative number.

8. **(C)**

I.

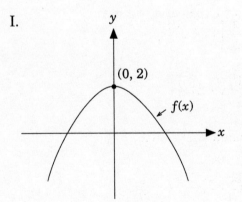

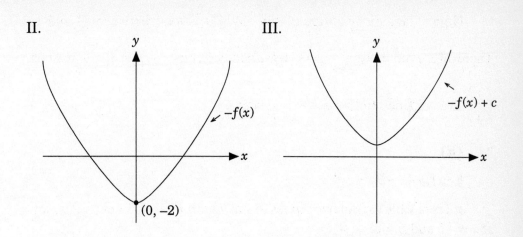

We see that in order for the graph of $f(x)$ to not intersect the x-axis, $-f(x) + c$ must lie completely above the axis. Since the lowest point on the graph $-f(x)$ is the point $(0, -2)$, this point must be raised (along with the rest of the graph) to above the x-axis. This can be accomplished by adding $c > 2$.

9. **(B)**

$g'(x) = 2\,(x - 2)\,f(x) + (x - 2)^2\,f'(x)$, by the product rule.

$\Rightarrow g'(2) = 2(0)\,f(2) + (2 - 2)^2\,f'(2)$

$= 0 + 0 = 0.$

10. **(D)**

$\displaystyle \lim_{h \to 0} \frac{f(2 + h) - f(2)}{h} = f'(2)$, by the definition of derivative.

But $\displaystyle f'(x) = \frac{d}{dx}\left((x + 2)^{\frac{1}{2}} \right)$

$\displaystyle = \frac{1}{2}(x + 2)^{-\frac{1}{2}},$

by the power rule and chain rule,

$\displaystyle \Rightarrow f'(2) = \frac{1}{2}(2 + 2)^{-\frac{1}{2}}$

$$= \frac{1}{2}(4)^{-\frac{1}{2}}$$

$$= \frac{1}{4}$$

11. **(E)**

$f'(x) = 4x - 3$

$g'(x) = 2x + 2$

Therefore, $f'(a) = g'(a)$

$$\Rightarrow 4a - 3 = 2a + 2$$

$$\Rightarrow 2a = 5$$

$$\Rightarrow a = \frac{5}{2}$$

12. **(A)**

$y = A \sin x + B \cos x$

$$\Rightarrow \frac{dy}{dx} = A \cos x - B \sin x$$

$$\Rightarrow \frac{d^2y}{dx^2} = \frac{d}{dx}(A \cos x - B \sin x)$$

$$= -A \sin x - B \cos x$$

$$= -(A \sin x + B \cos x)$$

$$= -y$$

Therefore, $y + \dfrac{d^2y}{dx^2} = y - y = 0$

13. **(C)**

$$f'(x) = \frac{dy}{dx}$$

$$= \left(\frac{3}{2}\right)\left(\frac{2}{3}\right)x^{\frac{3}{2}-1}$$

$$= x^{\frac{1}{2}}$$

by the power rule for differentiation.

$\Rightarrow f'(x_0)$ must equal the slope of the line $y = 2.5x$

$\Rightarrow f'(x_0) = 2.5$

$\Rightarrow x_0^{\frac{1}{2}} = 2.5$

$\Rightarrow x_0 = 6.25$

14. **(A)**

By implicit differentiation,

$$8x + 2x\frac{dy}{dx} + 2y - y^3 - 3xy^2\frac{dy}{dx} = 0$$

$$\Leftrightarrow (3xy^2 - 2x)\frac{dy}{dx} = 8x + 2y - y^3,$$

after moving the terms containing $\dfrac{dy}{dx}$ to one side,

$$\Rightarrow \frac{dy}{dx} = \frac{8x + 2y - y^3}{3xy^2 - 2x}.$$

Therefore, when $x = 1$ and $y = -1$,

$$\frac{dy}{dx} = \frac{8 - 2 - (-1)^3}{3 \times 1(-1)^2 - 2 \times 1}$$

$$= \frac{8 - 2 + 1}{1}$$

$$= 7.$$

15. **(D)**

	$x < 1$		$1 < x < 2$		$2 < x$
$(x - 1)$	Negative	**0**	Positive		Positive
$(x - 2)$	Negative		Negative	**0**	Positive
$(x - 1)(x - 2)$	Positive	**0**	Negative		Positive

$x = 1$ at the first divider, $x = 2$ at the second divider.

As the chart shows, when $1 < x < 2$, $(x - 1)(x - 2) < 0$

$\Rightarrow y = \sqrt{(x-1)(x-2)}$ is undefined. Otherwise, y is defined.

16. **(E)**

Since $f(1) = 0$ and $f(4) = 0$, by the mean value theorem (or by Rolle's theorem), there is an $x_0 \in (1, 4)$, such that

$$f'(x_0) = \frac{f(4) - f(1)}{4 - 1} = 0$$

17. **(C)**

$$\frac{dy}{dx} = 3\cos^2 x - 3\sin^2 x$$

$$= 3(\cos^2 x - \sin^2 x)$$

$$= 3\cos(2x),$$

since $\cos(2x) = \cos^2 x - \sin^2 x$

$\Rightarrow y = \int 3\cos(2x)\, dx$

By the method of substitution, if we let

$2x = u$

$\Rightarrow 2dx = du$

$\Rightarrow dx = \dfrac{du}{2}$

$\Rightarrow \int 3\cos(2x)\, dx = 3\int \cos u \left(\dfrac{du}{2} \right)$

$$= \dfrac{3}{2}\sin u + c, \quad \text{where} \quad u = 2x$$

$$= \dfrac{3}{2}\sin(2x) + c.$$

18. **(A)**

$\dfrac{x - \tan x}{x - \sin x}$ is an indeterminate form of the type $\dfrac{0}{0}$.

Also: $\dfrac{(x - \tan x)'}{(x - \sin x)'} = \dfrac{1 - \sec^2 x}{1 - \cos x}$ which is again of the $\dfrac{0}{0}$ type.

Therefore, $\dfrac{\left(1 - \sec^2 x\right)'}{(1 - \cos x)'} = -\dfrac{2(\sec x)(\sec x)(\tan x)}{\sin x}$, by chain rule

$$= -\dfrac{2\left(\dfrac{1}{\cos x}\right) \times \dfrac{1}{\cos x} \times \dfrac{\sin x}{\cos x}}{\sin x}$$

$$= -\dfrac{2}{\cos^3 x}.$$

Moreover, $\lim\limits_{x \to 0} -\dfrac{2}{\cos^3 x} = -2$, since $\lim\limits_{x \to 0} \cos x = 1$.

Hence, by L'Hôpital's rule

$$\lim_{x \to 0} \frac{x - \tan x}{x - \sin x} = \lim_{x \to 0} \frac{1 - \sec^2 x}{1 - \cos x}$$

$$= \lim_{x \to 0} -\frac{2}{\cos^3 x}$$

$$= -2$$

19. **(C)**

$$\lim_{n \to \infty} \frac{6n^2}{200 - 4n + kn^2} = \lim_{n \to \infty} \frac{\dfrac{6n^2}{n^2}}{\dfrac{200}{n^2} - \dfrac{4}{n} + k},$$

by dividing both the numerator and the denominator by n^2.

Therefore,

$$\lim_{n \to \infty} \frac{6n^2}{200 - 4n + kn^2} = \lim_{n \to \infty} \frac{6}{\dfrac{200}{n^2} - \dfrac{4}{n} + k}$$

$$= \frac{6}{k}, \quad \text{since} \quad \frac{200}{n^2} \to 0 \quad \text{and} \quad \frac{4}{n} \to 0.$$

From what is given, $\dfrac{6}{k} = \dfrac{1}{2}$

$$\Rightarrow k = 12$$

20. **(B)**

$$\lim_{n\to\infty}\left(1+\frac{1}{n}\right)^{kn} = \lim_{n\to\infty}\left[\left(1+\frac{1}{n}\right)^n\right]^k$$

$$= \left[\lim_{n\to\infty}\left(1+\frac{1}{n}\right)^n\right]^k, \text{ by property of limit of powers}$$

$$= e^k, \quad \text{since} \quad \lim_{n\to\infty}\left(1+\frac{1}{n}\right)^n = e.$$

But we are given that

$$\lim_{n\to\infty}\left(1+\frac{1}{n}\right)^{kn} = \frac{1}{e^2}$$

$$= e^{-2}$$

$$\Rightarrow e^k = e^{-2}$$

$$\Rightarrow k = -2$$

21. **(D)**

$$y = -\frac{1}{\sqrt{x^2+1}}$$

$$= -\left(x^2+1\right)^{-\frac{1}{2}}$$

$$\Rightarrow \frac{dy}{dx} = (-1)\left(-\frac{1}{2}\right)\left(x^2+1\right)^{-\frac{3}{2}}(2x), \text{ by the chain rule,}$$

$$= \frac{x}{\left(x^2+1\right)^{\frac{3}{2}}}$$

22. **(E)**

$$\frac{dy}{dx} = \frac{1}{(x+1)(x+2)}\left[\frac{d}{dx}((x+1)(x+2))\right],$$

by the chain rule

$$= \frac{1}{(x+1)(x+2)}((x+2)+(x+1)),$$

by the product rule

$$= \frac{1}{x+1} + \frac{1}{x+2}.$$

Alternatively, we can use the fact that $\ln(ab) = \ln(a) + \ln(b)$, so that

$y = \ln[(x+1)(x+2)]$

$\quad = \ln(x+1) + \ln(x+2)$

$\Rightarrow \dfrac{dy}{dx} = \dfrac{1}{x+1} + \dfrac{1}{x+2}.$

23. **(B)**

$$f'(x) = kae^{kx}$$

$$\Rightarrow \frac{f'(x)}{f(x)} = \frac{kae^{kx}}{ae^{kx}}$$

$$= k$$

$$\Rightarrow k = -\frac{5}{2}$$

24. **(B)**

$$\frac{\text{height}}{s} = \sin 60°$$

$$\Leftrightarrow \text{height} = s(\sin 60°)$$

$$= s\frac{\sqrt{3}}{3}$$

$$\Rightarrow \text{Area} = \frac{1}{2}h(S)$$

$$= \left(\frac{1}{2}\right)\frac{\sqrt{3}(s)(s)}{2}, \quad \text{substituting for } h$$

$$= \frac{\sqrt{3}s^2}{4}$$

$$\Rightarrow s\frac{dA}{ds} = \frac{\sqrt{3}S}{2}$$

Therefore, when $s = 2$, $\dfrac{dA}{ds} = \dfrac{2\sqrt{3}}{2}$

$$= \sqrt{3}$$

$$\approx 1.73$$

25. **(D)**

$$f(x) = e^{\frac{x^3}{3} - x}$$

$$\Rightarrow f'(x) = (x^2 - 1)e^{\frac{x^3}{3} - x}, \text{ by the chain rule.}$$

We see $f(x) = e^{\frac{x^3}{3} - x} > 0$ for every real number x, and

$$x^2 - 1 = (x + 1)(x - 1)$$

$$\Rightarrow x^2 - 1 < 0 \quad \text{when} \quad x \in (-1, 1) \quad \text{and}$$

$$x^2 - 1 > 0 \quad \text{when} \quad |x| > 1.$$

Hence,

$$f'(x) = (x^2 - 1) \, e^{\frac{x^3}{3} - x} < 0 \quad \text{for} \quad x \in (-1, 1) \quad \text{and}$$

$$f'(x) = (x^2 - 1) \, e^{\frac{x^3}{3} - x} > 0 \quad \text{for} \quad |x| > 1.$$

(D) is the answer.

26. **(C)**

Let $u = x^3 + 3x + 1$

Then $du = 3x^2 dx + 3dx = 3(x^2 + 1)dx$ so the integrand is:

$$\frac{x^2 + 1}{x^3 + 3x + 1} dx = \frac{1}{3} \times \frac{3(x^2 + 1)dx}{x^3 + 3x + 1} = \frac{1}{3} \times \frac{du}{u}$$

Also, if $x = 1$ then $u = (1)^3 + 3(1) + 1 = 5$,

and, if $x = 2$ then $u = (2)^3 + 3(2) + 1 = 15$.

$$\int_1^2 \frac{x^2 + 1}{x^3 + 3x + 1} dx = \int_5^{15} \frac{1}{3} \times \frac{du}{u}$$

$$= \frac{1}{3} \ln|u| \Big|_5^{15}$$

$$= \frac{1}{3} \ln 15 - \frac{1}{3} \ln 5$$

$$= \frac{1}{3} (\ln 15 - \ln 5)$$

$$= \frac{1}{3} \left(\ln \frac{15}{5} \right)$$

$$= \frac{1}{3} \ln 3 = 0.366$$

27.   **(D)**

The area of a region bounded above by the graph of a function and below by the x-axis is the integral of the function. Since the given region is bounded above by two functions, its area is the sum of the integrals of the two functions.

Let A_1 be the area of the region bounded by f, and let A_2 be the area of the region bounded by g:

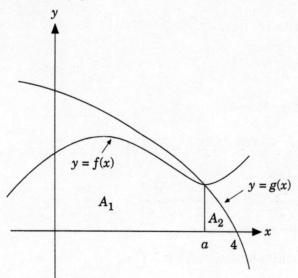

The total area is their sum:

$$A = A_1 + A_2$$

$$= \int_0^a f(x)dx + \int_a^4 g(x)dx$$

28. **(B)**

The Mean Value Theorem states that the equation

$$f'(c) = \frac{f(b) - f(a)}{b - a}$$

holds for some c between a and b. Here $a = 1$ and $b = 5$ are given and $f(x) = \sqrt{x - 1}$. The right-hand side of the equation is:

$$\frac{f(b) - f(a)}{b - a} = \frac{f(5) - f(1)}{5 - 1}$$

$$= \frac{\sqrt{5 - 1} - \sqrt{1 - 1}}{4}$$

$$= \frac{\sqrt{4} - \sqrt{0}}{4} = \frac{2 - 0}{4}$$

$$= \frac{1}{2}$$

This is the mean value of the derivative function f' over the interval $1 \le x \le 5$.

The derivative function is:

$$f'(x) = \frac{d}{dx} \sqrt{x - 1}$$

$$= \frac{1}{2\sqrt{x - 1}}$$

Hence f' attains its mean value at any c for which

$$\frac{1}{2\sqrt{c - 1}} = \frac{1}{2}$$

Solve this equation for c:

Cross multiply: $2 = 2\sqrt{c - 1}$

Divide by 2: $1 = \sqrt{c - 1}$

Square both sides: $1 = c - 1$

Add 1 to both sides: $c = 2$

29. **(C)**

$$f(x) = x - \frac{1}{x}$$

$$\Rightarrow f\left(\frac{1}{x}\right) = \frac{1}{x} - \frac{1}{\frac{1}{x}}$$

$$= \frac{1}{x} - x$$

$$= -\left(x - \frac{1}{x}\right) \qquad \text{factoring out } -1.$$

$$= -f(x), \qquad \text{so (A) is true.}$$

$$f\left(\frac{1}{x}\right) = -f(x) = -x + \frac{1}{x}$$

$$= -x - \frac{1}{-x} = f(-x), \qquad \text{so (B) is true.}$$

$$f(-x) = (-x) - \frac{1}{(-x)}$$

$$= -x + \frac{1}{x}$$

$$= -\left(x - \frac{1}{x}\right)$$

$$= -f(x), \qquad \text{so (C) is false.}$$

30. **(B)**

$x + y = 20$

$\Rightarrow y = 20 - x$

$\Rightarrow xy = x(20 - x)$

$= 20x - x^2$

Now let $f(x) = 20x - x^2$

$\Rightarrow f'(x) = 20 - 2x$

$\Rightarrow f'(x) = -2(x - 10)$

$f'(x) = 0 \Rightarrow 0 = -2(x - 10)$

$\Rightarrow x = 10$

We see that $f''(x) = -2 < 0$, so we have a maximum at the critical point $x = 10$. Since $x + y = 20$, we see $y = 10$.

31. **(B)**

$f(x) = 2\sqrt{x}$

$= 2x^{\frac{1}{2}}$

$\Rightarrow f'(x) = (2)\left(\frac{1}{2}\right)x^{\frac{1}{2} - 1}$

$= \frac{1}{\sqrt{x}}$

We are given that $f'(x_0) = 2f'(4)$

$\Rightarrow \dfrac{1}{\sqrt{x_0}} = 2\dfrac{1}{\sqrt{4}}$

$\Rightarrow \dfrac{1}{\sqrt{x_0}} = 1$

$\Rightarrow x_0 = 1$

32. **(A)**

Draw the graphs of $f(x)$ and $g(x)$

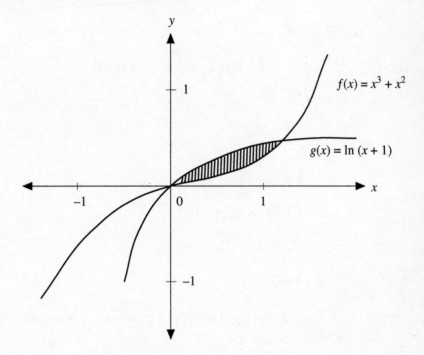

Reset viewing window to $[0, 1] \bullet [0, 1]$ and trace to the intersection point of $f(x)$ and $g(x)$, which should turn out to be $x = 0.5264$, $y = 0.4229$.

The area enclosed is the integral $\int_0^{0.5264} \ln (x + 1) - (x^3 + x^2)$, using your calculator, which can easily be computed. The number is 0.0513.

33. **(B)**

Draw the graphs of $y = \sin 3x \cos x$.

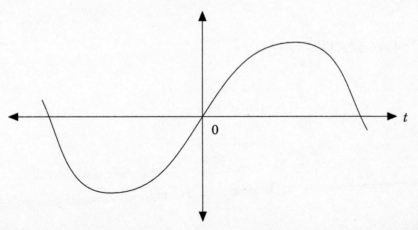

Tracing the first value of x when $y = 0$ gives the x-intercept 1.03.

Then the area is the integral

$$\int_0^{1.03} \sin 3x \cos x$$

or *fnInt* (sin 3x cos x, x, 0, 1.03) which equals 0.56.

34. **(D)**

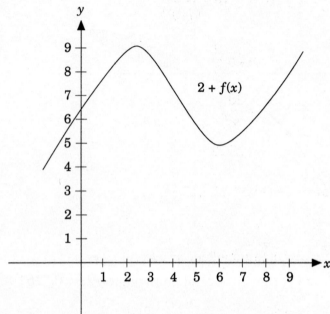

As you can see from the graph on the previous page, lifting the graph vertically upwards or downwards does not change the nature of the concavity of the inflection points.

35. **(D)**

$$f(x) = g(x) - \frac{1}{g(x)}$$

$$\Rightarrow f'(x) = \frac{d}{dx}(f(x)) = g'(x) - \frac{d}{dx}\left(\frac{1}{g(x)}\right)$$

$$= g'(x) - \left(\frac{0 \times g(x) - g'(x) \times 1}{[g(x)]^2}\right), \quad \text{by the quotient rule.}$$

$$= g'(x) - \left(-\frac{g'(x)}{[g(x)]^2} \right)$$

$$= g'(x) + \frac{g'(x)}{[g(x)]^2}$$

As a result, $f'(0) = g'(0) + \dfrac{g'(0)}{[g(0)]^2}$

$$= 2 + \frac{2}{9}$$

$$= \frac{20}{9}$$

$$\approx 2.222$$

Calculator: $20 \div 9 = \approx 2.222$

36. **(C)**

   Let $s(t)$ = distance travelled in time t.

   $\Rightarrow$ acceleration $= \dfrac{d^2 s}{dt^2} = (4t+1)^{\frac{1}{2}}$ and

$$v(t) = \frac{ds}{dt} = \int a(t)dt$$

$$= \int_0^t (4t+1)^{\frac{1}{2}} dt$$

$$= \frac{1}{4} \times \frac{2}{3} \times (4t+1)^{\frac{3}{2}} \Big|_0^t$$

$$v(t) - v(0) = \frac{1}{6}\left((4t+1)^{\frac{3}{2}} - 1 \right)$$

$$\Rightarrow v(t) = \frac{1}{6}\left((4t+1)^{\frac{3}{2}} - 1 \right) - \frac{13}{3}$$

or $v(t) = v(t) = \frac{1}{6}(4t+1)^{\frac{3}{2}} - \frac{9}{2}$.

Integrating this yields:

$$\Rightarrow s(t) = \frac{1}{60}(4t+1)^{\frac{5}{2}} - \frac{9}{2}t + C$$

$$\Rightarrow s(2) - s(0) = \left(\frac{1}{60}(9)^{\frac{5}{2}} - 9 + C\right) - \left(\frac{1}{60} + C\right)$$

$$= \frac{3^5}{60} - 9 - \frac{1}{60}$$

$$= \frac{243}{60} - 9 - \frac{1}{60}$$

$$= 4 + \frac{2}{60} - 9$$

$$= -\frac{149}{30}$$

37. **(A)**

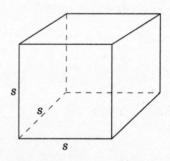

Let the edge of the cube at time t be $S(t)$.

$$\Rightarrow V = S^3$$

$$\Rightarrow \frac{dV}{dt} = 3[S]^2 \frac{dS}{dt}, \text{ by the chain rule.}$$

But we are given that $\frac{dV}{dt}$ 300 in³/ min.

So, $300 \text{ in}^3/\text{min.} = 3S^2 \dfrac{dS}{dt}$

$$\Rightarrow \dfrac{dS}{dt} = \dfrac{300}{3S^2} \text{ in}^3/\text{min.}$$

Therefore, when the edge is 20 inches long,

$$\dfrac{dS}{dt} = \dfrac{300 \text{ in}^3/\text{min.}}{(3)(20)(20) \text{ in}^2}$$

$$= \dfrac{1}{4} \text{ in/min.}$$

38. **(E)**

Using your calculator,

$$fnInt\left(\dfrac{6(x\wedge 3+1)}{x+1}, \ x, \ -1, \ 1 \right),$$

which gives 16.

39. **(C)**

$f(x) = x^3 - 2x$

$\Rightarrow f'(x) = 3x^2 - 2$

Therefore, $f'(x) = 0$

$$\Rightarrow 3x^2 - 2 = 0$$

$$\Rightarrow x = \pm\sqrt{\dfrac{2}{3}}$$

Also, $f''(x) = 6x$

$$\Rightarrow f''\left(\sqrt{\dfrac{2}{3}}\right) = 6\sqrt{\dfrac{2}{3}} > 0$$

and $f''\left(-\sqrt{\dfrac{2}{3}}\right)=-6\sqrt{\dfrac{2}{3}}<0$.

Hence, f has a relative Max. at $x=-\sqrt{\dfrac{2}{3}}$ and a relative Min. at $x=\sqrt{\dfrac{2}{3}}$ by the second derivative test.

40. **(A)**

You can directly solve this problem by using the calculator. For example,

$$\text{der }1\left(256x^{\wedge}(-0.5)+64x^{\wedge}0.5+3x^{\wedge}\left(\dfrac{2}{3}\right),\ x,\ 64\right)$$

should get 4.25.

41. **(B)**

Draw the graph of $y = x^2(1 - x^{-1})$.

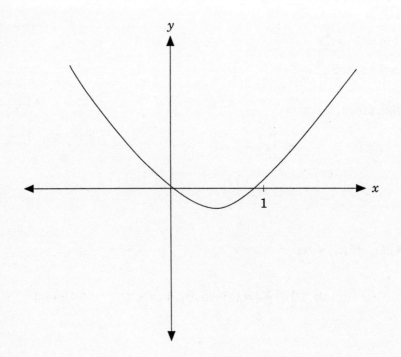

Set the viewing window to [0, 1] • [−1, 1]. By tracing y to the lowest value, you can get $y = -0.25$.

42. **(B)**

$$\int_a^b f(x)\, dx = \int_a^b f(x)\, dx + \int_b^c f(x)\, dx + \int_c^d f(x)\, dx.$$

Since $f(x)$ is non-negative in $[a, b]$ and $[c, d]$ the integral of $f(x)$ in $[a, b]$ and $[c, d]$ corresponds with the areas of regions A and C, respectively.

Since $f(x)$ is ≤ 0 in $[b, c]$, the integral is actually the negative of the area of region B.

Hence, $\int_a^d f(x)\, dx = 3 - \left(1\dfrac{1}{2}\right) + 2$

$$= 3\dfrac{1}{2}$$

$$= \dfrac{7}{2}$$

43. **(C)**

Use integration by parts:

Let $u = x$ and $dv = \cos(4x)\, dx$

$\Rightarrow du = dx$ and $v = \dfrac{1}{4}\sin(4x)$

$\Rightarrow \int x\cos(4x)\, dx = \dfrac{x}{4}\sin(4x) - \int \dfrac{1}{4}\sin(4x)\, dx$

$$= \dfrac{x}{4}\sin(4x) + \dfrac{1}{16}\cos(4x) + c.$$

44. **(C)**

First find the derivatives of the two functions and evaluate them at $t = 2$:

$t = 2$:

$$x = t^3 - 3t \quad \Rightarrow \quad \frac{dx}{dt} = 3t^2 - 3$$

$$\Rightarrow \left. \frac{dx}{dt} \right|_{t=2} = 3(2)^2 - 3 = 9$$

$$y = \left(t^2 + 1\right)^2 \quad \Rightarrow \quad \frac{dy}{dt} = 2\left(t^2 + 1\right) \cdot 2t$$

$$\Rightarrow \left. \frac{dy}{dt} \right|_{t=2} = 2\left((2)^2 + 1\right) \cdot 2(2) = 40$$

Then use the fact that

$$\frac{dy}{dx} = \frac{\left(\dfrac{dy}{dt}\right)}{\left(\dfrac{dx}{dt}\right)};$$

$$\left. \frac{dy}{dx} \right|_{t=2} = \frac{\left. \dfrac{dy}{dt} \right|_{t=2}}{\left. \dfrac{dx}{dt} \right|_{t=2}} = \frac{40}{9}$$

45.   **(D)**

The normal line is the line that is perpendicular to the curve at the given point. Its equation is $y = y_0 + m(x - x_0)$ where (x_0, y_0) is the given point and m is the slope. At the point where $x = 1$,

$$y = x^4 - 3x^2 + 1$$

$$= (1)^4 - 3(1)^2 + 1$$

$$= -1$$

Thus, $(x_0, y_0) = (1, -1)$. The slope m of the normal line is the negative reciprocal of the slope of the tangent line, which is the value of the derivative at the given point;

$$\text{i.e.,} \quad m = \frac{-1}{\left. \dfrac{dy}{dx} \right|_{x=1}}$$

Since $\dfrac{dy}{dx} = \dfrac{d}{dx}\left(x^4 - 3x^2 + 1\right)$

$$= 4x^3 - 6x,$$

$$m = \dfrac{-1}{\left(4x^3 - 6x\right)\big|_{x=1}}$$

$$= \dfrac{-1}{(4-6)}$$

$$= \dfrac{-1}{-2}$$

$$= \dfrac{1}{2}$$

Thus, the equation of the normal line is:

$$y = y_0 + m(x - x_0)$$

$$y = -1 + \frac{1}{2}(x-1)$$

$$2y = -2 + (x-1)$$

$$2y = x - 3$$

$$x - 2y - 3 = 0$$

$$\boxed{\textbf{SECTION II}}$$

1. (A)

$$\lim_{x\to\frac{\pi}{4}}\left(\frac{1}{2}+\frac{1}{2}\cos(2x)\right)=\lim_{x\to\frac{\pi}{4}}\frac{1}{2}+\lim_{x\to\frac{\pi}{4}}\frac{1}{2}\cos(2x),\text{ by addition rule.}$$

$$=\frac{1}{2}+\frac{1}{2}\lim_{x\to\frac{\pi}{4}}\cos(2x),$$

since $\lim_{x\to a}c\,f(x)=c\lim_{x\to a}f(x)$

$$=\frac{1}{2}+\frac{1}{2}\times\cos\left(2\times\frac{\pi}{4}\right),\text{ since }\cos x\text{ is a continuous function.}$$

$$=\frac{1}{2}+\frac{1}{2}\cos\frac{\pi}{2}$$

$$=\frac{1}{2}+\frac{1}{2}\times 0,\text{ since }\cos\frac{\pi}{2}=0,$$

$$=\frac{1}{2}$$

(B)

$$\text{Average value }=\frac{1}{\pi-0}\int_0^\pi\left(\frac{1}{2}+\frac{1}{2}\cos(2x)\right)dx$$

$$=\frac{1}{\pi}\left(\int_0^\pi\frac{1}{2}\,dx+\frac{1}{2}\int_0^\pi\cos(2x)\,dx\right)$$

$$=\frac{1}{\pi}\left(\frac{1}{2}\times\pi+\frac{1}{2}\times\frac{1}{2}\sin(2x)\Big|_0^\pi\right)$$

$$=\frac{1}{\pi}\left(\frac{\pi}{2}+\frac{1}{4}(\sin 2\pi-\sin 0)\right)$$

$$= \frac{1}{2},$$

since $\sin 2\pi = \sin 0 = 0$

(C)

First, $\quad f(b) = \dfrac{1}{2} + \dfrac{1}{2}\cos (2b)$

and $\quad f(a) = \dfrac{1}{2} + \dfrac{1}{2}\cos (2a).$

$$\Rightarrow f(b) - f(a) = \frac{1}{2}(\cos (2b) - \cos (2a)).$$

By the Mean Value Theorem,

$$f(b) - f(a) = (b - a) f'(c) \text{ for some } a < c < b.$$

But, $f'(c) = -\sin (2c),$

since $f'(x) = \dfrac{1}{2} \times 2(-\sin 2x)$, by the chain rule.

$$\Rightarrow | f(b) - f(a)| = |- \sin(2c)| \, | b - a|$$
$$\Rightarrow | f(b) - f(a)| \le | b - a|, \text{ since } |- \sin (2c)| \le 1.$$

2. (A)

Use a viewing window of $[-5, \ 5] \bullet [-5, \ 40]$ and draw the graphs of $f(x)$ and $g(x)$.

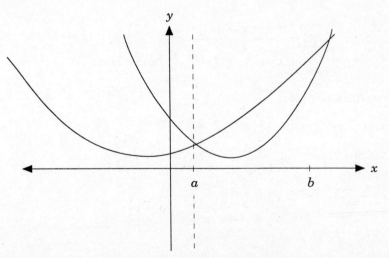

By tracing on the graphs to the integrational points, you can find points $a = 0.268...$ and $b = 3.732... \left(2 \pm \sqrt{3}\right)$

(B)

Draw the graphs of $f'(x)$ and $g'(x)$.

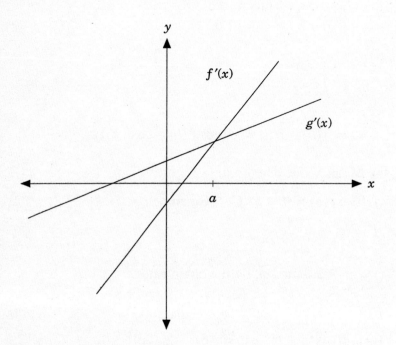

$f'(x) = 4x{-}2$

$g'(x) = 2x + 2$

if $f'(a) = g'(a)$ then $a = 2$.

(C)

Finding $\int_{0.268}^{0.3732} ((x^2 + 2x + 4){-}(2x^2 - 2x + 5))dx$

by using the calculator.

$fnInt\ (-x \wedge 2 + 4x - 1, x, 0.2, 4.81)$

results in 4.49.

3.   (A)

(i)

f is an even function

$\Rightarrow f(x) = f(-x)$ for every x

$\Rightarrow f'(x) = -f'(-x)$, by chain rule

Therefore, $f'(-x) = -f'(x)$

$\Rightarrow f'(2) = -f'(-2)$

$\Rightarrow f'(-2) = -f'(2)$

$\Rightarrow f'(-2) = -5$, since $f'(2) = 5$.

(ii)

$f'(x) = -f'(-x)$

$\Rightarrow f'(0) = -f'(-0)$

$\Rightarrow f'(0) = -f'(0)$

$\Rightarrow f'(0) + f'(0) = 0$, adding $f'(0)$ to both sides.

$\Rightarrow 2f'(0) = 0$

$\Rightarrow f'(0) = 0$, multiplying both sides by $\dfrac{1}{2}$.

(B)

Slope of $L_1 = f'(2) = 5$

Slope of $L_2 = f'(-2) = -5$

Moreover, L_1 passes through $(2, 1)$ and L_2 passes through $(-2, 1)$, since $f(2) = f(-2) = 1$, because f is an even function.

Therefore, the point slope form of the equation of

L_1 is $y - 1 = 5(x - 2)$ and that of

L_2 is $y - 1 = -5(x + 2)$.

$\Rightarrow y = 5(x - 2) + 1$

and $y = -5(x + 2) + 1$

Solving these two equations simultaneously, we have:

$5(x - 2) + 1 = -5(x + 2) + 1$

$\Rightarrow 5(x - 2) + 5(x + 2) = 0$

$\Rightarrow 10x = 0$

$\Rightarrow x = 0$

$\Rightarrow y = 5(x - 2) + 1$

$\quad = 5(0 - 2) + 1$

$\quad = 5(-2) + 1$

$\quad = -10 + 1$

$\Rightarrow y = -9$

So, $P = (0, -9)$

4. (A)

h is the constant function $h(x) = -2$.

By similar reasoning, $g(x) = -5$.

$\qquad \Rightarrow h(x) - g(x) = -2 - (-5) = 3$, a positive constant.

Therefore, $(h - g)f = 3f$.

Since $\dfrac{d}{dx}(3f) = 3f'$ and $\dfrac{d^2}{dx^2}f = 3f''$, then $3f$, like f, is concave upward in the intervals

$$\left(-\frac{1}{4}, \ 3\right) \cup (6, \ 9);$$

and $3f$ is concave downward in the intervals

$$\left(-5, \ -\frac{1}{4}\right) \cup (3, \ 6).$$

(B)

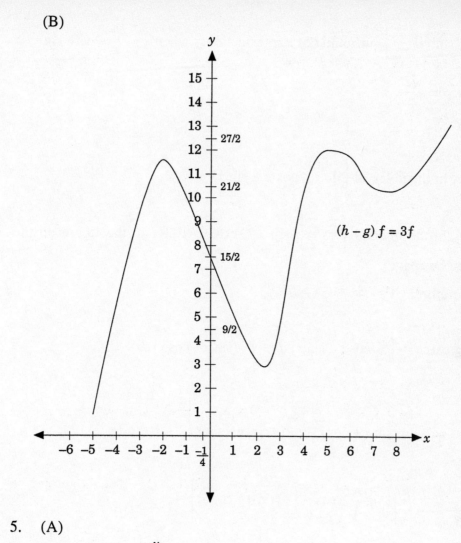

$(h - g) f = 3f$

5. (A)

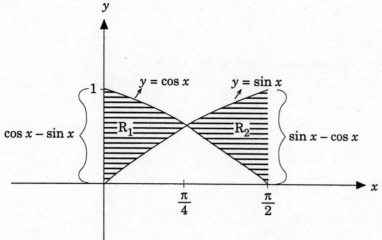

In $\left[0, \dfrac{\pi}{2}\right]$ sin x and cos x intersect only when $x = \dfrac{\pi}{4}$ where $\sin\dfrac{\pi}{4} =$

$\cos\dfrac{\pi}{4} = \dfrac{\sqrt{2}}{2}$.

(B)

In the inverval $\left[0, \dfrac{\pi}{4}\right]$, cos $x \geq$ sin x.

In the interval $\left[\dfrac{\pi}{4}, \dfrac{\pi}{2}\right]$, sin $x \geq$ cos x. (Refer to the figure on the previous page).

Therefore,

$$\text{Area} = \int_0^{\frac{\pi}{4}} (\cos x - \sin x)\, dx + \int_{\frac{\pi}{4}}^{\frac{\pi}{2}} (\sin x - \cos x)\, dx$$

$$= (\sin x + \cos x)\Big|_0^{\frac{\pi}{4}} + (-\cos x - \sin x)\Big|_{\frac{\pi}{4}}^{\frac{\pi}{2}}$$

$$= \left[\left(\sin\frac{\pi}{4} + \cos\frac{\pi}{4}\right) - (\sin 0 + \cos 0)\right] +$$

$$\left[\left(-\cos\frac{\pi}{2} - \sin\frac{\pi}{2}\right) - \left(-\cos\frac{\pi}{4} - \sin\frac{\pi}{4}\right)\right]$$

$$= \left[\frac{\sqrt{2}}{2} + \frac{\sqrt{2}}{2} - (1)\right] + \left[-1 - \left(-\frac{\sqrt{2}}{2} - \frac{\sqrt{2}}{2}\right)\right],$$

since $\quad \sin 0 = \cos\dfrac{\pi}{2} = 0.$

$$= \sqrt{2} - 1 - 1 + \sqrt{2}$$

$$= 2\sqrt{2} - 2$$

$$= 2\left(\sqrt{2} - 1\right)$$

(C)

To find volume, we note that in R_1 $\sin x \leq \cos x$ (Refer to figure above).

$$\Rightarrow dV = \pi(\cos^2 x - \sin^2 x)\, dx$$

In R_2 $\sin x \geq \cos x$

$$\Rightarrow dV = \pi(\sin^2 x - \cos^2 x)\, dx$$

Therefore,

$$\text{volume} = \int_0^{\frac{\pi}{4}} \pi\left(\cos^2 x - \sin^2 x\right) dx + \int_{\frac{\pi}{4}}^{\frac{\pi}{2}} \pi\left(\sin^2 x - \cos^2 x\right) dx$$

$$= 2\pi \int_0^{\frac{\pi}{4}} \cos 2x\, dx$$

$$= \pi$$

6. (A)

$$f'(x) = 3x^2 + 2ax + b.$$

Since f has a relative minimum at $x = 4$, then

$$f'(4) = 3(4)^2 + 2a\,(4) + b = 0$$

$$\Rightarrow 48 + 8a + b = 0 \qquad\qquad (1)$$

(must also check that $f''(4) > 0$, which it is)

Since f has an inflection point at $x = 1$

$$\Rightarrow f''(1) = 0 \quad \text{but} \quad f''(x) = 6x + 2a$$

$$f''(1) = 0 \Rightarrow 6 + 2a = 0$$

$$\Rightarrow a = -3 \qquad\qquad (2)$$

We substitute equation (2) into equation (1) to find b:

$$48 + 8(-3) + b = 0$$

$$24 + b = 0$$

$$b = -24.$$

(B)

When we plug $a = -3$ and $b = -24$ into

$$f(x) = x^3 + ax^2 + bx + c \quad \text{we get}$$

$$f(x) = x^3 + 3x^2 + 24x + c$$

But, $f(0) = 1$

$$\Rightarrow 1 = f(0) = 0^3 - 3(0)^2 - 24(0) + c = c$$

Hence, $f(x) = x^3 - 3x^2 - 24x + 1$

$$\Rightarrow f'(x) = 3x^2 - 6x - 24$$

So, $f'(x) = 0$

$$\Rightarrow 3x^2 - 6x - 24 = 0$$

$$\Rightarrow x^2 - 2x - 8 = 0 \quad \text{(multiplying both sides by } \frac{1}{3})$$

$$\Rightarrow (x - 4)(x + 2) = 0$$

$$\Rightarrow x = 4 \text{ or } x = -2$$

Moreover, $f''(x) = 6x - 6$

Plugging in the critical points $x = 4$, $x = -2$, we see that

$$\Rightarrow f''(4) = 18 > 0 \text{ and } f''(-2) = -18 < 0$$

Hence, f has a relative Max. at $x = -2$ and a relative Min. at $x = 4$.

So, the relative Maximum of f is

$$f(-2) = -8 - 12 + 48 + 1$$

$$= 29.$$

Advanced Placement Examination in Calculus AB

EXAM V

ADVANCED PLACEMENT CALCULUS AB EXAM V

SECTION I

PART A

Time: 55 minutes
28 questions

DIRECTIONS: Each of the following problems is followed by five choices. Solve each problem, select the best choice, and blacken the correct space on your answer sheet. Calculators may not be used for this section of the exam.

NOTE: Unless otherwise specified, the domain of function f is assumed to be the set of all real numbers x for which $f(x)$ is a real number.

1. If $3x^2 - x^2y^3 + 4y = 12$ determines a differentiable function such that $y = f(x)$, then $\dfrac{dy}{dx} =$

(A) $\dfrac{-3x + 2xy^3}{2}$

(B) $\dfrac{-6x + 2xy^3}{-3x^2y^2 + 4}$

(C) $\dfrac{-3x + 2xy^3 + 6}{2}$

(D) $\dfrac{-6x + 2xy^3 + 3x^2y^2}{4}$

(E) $\dfrac{-6x + 2xy^3}{3x^2y^2 + 4}$

2. $\int_1^4 \dfrac{5x^2 - x}{2\sqrt{x}}\, dx =$

(A) 29

(D) $\dfrac{311}{12}$

(B) $\dfrac{113}{6}$

(E) $\dfrac{100}{3}$

(C) $\dfrac{86}{3}$

3. The area in the first quadrant that is enclosed by the graphs of $x = y^3$ and $x = 4y$ is

(A) 4

(D) 1

(B) 8

(E) 0

(C) −4

4. For what value of c is $f(x) = \begin{cases} 3x^2 + 2, & x \geq -1 \\ -cx + 5, & x < -1 \end{cases}$ continuous?

(A) 3

(D) None

(B) −3

(E) 0

(C) 6

5. $\displaystyle \lim_{x \to \infty} \sqrt[3]{\dfrac{8 + x^2}{x(x+1)}} =$

(A) 0

(D) 1

(B) 2

(E) Does not exist

(C) $\sqrt[3]{9}$

6. If $y = \tan(\text{arcsec } x)$, then $\dfrac{dy}{dx} =$

   (A) $\sqrt{x^2 - 1}$

   (D) $\dfrac{x}{\sqrt{x^2 - 1}}$

   (B) $\dfrac{x}{\sqrt{1 + x^2}}$

   (E) $\dfrac{x}{\sqrt{1 - x^2}}$

   (C) $\dfrac{\sqrt{x^2 - 1}}{x}$

7. Let $f(x) = 2x^5 - x^3 + x^2 + 2$ and $g(x) = f^{-1}(x)$. If $f(1) = 4$ then $g'(4) =$

   (A) 9

   (D) $\dfrac{1}{2,002}$

   (B) $\dfrac{1}{9}$

   (E) $\dfrac{1}{2,376}$

   (C) $\dfrac{1}{4}$

8. $\lim\limits_{x \to 0^-} (1 - x)^{\frac{2}{x}} =$

   (A) e^{-2}

   (D) e^2

   (B) -2

   (E) Does not exist

   (C) 2

9. If $f(x) = |x|$ for all real numbers x, then $f'(x)$ is a real number for

   (A) $x < 0$ only

   (D) $x \neq 0$ only

   (B) $x > 0$ only

   (E) All real numbers x

   (C) $x = 0$ only

10. Note that $\sin\dfrac{\pi}{2} \neq \sin\left(\dfrac{\pi}{2}\right)^{\circ}$ since $\sin\dfrac{\pi}{2} = 1$ and $\sin\left(\dfrac{\pi}{2}\right)^{\circ} = \sin(1.578)^{\circ}$

$\cong 0.03$. Find $\dfrac{d}{dx}\sin(x^{\circ})$ when x° is measured in degrees, and x in radians.

(A) $\cos(x^{\circ})$

(D) $\dfrac{\pi}{180}\cos(x^{\circ})$

(B) $\dfrac{\pi}{2}\cos(x^{\circ})$

(E) $\dfrac{\pi}{180}\cos x$

(C) $\cos\left(\dfrac{\pi x}{180}\right)$

11. $\displaystyle\int \dfrac{\log\left(x^{3}\times10^{x}\right)}{x}\,dx =$

(<u>Note</u>: log stands for $\log_{10}$ and ln stands for $\log_{e}$)

(A) $\dfrac{3\ln 10}{2}(\log x)^{2} + x + C$

(B) $\dfrac{3}{2\ln 10}(\ln x)^{2} + x + C$

(C) $\dfrac{6\log x}{\ln 10} + x + C$

(D) $\dfrac{3(\log x)^{2}}{\ln 10} + x + C$

(E) $3\ln 10(\ln x^{2}) + x + C$

12. $f(x) = 2x^3 - 9x^2 + 12x - 3$ is decreasing for

(A) $x < 2$

(D) $1 < x$

(B) all values of x

(E) $1 < x < 2$

(C) $x < 1$ and $x > 2$

13. The equation of the horizontal asymptote of $f(x) = \dfrac{|x|}{|x+1|+x}$ is:

(A) $y = \dfrac{1}{2}$

(D) $y = -1$

(B) $y = 0$

(E) $x = 0$

(C) $y = 1$

14. Find the point on the parabola $y = x^2$ which is closest to the point $(6, 3)$.

(A) $(1\dfrac{1}{2}, 2\dfrac{1}{4})$

(D) $(3, 9)$

(B) $(2\dfrac{1}{2}, 6\dfrac{1}{4})$

(E) $(1\dfrac{3}{4}, 3\dfrac{1}{16})$

(C) $(2, 4)$

15. $\displaystyle\lim_{x \to -1} \dfrac{\sqrt{x^2 + 3} - 2}{x + 1} =$

(A) 0

(D) 2

(B) -2

(E) Does not exist

(C) $-\dfrac{1}{2}$

16. The area bounded by the parabola $y^2 = 2x - 2$ and the line $y = x - 5$
    is

(A) 22

(D) $\dfrac{52}{3}$

(B) 18

(E) $\dfrac{26}{3}$

(C) $\dfrac{14}{3}$

17. Population growth in a certain bacteria colony is best described by
    the equation $y = t^2 e^{3t^2 + \sqrt{t}}$, where t is in hours. The rate of growth of
    the colony at $t = 1$ is

(A) 464.084

(D) 300.290

(B) 245.692

(E) 545.982

(C) 409.486

18. $\displaystyle\int \dfrac{e^{2x}}{e^x - 3} \, dx =$

(A) $\left(e^x + 3\right) + 3\ln\left|e^x + 3\right| + C$

(B) $e^x - 3\ln\left|e^x - 3\right| + C$

(C) $\left(e^x - 3\right) + 3\ln\left|e^x - 3\right| + C$

(D) $\left(e^x - 3\right) - \dfrac{3}{\left(e^x - 3\right)^2} + C$

(E) $\left(e^x - 3\right) + \dfrac{3}{\left(e^x - 3\right)^2} + C$

19. If $xy - x = 2y - 5$, then which of the following must be true?

    I.   The relation is a function of x.

    II.   The domain is $\{x \mid x \ne 2\}$.

    III. The range is all reals.

(A) I only   (D) I and III only

(B) II only   (E) I, II, and III

(C) I and II only

20. If $h(x) = \sqrt{x^2 - 4}$, $x \le -2$, then $h^{-1}(x) =$

(A) $\sqrt{x^2 + 4}$ (D) $\sqrt{x + 4}$

(B) $-\sqrt{x^2 + 4}$ (E) $-\sqrt{x^2 - 4}$

(C) $-\sqrt{x + 4}$

21. Which of the following is the graph of $y = 1 + 2^{x+3}$?

(A)

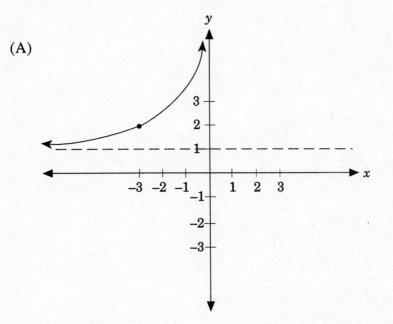

(B)

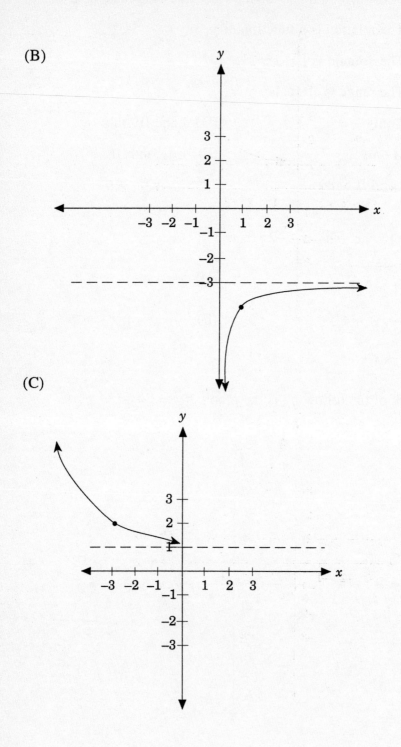

(C)

(D)

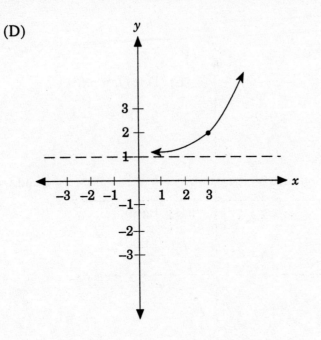

(E)

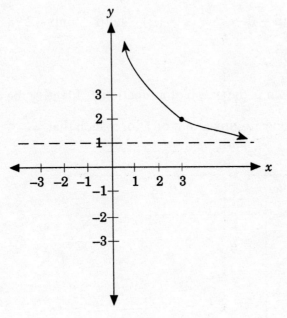

22. $\lim\limits_{x \to 0} \dfrac{\sin 2x}{x\cos x} =$

    (A) 0   (D) 2

    (B) 1   (E) Does not exist

    (C) $\dfrac{1}{2}$

23. Find the area bounded by the curve $xy = 4$, the x–axis, $x = e$ and $x = 2e$.

    (A) 4.000   (D) 1.386

    (B) 0.693   (E) 2.000

    (C) 2.773

24. $\dfrac{\cos 2\beta - \sin 2\beta}{\sin \beta \cos \beta} =$

    (A) $\cot\beta - \tan\beta - 2$ (D) $\tan\beta + \cot\beta - 2$

    (B) $\cot\beta + \tan\beta + 2$ (E) $-\cot\beta - \tan\beta - 2$

    (C) $\tan\beta - \cot\beta - 2$

25. The figure shown is the graph of a function f. Identify the equation which corresponds to this graph of f for x such that $-\dfrac{\pi}{3} \le x \le \dfrac{11\pi}{3}$.

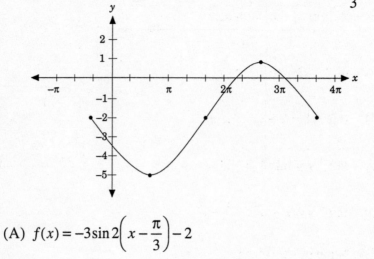

    (A) $f(x) = -3\sin 2\left(x - \dfrac{\pi}{3}\right) - 2$

(B) $f(x) = -3\sin\dfrac{1}{2}\left(x - \dfrac{\pi}{3}\right) + 2$

(C) $f(x) = 3\sin\dfrac{1}{2}\left(x + \dfrac{\pi}{3}\right) - 2$

(D) $f(x) = -3\sin\dfrac{1}{2}\left(x + \dfrac{\pi}{3}\right) - 2$

(E) $f(x) = 3\sin\dfrac{1}{2}\left(x - \dfrac{\pi}{3}\right) - 2$

26. Data suggests that between the hours of 1:00 P.M. and 3:00 P.M. on Sunday, the speed of traffic along a street is approximately $S(t) = 3t^2 + 10t$ miles per hour, where t is the number of hours past noon. Compute the average speed of the traffic between the hours of 1:00 P.M. and 3:00 P.M.

(A) 70   (D) 44

(B) 66   (E) 22

(C) 33

27. The solution of the equation $(x+1)\dfrac{dy}{dx} = x\left(y^2 + 1\right)$ is

(A) $\ln|y+1| = \tan^{-1} x + C$

(B) $\ln|y+1| = x - \tan^{-1} x + C$

(C) $\tan^{-1} y = \ln|x+1| + C$

(D) $\tan^{-1} y = x - \ln|x+1| + C$

(E) None of the above

28.   What are all the values of x for which the series

$$1+\frac{x^2}{2!}+\frac{x^4}{4!}\ldots+\frac{x^{2n}}{(2n)!}+\ldots \text{ converges?}$$

(A) $-1 \leq x \leq 1$ (D) $-1 < x < 1$

(B) $0 \leq x \leq 1$ (E) All values of x

(C) $0 < x < 2$

PART B

Time: 50 minutes
17 questions

DIRECTIONS: Calculators may be used for this section of the test. Each of the following problems is followed by five choices. Solve each problem, select the best choice, and blacken the correct space on your answer sheet.

NOTES:
1. Unless otherwise specified, answers can be given in unsimplified form.

2. The domain of function f is assumed to be the set of all real numbers x for which $f(x)$ is a real number.

29. If $y = \dfrac{2(x-1)^2}{x^2}$, then which of the following must be true?

I. The range is $\{y \mid y \geq 0\}$.

II. The y–intercept is 1.

III. The horizontal asymptote is $y = 2$.

(A) I only

(B) II only

(C) III only

(D) I and II only

(E) I and III only

30. If $g(x + 3) = x^2 + 2$, then $g(x)$ equals

(A) $\sqrt{x-3}$

(B) $(x-3)^2 + 2$

(C) $(x-3)^2 - 2$

(D) $\sqrt{x-3} + 2$

(E) $\sqrt{x-3} - 2$

31. The slope of the tangent line to the graph $y = \dfrac{x^2}{\sqrt[3]{3x^2 + 1}}$ at $x = 1$ is approximately

   (A) 0.945

   (B) 2.381

   (C) 1.890

   (D) 1.191

   (E) 1.575

32. If x and y are functions of t which satisfy the relation $x^4 + xy + y^4 = 1$, then $\dfrac{dy}{dt} =$

   (A) $\left(\dfrac{4x + y}{x + 4y^3} \right) \dfrac{dx}{dt}$

   (B) $-\left(\dfrac{4x^3 + y}{x + 4y^3} \right) \dfrac{dx}{dt}$

   (C) $-\left(\dfrac{x + 4y^3}{4x^3 + y} \right) \dfrac{dx}{dt}$

   (D) $-\left(\dfrac{4x^3 + y}{x + 4y} \right) \dfrac{dx}{dt}$

   (E) $\left(-\dfrac{4x^3 + y}{x + 4y^3} \right) \dfrac{dx}{dt}$

33. If $g(u) = \sqrt{u^3 + 2}$, $f(1) = 2$ and $f'(1) = -5$, then $\dfrac{d}{dx}\left(g(f(x)) \right)$ at $x = 1$ is approximately

   (A) 9.487

   (B) 18.974

   (C) −4.330

   (D) −9.487

   (E) 4.330

34. If $y = \dfrac{1}{\sin(t + \sqrt{t})}$, then $y'(1)$, in radians, is approximately

(A) –0.002

(D) 410.267

(B) –1,641.070

(E) –0.070

(C) 0.755

35. Find $\displaystyle\int \arctan x \, dx$ using integration by parts.

(A) $\arctan x + \ln(1 + x^2) + C$

(B) $x \arctan x + C$

(C) $\dfrac{1}{\left(1 + x^2\right)} + C$

(D) $x \arctan x - \dfrac{1}{2}\ln(1 + x^2) + C$

(E) $\ln(1 + x^2) + x \arctan x + C$

36. If $y = -\ln\left|\dfrac{1 + \sqrt{1 - x^2}}{x}\right|$ then $\dfrac{dy}{dx} =$

(A) $\dfrac{1}{x\sqrt{1 - x^2}}$

(D) $\dfrac{1}{\sqrt{1 - x^2}}$

(B) $\dfrac{1}{x} - \dfrac{1}{\sqrt{1 - x^2}}$

(E) $\dfrac{x}{\sqrt{1 - x^2}}$

(C) $\dfrac{x + 1}{x\sqrt{1 - x^2}}$

37. Let $F = \dfrac{6000k}{k\sin\theta + \cos\theta}$ where k is a constant. For which value of

 θ is $\dfrac{dF}{d\theta} = 0$ for $\dfrac{-\pi}{2} < \theta < \dfrac{\pi}{2}$?

 (A) $\theta = \arctan\dfrac{1}{k}$ (D) $\theta = \arctan k$

 (B) $\theta = 0$ (E) $\theta = \operatorname{arccot} k$

 (C) $\theta = \dfrac{\pi}{2}$

38. If $f(x) = \dfrac{1}{\sin(x + \sqrt{x})}$, calculate $\displaystyle\int_0^1 f(x)$.

 (A) 2.57   (D) 98.10

 (B) 10.26   (E) 1.65

 (C) −3.10

39. $f(x) = \left(x^2 - 3\right)^{\frac{2}{3}}$ is increasing for which values of x?

 (A) $-\sqrt{3} \le x \le \sqrt{3}$

 (B) $x \le -\sqrt{3}$ or $x > \sqrt{3}$

 (C) $-3 \le x \le 3$

 (D) $-\sqrt{3} < x < 0$ or $x > \sqrt{3}$

 (E) $f(x)$ is never increasing.

40. If $y = \tan(\arccos x)$ then $\dfrac{dy}{dx} =$

(A) $\dfrac{-1}{x^2\sqrt{1-x^2}}$

(D) $\dfrac{1}{x\sqrt{1-x^2}}$

(B) $\dfrac{1}{x^2\sqrt{1-x^2}}$

(E) $\dfrac{-1}{x^2\sqrt{x^2-1}}$

(C) $\dfrac{-1}{x\sqrt{1-x^2}}$

41. Which of the following statements is true?

(A) $\log_{\frac{1}{2}} 2 < \log_{\frac{1}{\sqrt{2}}} 2$

(B) $\log_3 (2 + 4) = \log_3 2 + \log_3 3$

(C) $\log_{10} 2 > \log_{10} 4$

(D) $\log_{\frac{1}{5}} (5\sqrt{5}) = \dfrac{2}{3}$

(E) $\log_{\frac{1}{2}} 2 - \log_{\frac{1}{2}} 4 = \log_{\frac{1}{2}} 2$

42. Let $f(x) = (x^2 - 3)^2$. The local minimum of $f'(x)$ is

(A) 7.99

(D) –7.99

(B) 5.80

(E) 6.28

(C) 3.25

43. $f(x) = \dfrac{x^2}{e^x}$.

$\displaystyle\int_0^5 \dfrac{x^2}{e^x}\, dx$ is

(A) 2.25   (D) 1.75

(B) 1.30   (E) 12.50

(C) 7.10

44. The equation of the line tangent to the curve $x(t) = t^2$, $y(t) = t^3 - 1$ at the point $(4, 7)$ is

(A) $x - 3y = -5$ (D) $4x + 7y = 12$

(B) $3x - y = 5$ (E) $x^2 + y^3 = 1$

(C) $4x - 7y = 0$

45. $\displaystyle\int \dfrac{1}{(x+3)(x+4)}\, dx =$

(A) $\ln\dfrac{|x+3|}{|x+4|} + C$

(B) $\ln\dfrac{|x+4|}{|x+3|} + C$

(C) $\ln\dfrac{|x-4|}{|x-3|} + C$

(D) $\left(\ln|x+3|\right)\left(\ln|x+4|\right) + C$

(E) $\ln|(x+3)(x+4)| + C$

SECTION II

Time: 1 hour and 30 minutes

6 problems*

DIRECTIONS: Show all your work. Grading is based on the methods used to solve the problems as well as the accuracy of your final answers. Please make sure all procedures are clearly shown. For some problems or parts of problems it will be necessary to use a calculator.

NOTES:

1. Unless otherwise specified, answers can be given in unsimplified form.

2. The domain of function f is assumed to be the set of all real numbers x for which $f(x)$ is a real number.

---

1. Let f be the function given by $f(x) = \dfrac{x^2 - 4}{1 - x^2}$.

    (A) Find the domain of f.

    (B) Find the range of f.

    (C) Find the equations for each vertical and each horizontal asymptote.

    (D) Find the critical points.

---

* The practice tests in this book incorporate Section II free-response solutions that approximate the content breakdown you will encounter on the AP exam. The overall timing and formatting of the practice tests in this book mirror the actual test; examinees should note, however, that this section is split into two parts on the AP exam. Furthermore, prospective examinees should pay attention to restrictions on calculator use. For details, consult current official College Board materials in print or on the Web.

2. At a child's party, there is a contest to see which child can run the fastest from a point 20 feet from a fence, to the fence, and then to a point 30 feet from the fence as in the figure shown. Find the point on the fence to where the children should run in order to minimize the distance by using the following:

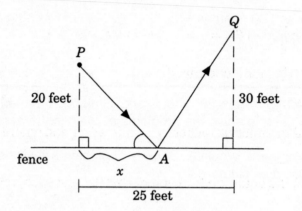

(A) Express $\overline{PA}$ and $\overline{QA}$ in terms of x.

(B) Find x.

3. The current I in a circuit is given by $I(t) = 20\sin(311t) + 40\cos(311t)$. Let $\cos\theta = \dfrac{1}{\sqrt{5}}$ and $\sin\theta = \dfrac{2}{\sqrt{5}}$.

(A) Verify, by use of the sum formula for the sine function, that $I(t) = 20\sqrt{5}\sin(311t + \theta)$.

(B) Determine the peak current (the maximum value of I) by the second derivative test.

4. Use the information below to answer the following questions about $y = f(x)$:

$$\lim_{x \to 2^-} f(x) = -\infty, \qquad \lim_{x \to 2^+} f(x) = \infty, \qquad \lim_{x \to -1^-} f(x) = \infty$$

$$\lim_{x \to -1^+} f(x) = -\infty, \qquad \lim_{x \to \infty} f(x) = 0, \qquad \lim_{x \to -\infty} f(x) = 0$$

Interval	$(-\infty, -4)$	$(-4, 0)$	$(0, \infty)$
sign of $f'(x)$	$-$	$+$	$-$

$f(-4) = -\dfrac{2}{3}, \quad f(0) = -6, \quad f(-2) = 0$

$f(2)$ and $f(-1)$ are undefined.

(A) Find the intervals where f is increasing and where f is decreasing.

(B) Find the equation for each horizontal and each vertical asymptote.

(C) Find the local maximum and minimum values of f.

(D) Sketch f. Label asymptotes, local extrema, and intercepts.

5. Let $f(x) = \dfrac{2}{3}x^{\frac{3}{2}}$ and suppose that the line $y = cx + d$ is tangent to $f(x)$ at x_0.

(A) If $x_0 = 2$, find c and d.

(B) If $c = 1$, find x_0 and d.

(C) Find $\displaystyle\int_0^3 \dfrac{2}{3}x^{\frac{3}{2}}dx$.

6. A projectile is fired directly upward from the ground with an initial velocity of 112 feet/second, and its distance above the ground after t seconds is $s(t) = 112t - 16t^2$ feet.

(A) What are the velocity and acceleration of the projectile at $t = 3$ seconds?

(B) At what time does the projectile reach its maximum height?

(C) What is the velocity at the moment of impact?

(D) The projectile travels (up and back) 392 feet. A bug traverses the

arc of the curve $y = \dfrac{\sqrt{\left(x^2 - 2\right)^3}}{3}$ from $x = 1$ foot to $x = 10$ feet.

Which distance is longer, the path of the projectile or the path traversed by the bug?

ADVANCED PLACEMENT CALCULUS AB EXAM V

ANSWER KEY

Section I

1.	(B)	12.	(E)	23.	(C)	34.	(C)
2.	(C)	13.	(A)	24.	(A)	35.	(D)
3.	(A)	14.	(C)	25.	(D)	36.	(A)
4.	(E)	15.	(C)	26.	(C)	37.	(D)
5.	(D)	16.	(B)	27.	(D)	38.	(E)
6.	(D)	17.	(A)	28.	(E)	39.	(D)
7.	(B)	18.	(C)	29.	(E)	40.	(A)
8.	(A)	19.	(C)	30.	(B)	41.	(B)
9.	(D)	20.	(B)	31.	(A)	42.	(A)
10.	(D)	21.	(A)	32.	(B)	43.	(D)
11.	(B)	22.	(D)	33.	(D)	44.	(B)
						45.	(A)

Section II

See Detailed Explanations of Answers.

DETAILED EXPLANATIONS OF ANSWERS

$$\boxed{\text{SECTION I}}$$

1. **(B)**

$$\frac{d}{dx}\left(3x^2 - x^2y^3 + 4y\right) = \frac{d}{dx}(12)$$

$$6x - 2xy^3 - x^2 3y^2 y' + 4y' = 0$$

$$6x - 2xy^3 + y'\left(-3x^2y^2 + 4\right) = 0$$

$$y'\left(-3x^2y^2 + 4\right) = -6x + 2xy^3$$

$$y' = \frac{-6x + 2xy^3}{-3x^2y^2 + 4}$$

$$\frac{dy}{dx} = \frac{-6x + 2xy^3}{-3x^2y^2 + 4}$$

2. **(C)**

$$\int_1^4 \frac{5x^2 - x}{2\sqrt{x}}\, dx = \int_1^4 \frac{5x^2 - x}{2x^{\frac{1}{2}}}\, dx$$

$$= \int_1^4 \left(\frac{5x^{\frac{3}{2}}}{2} - \frac{x^{\frac{1}{2}}}{2} \right) dx$$

$$= \left(x^{\frac{5}{2}} - \frac{1}{3}x^{\frac{3}{2}} \right) \Big|_1^4$$

$$= \left(2^5 - 1^5 \right) - \frac{1}{3}\left(2^3 - 1^3 \right)$$

$$= (31) - \frac{7}{3}$$

$$= \frac{86}{3}$$

3. **(A)**

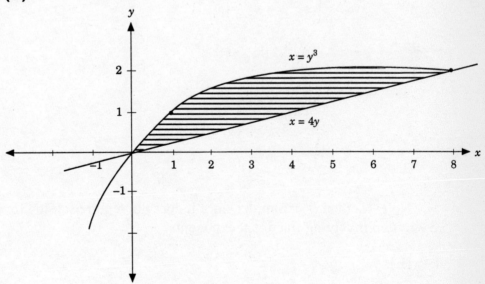

(i) $A = \int_0^2 \left(4y - y^3\right) dy$

$= \left(2y^2 - \dfrac{y^4}{4}\right)\Big|_0^2$

$= 2(2)^2 - \dfrac{1}{4}(2)^4$

$= 8 - 4$

$= 4$

or (ii) $A = \int_0^8 \left(\sqrt[3]{x} - \dfrac{x}{4}\right) dx$

$= \int_0^8 \left(x^{\frac{1}{3}} - \dfrac{1}{4}x\right) dx$

$= \left(\dfrac{3}{4} x^{\frac{4}{3}} - \dfrac{1}{8} x^2\right)\Big|_0^8$

$= \dfrac{3}{4}(8)^{\frac{4}{3}} - \dfrac{1}{8}(8)^2$

$= \dfrac{3}{4}(16) - 8$

$= 4$

Note: Method (i) is simpler since it does not require solving for y or integration involving fractional exponents.

4. **(E)**

$f(x)$ is continuous for $x > -1$ and $x < -1$ since polynomials are continuous for all reals.

For $x = -1$, $3x^2 + 2 = 5$.

For $c = 0$,

$$\lim_{x \to -1^-}(-cx + 5) = \lim_{x \to -1^-}(5) = 5$$

Therefore, if $c = 0$ then for all values of x_0 we have

$$\lim_{x \to x_0} f(x) = f(x_0)$$

The graph of $f(x)$ with $c = 0$ is sketched below:

$$f(x) = \begin{cases} 3x^2 + 2 & x \geq -1 \\ 5 & x < -1 \end{cases}$$

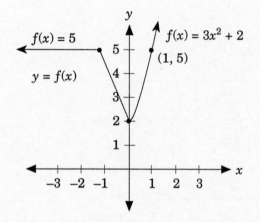

5.   **(D)**

$$\lim_{x \to \infty} \sqrt[3]{\frac{8 + x^2}{x(x + 1)}} = \lim_{x \to \infty} \sqrt[3]{\frac{8 + x^2}{x^2 + x}}$$

$$= \lim_{x \to \infty} \sqrt[3]{\frac{(8 + x^2)\dfrac{1}{x^2}}{(x^2 + x)\dfrac{1}{x^2}}}$$

$$= \lim_{x \to \infty} \sqrt[3]{\frac{\left(\dfrac{8}{x^2}\right) + 1}{1 + \dfrac{1}{x}}}$$

$$= 3\sqrt{\lim_{x\to\infty} \frac{\left(\dfrac{8}{x^2}\right)+1}{1+\dfrac{1}{x}}}$$

$$= 3\sqrt{\frac{\lim\left(\dfrac{8}{x^2}\right)+\lim(1)}{\lim(1)+\lim\left(\dfrac{1}{x}\right)}}$$

$$= 3\sqrt{\frac{0+1}{1+0}}$$

$$= 3\sqrt[3]{1}$$

$$= 1$$

Note: $\displaystyle \lim_{x\to\infty}\left[3\sqrt{\frac{\dfrac{8}{x^2}+1}{1+\dfrac{1}{x}}}\right] = 3\sqrt{\lim_{x\to\infty}\frac{\dfrac{8}{x^2}+1}{1+\dfrac{1}{x}}}$

because $f(x) = \sqrt[3]{x}$ is continuous for all reals and $\displaystyle\lim_{x\to\infty}\frac{\dfrac{8}{x^2}+1}{1+\dfrac{1}{x}}$ exists.

6. **(D)**

   Let $\theta = \text{arcsec } x$.

   By the identity $\tan^2\theta + 1 = \sec^2\theta$, we have

   $$\tan^2(\text{arc sec } x) + 1 = \sec^2(\text{arcsec } x)$$

   $$\Rightarrow y^2 + 1 = x^2$$

   $$\Rightarrow y = \pm\sqrt{x^2 - 1}$$

   Hence, $y = \pm\left(x^2 - 1\right)^{\frac{1}{2}}$

   therefore, $y' = \dfrac{\pm x}{\sqrt{x^2 - 1}}$.

7. **(B)**

Since $g(x) = f^{-1}(x)$ then $f(g(x)) = x$

Differentiating both sides with respect to x gives:

$$\frac{d}{dx} f(g(x)) = \frac{d}{dx}(x)$$

Using the chain rule, we obtain $f'(g(x)) \times g'(x) = 1$

Hence, $g'(x) = \dfrac{1}{f'(g(x))}$.

Since $f(1) = 4$ and $g(4) = 1$

therefore, $g'(4) = \dfrac{1}{f'(g(4))}$

$$= \frac{1}{f'(1)}$$

Since $f'(x) = 10x^4 - 3x^2 + 2x$

$$f'(1) = 10 - 3 + 2$$

$$= 9$$

therefore, $g'(4) = \dfrac{1}{9}$

8. **(A)**

$$\lim_{x \to 0^-} (1-x)^{\frac{2}{x}}$$

Let $\quad y = (1-x)^{\frac{2}{x}}$

$$\ln y = \ln(1-x)^{\frac{2}{x}}$$

$$= \frac{2}{x}\ln(1-x)$$

$$= \frac{2\ln(1-x)}{x}$$

By L'Hôpital's Rule, $\displaystyle\lim_{x\to 0^-} \ln y = \lim_{x\to 0^-} \frac{2\ln(1-x)}{x}$

$$= \lim_{x\to 0^-} \frac{2\left(\dfrac{1}{1-x}\right)(-1)}{1}$$

$$= \lim_{x\to 0^-} -\frac{2}{1-x}$$

$$= -2$$

Therefore, $\displaystyle\lim_{x\to 0^-} \ln y = -2$

$$\lim_{x\to 0^-} (1-x)^{\frac{2}{x}} = \lim_{x\to 0^-} y$$

$$= \lim_{x\to 0^-} e^{\ln y}$$

$$= e^{\lim_{x\to 0^-} \ln y}$$

$$= e^{-2}$$

9. **(D)**

We know that $f(x) = |x| = \begin{cases} x & \text{if} \quad x \geq 0 \\ -x & \text{if} \quad x < 0 \end{cases}$

Hence, $f'(x) = \begin{cases} 1 & \text{if} \quad x > 0 \\ -1 & \text{if} \quad x < 0 \end{cases} = \dfrac{x}{|x|}$, for $x \neq 0$

Therefore, $f'(x)$ is a real number for all $x \neq 0$.

10. **(D)**

Since (degrees) $= \left(\dfrac{\text{degrees}}{\text{radians}}\right)$ (radians), or $x° = \dfrac{360}{2\pi}x$, we have

$$\frac{d}{dx}\sin(x^\circ) = \frac{d}{dx}\sin\left(\frac{180}{\pi}x\right)$$

$$= \frac{180}{\pi}\cos\left(\frac{180}{\pi}x\right)$$

$$= \frac{180}{\pi}\cos(x^\circ)$$

11. **(B)**

$$\int \frac{\log\left(x^3 \times 10^x\right)}{x}\,dx = \int \frac{\log x^3 + \log 10^x}{x}\,dx$$

$$= \int \frac{3\log x + x}{x}\,dx$$

$$= \int \left(\frac{3\log x}{x} + 1\right)dx$$

$$= \int \left(1 + A\frac{\ln x}{x}\right)dx \quad \text{where} \quad A = \frac{3}{\ln 10}$$

$$= x + \frac{A}{2}(\ln x)^2 + C$$

$$= x + \frac{3}{2\ln 10}(\ln x)^2 + C$$

12. **(E)**

We see that

$$f'(x) = 6x^2 - 18x + 12 = 6(x-1)(x-2)$$

$f'(x) > 0$ for $x > 2$ or $x < 1$

$f'(x) < 0$ for $1 < x < 2$

13. **(A)**

$$\lim_{x \to +\infty} \frac{|x|}{|x+1|+x} = \lim_{x \to +\infty} \frac{x}{x+1+x}$$

$$= \lim_{x \to +\infty} \left(\frac{x}{2x+1} \right) \left(\frac{\frac{1}{x}}{\frac{1}{x}} \right)$$

$$= \lim_{x \to +\infty} \frac{1}{2 + \frac{1}{x}}$$

$$= \frac{1}{2}$$

$$\lim_{x \to -\infty} \frac{|x|}{|x+1|+x} = \lim_{x \to -\infty} \frac{-x}{-(x+1)+x}$$

$$= \lim_{x \to -\infty} \frac{-x}{-1}$$

$$= \lim_{x \to -\infty} x$$

$$= -\infty$$

Thus $y = \dfrac{1}{2}$ is a horizontal asymptote.

14. **(C)**

We want to minimize the distance $D = \sqrt{(x-6)^2 + (y-3)^2}$ from a point (x, y) to the point $(6, 3)$ subject to $y = x^2$.

We can do this more easily if we square both sides to remove the square root sign.

We have $D^2 = (x-6)^2 + (y-3)^2$

We can now replace y with x^2 since the point is on the parabola $y = x^2$.

We expand to get: $D^2 = (x-6)^2 + (x^2-3)^2$

$$= x^2 - 12x + 36 + x^4 - 6x^2 + 9$$

$$= x^4 - 5x^2 - 12x + 45.$$

We now take the derivative and set it equal to zero:

$$4x^3 - 10x - 12 = 0$$

Dividing by 2 gives $0 = 2x^3 - 5x - 6$

$$0 = (x-2)(2x^2 + 4x + 3)$$

The roots of $2x^2 + 4x + 3 = 0$ are

$$x = \frac{-4 \pm \sqrt{16-24}}{4},$$

which are not real numbers.

So $x = 2$ and $y = x^2 = 4$. The point on the parabola is then $(2, 4)$.

15. **(C)**

Apply L'Hôpital's rule.

$$\lim_{x \to -1} \frac{\sqrt{x^2+3}-2}{x+1} = \lim_{x \to -1} \frac{\frac{1}{2}(x^2+3)^{-\frac{1}{2}}(2x)}{1}$$

$$= \lim_{x \to -1} \frac{x}{\sqrt{x^2+3}}$$

$$= -\frac{1}{\sqrt{4}}$$

$$= -\frac{1}{2}$$

16. **(B)**

$$y^2 = 2x - 2 \qquad y = x - 5$$

To find the points of intersection, replace y with $x - 5$ in $y^2 = 2x - 2$

$$(x-5)^2 = 2x - 2$$

$$x^2 - 10x + 25 = 2x - 2$$

$$x^2 - 12x + 27 = 0$$

$$(x-9)(x-3) = 0$$

$$x = 9 \Rightarrow y = 9 - 5 = 4, \qquad (x,\ y) = (9,\ 4)$$

$$x = 3 \Rightarrow y = 3 - 5 = -2, \qquad (x,\ y) = (3,\ -2)$$

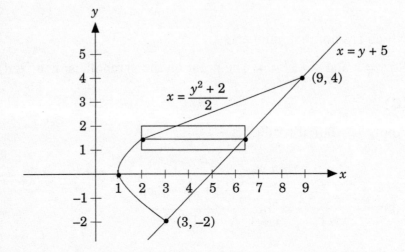

$$A = \int_{-2}^{4} \left[(y+5) - \left(\frac{y^2 + 2}{2} \right) \right] dy$$

$$= \frac{1}{2} \int_{-2}^{4} \left(2y + 10 - y^2 - 2 \right) dy$$

$$= \frac{1}{2} \int_{-2}^{4} \left(-y^2 + 2y + 8 \right) dy$$

$$= \frac{1}{2} \left[-\frac{y^3}{3} + y^2 + 8y \right] \Big|_{-2}^{4}$$

$$= \frac{1}{2} \left[-\frac{1}{3}(64+8) + (16-4) + 8(4+2) \right]$$

$$= \frac{1}{2} \left[-\frac{72}{3} + 12 + 48 \right]$$

$$= \frac{1}{2}[36]$$

$$= 18$$

17. **(A)**

$$y = t^2 e^{3t^2 + \sqrt{t}} = t^2 (e^{3t^2 + t^{\frac{1}{2}}})$$

$$y' = 2t(e^{3t^2 + t^{\frac{1}{2}}}) + (e^{3t^2 + t^{\frac{1}{2}}})(6t + \frac{1}{2}t^{-\frac{1}{2}})t^2$$

$$y'(1) = 2(1)(e^{3+1}) + e^{3+1}(6 + \frac{1}{2}(1)) \times 1$$

$$= 2e^4 + 6.5e^4$$

$$= 8.5e^4$$

$$\approx 464.084$$

18. **(C)**

$$\int \frac{e^{2x}}{e^x - 3} \, dx$$

Let $\quad u = e^x - 3 \Rightarrow u + 3 = e^x$

$\quad\quad du = e^x \, dx$

$$\int \frac{e^x(e^x dx)}{e^x-3} = \int \frac{(u+3)}{u}\,du$$

$$= \int \left(1+\frac{3}{u}\right)du$$

$$= u+3\ln|u|+C$$

$$= \left(e^x-3\right)+3\ln\left|e^x-3\right|+C$$

19. **(C)**

$$xy-x=2y-5$$

$$xy-2y=x-5$$

$$y(x-2)=x-5$$

$$y=\frac{x-5}{x-2}.$$

y is a function of x with domain $\{x \mid x \neq 2\}$.

To determine the range we solve for x

$$x=\frac{2y-5}{y-1}$$

$$=2-\frac{3}{y-1}$$

y can assume all values except $y = 1$.

Hence, only I and II are true.

20. **(B)**

$$y=h(x)=\sqrt{x^2-4}$$

Solving for x we get $x=\pm\sqrt{y^2+4}$.

Since $x \leq -2$ we take $x = h^{-1}(y) = -\sqrt{y^2 + 4}$.

Therefore, $h^{-1}(x) = -\sqrt{x^2 + 4}$

21. **(A)**

$$y = 1 + 2^{x+3}$$

$$y' = 2^{x+3} \ln 2$$

Since $y' > 0$, y is always increasing. Graphs (A), (B), and (D) are increasing. The ordered pair $(-3, 2)$ is a point on the graph, and (A) is the only one of these graphs which includes $(-3, 2)$.

22. **(D)**

$$\lim_{x \to 0} \frac{\sin 2x}{x \cos x} = \lim_{x \to 0} \frac{2 \sin x \cos x}{x \cos x}$$

$$= 2 \lim_{x \to 0} \frac{\sin x}{x}.$$

Apply L'Hôpital's rule:

$$= 2 \lim_{x \to 0} \frac{\cos x}{1}$$

$$= 2(1)$$

$$= 2$$

Note: $\lim_{x \to 0} \dfrac{\sin x}{x} = 1$ is also a well–known theorem.

23. **(C)**

We write $xy = 4$ as $y = \dfrac{4}{x}$. We want to find the area between $y = \dfrac{4}{x}$ and $y = 0$ (the x-axis), with $x = e$ and $x = 2e$ as the limits of integration.

Hence,

$$A = \int_e^{2e} \left(\frac{4}{x} - 0 \right) dx$$

$$= 4 \int_e^{2e} \frac{dx}{x}$$

$$= 4 \ln x \Big|_e^{2e}$$

$$= 4(\ln 2e - \ln e)$$

$$= 4 \ln \frac{2e}{e}$$

$$= 4 \ln 2$$

$$= 2.77259\ldots$$

24. **(A)**

$$\frac{\cos 2\beta - \sin 2\beta}{\sin \beta \cos \beta} = \frac{\left(\cos^2 \beta - \sin^2 \beta \right) - \left(2 \sin \beta \cos \beta \right)}{\sin \beta \cos \beta}$$

$$= \frac{\cos^2 \beta}{\sin \beta \cos \beta} - \frac{\sin^2 \beta}{\sin \beta \cos \beta} - \frac{2 \sin \beta \cos \beta}{\sin \beta \cos \beta}$$

$$= \frac{\cos \beta}{\sin \beta} - \frac{\sin \beta}{\cos \beta} - 2$$

$$= \cot \beta - \tan \beta - 2$$

25. **(D)**

The graph has the form $A + B \sin k \, (x - x_0)$.

The average value of y is -2, therefore, $A = -2$.

The lows are confined to $-5 \le y \le 1$, therefore, $|B| = 3$. However, the phase dictates that $B = -3$.

The period is $\dfrac{11\pi}{3} - \left(-\dfrac{\pi}{3}\right) = 4\pi$, therefore, $2\pi k = 4\pi$, or $k = \dfrac{1}{2}$.

Finally, $-\dfrac{\pi}{3} - x_0 = 0$, therefore, $x_0 = -\dfrac{\pi}{3}$ (using the left-most point).

$P = 4\pi$

26. **(C)**

$$\text{Average Speed} = \frac{1}{3-1} \int_1^3 \left(3t^2 + 10t\right) dt = \frac{1}{2}\left(t^3 + 5t^2\right)\Big|_1^3$$

$$= \frac{1}{2}(27 + 45 - 1 - 5) = \frac{1}{2}(66) = 33 \text{ mph}$$

27. **(D)**

Change the equation to differential form, then separate the variables and integrate.

$$(x+1)dy = x\left(y^2 + 1\right)dx$$

$$\int \frac{dy}{y^2 + 1} = \int \frac{x\,dx}{x+1}$$

Let $u = x + 1$, $du = dx$

Then $\displaystyle\int \frac{x\,dx}{x+1} = \int \frac{u-1}{u}\,du = \int \left(1 - \frac{1}{u}\right) du$

$$= u - \ln|u| + C'$$

$$= (x+1) - \ln|x+1| + C'$$

$$= x - \ln|x+1| + C$$

$$\Rightarrow \tan^{-1} y = x - \ln|x+1| + C$$

28.　　**(E)**

$$\frac{u_n + 1}{u_n} = \frac{x^{2n+2}}{(2n+2)!} \times \frac{(2n)!}{x^{2n}} = \frac{(2n)! x^2}{(2n+2)!}$$

$$= \frac{x^2}{(2n+1)(2n+2)}$$

$$\lim_{n \to \infty} \frac{x^2}{(2n+1)(2n+2)} = 0$$

Hence the series converges for all values of x.

29. **(E)**

$$y = \frac{2(x-1)^2}{x^2}$$

(i)　The function is positive and continuous for all values of $x \neq 0$.
Since $\lim_{x \to 0^+} f(x) \to +\infty$ and $f(1) = 0$, the range is $0 \leq y$.

(ii)　At $x = 0$, y is undefined, hence there is no y-intercept.

Note: $x = 1$ is an x-intercept.

(iii)　$\lim_{x \to \pm\infty} \dfrac{2(x-1)^2}{x^2} = \lim_{x \to \pm\infty} \dfrac{2 \times 2(x-1)}{2x}$, applying L'Hôpital's rule,

$$= 2 \lim_{x \to \pm\infty} \frac{1}{1}$$

$$= 2$$

Therefore, $y = 2$ is a horizontal asymptote. Only I and III are true.

30. **(B)**

   $g(u + 3) = u^2 + 2$

   Let $x = u + 3$, i.e., $u = x - 3$

   Therefore, $g(x) = (x - 3)^2 + 2$

31. **(A)**

$$y = \frac{x^2}{\sqrt[3]{3x^2 + 1}}$$

$$= \frac{x^2}{(3x^2 + 1)^{\frac{1}{3}}}$$

$$y' = \frac{2x(3x^2 + 1)^{\frac{1}{3}} - \frac{1}{3}(3x^2 + 1)^{-\frac{2}{3}}(6x)x^2}{(3x^2 + 1)^{\frac{2}{3}}}$$

$$= \frac{2x(3x^2 + 1)^{\frac{1}{3}} - (3x^2 + 1)^{-\frac{2}{3}}2x^3}{(3x^2 + 1)^{\frac{2}{3}}}$$

$$y'(1) = \frac{2(3 + 1)^{\frac{1}{3}} - (3 + 1)^{-\frac{2}{3}}(2)}{(3 + 1)^{\frac{2}{3}}}$$

$$= \frac{2(4)^{\frac{1}{3}} - 2(4)^{-\frac{2}{3}}}{4^{\frac{2}{3}}} \times \frac{4^{\frac{2}{3}}}{4^{\frac{2}{3}}}$$

$$= \frac{2(4) - 2}{(4)^{\frac{4}{3}}}$$

$$= \frac{6}{4(4)^{\frac{1}{3}}}$$

$$= \frac{3}{2\sqrt[3]{4}} \times \frac{\sqrt[3]{2}}{\sqrt[3]{2}}$$

$$= \frac{3\sqrt[3]{2}}{2\sqrt[3]{8}}$$

$$= \frac{3\sqrt[3]{2}}{4}$$

Therefore, the slope of the tangent line at $x = 1$ is $\dfrac{3\sqrt[3]{2}}{4}$.

Calculator: $2\sqrt[3]{x} \times .75 \approx 0.945$

32. **(B)**

$x^4 + xy + y^4 = 1.$

Differentiate both sides with respect to t.

$$\frac{d}{dt}\left(x^4 + xy + y^4\right) = \frac{d}{dt}(1)$$

$$4x^3\frac{dx}{dt} + \frac{dx}{dt} \times y + \frac{dy}{dt} \times x + 4y^3\frac{dy}{dt} = 0$$

$$\frac{dy}{dt}\left(x + 4y^3\right) = -(4x^3 + y)\frac{dx}{dt}$$

$$\frac{dy}{dt} = -\left(\frac{4x^3 + y}{x + 4y^3}\right)\frac{dx}{dt}.$$

33. **(D)**

$g(u) = \sqrt{u^3 + 2}$,

$g'(u) = \dfrac{1}{2}\left(u^3 + 2\right)^{-\frac{1}{2}} 3u^2$

$\dfrac{d}{dx}\left(g(f(x))\right) = g'(f(x))f'(x)$

At $x = 1$ $\quad = g'(f(1))f'(1)$

$\qquad = g'(2)(-5)$

$\qquad = \dfrac{1}{2}(2^3 + 2)^{-\frac{1}{2}} 3(2^2)(-5)$

$\qquad = \dfrac{1}{2\sqrt{10}}\, 12\,(-5)$

$\qquad = -\dfrac{30}{\sqrt{10}} \times \dfrac{\sqrt{10}}{\sqrt{10}}$

$\qquad = -\dfrac{30\sqrt{10}}{10}$

$\qquad = -3\sqrt{10}$

$\qquad \approx -9.487$

Calculator: $+/- \; 3x \; 10\sqrt{x} \approx -9.487$

34. **(C)**

$y = \dfrac{1}{\sin(t + \sqrt{t})}$

$\quad = \left(\sin\left(t + t^{\frac{1}{2}}\right)\right)^{-1}$

$$y' = -1\left(\sin\left(t+t^{\frac{1}{2}}\right)\right)^{-2} \cos\left(t+t^{\frac{1}{2}}\right)\left(1+\frac{1}{2}t^{-\frac{1}{2}}\right)$$

Therefore, $y'(1) = -1(\sin 2)^{-2}\cos 2\left(1+\frac{1}{2}\right)$

$$= -\frac{3}{2}\frac{\cos 2}{\sin^2 2} \approx 0.755$$

Calculator: 2 cos + (2 sin x^2) = x +/− 1.5 ≈ .755

35. **(D)**

Let $u = \arctan x$, $dv = dx$. Then $du = \dfrac{1}{1+x^2}\,dx$ and $v = x$, so integra-

tion by parts gives:

$$\int \arctan x\,dx = x\arctan x - \int \frac{x}{1+x^2}\,dx$$

Now let $z = 1 + x^2$, $dz = 2x\,dx$.

Then $\displaystyle\int \frac{x}{1+x^2}\,dx = \frac{1}{2}\int \frac{dz}{z}$

$$= \frac{1}{2}\ln z + C$$

$$= \frac{1}{2}\ln\left(1+x^2\right) + C.$$

So, $\displaystyle\int \arctan x\,dx = x\arctan x - \frac{1}{2}\ln\left(1+x^2\right) + C.$

36. **(A)**

$$y = -\ln\left|\frac{1+\sqrt{1-x^2}}{x}\right| = \ln\left|\frac{x}{1+\sqrt{1-x^2}}\right|$$

$$= \ln|x-1|\ln|1+\sqrt{1-x^2}|$$

$$\frac{dy}{dx} = \frac{1}{x} - \frac{1}{1+\sqrt{1-x^2}} \frac{1}{2} \left(1-x^2\right)^{-\frac{1}{2}} (-2x)$$

$$= \frac{1}{x} + \frac{1}{\left(1+\sqrt{1-x^2}\right)} \frac{x}{\left(\sqrt{1-x^2}\right)}$$

$$= \frac{\left(1+\sqrt{1-x^2}\right)\sqrt{1-x^2} + x^2}{x\left(1+\sqrt{1-x^2}\right)\left(\sqrt{1-x^2}\right)}$$

$$= \frac{\sqrt{1-x^2} + \left(1-x^2\right) + x^2}{x\left(1+\sqrt{1-x^2}\right)\left(\sqrt{1-x^2}\right)}$$

$$= \frac{1+\sqrt{1-x^2}}{x\left(1+\sqrt{1-x^2}\right)\left(\sqrt{1-x^2}\right)}$$

$$= \frac{1}{x\sqrt{1-x^2}}$$

37. **(D)**

$$F = \frac{6,000k}{k\sin\theta + \cos\theta}$$

$$= 6,000k(k\sin\theta + \cos\theta)^{-1}$$

$$\frac{dF}{d\theta} = -6,000k(k\sin\theta + \cos\theta)^{-2}(k\cos\theta - \sin\theta)$$

$$= -\frac{6,000k(k\cos\theta - \sin\theta)}{(k\sin\theta + \cos\theta)^2}$$

$$\frac{dF}{d\theta} = 0 \Rightarrow k\cos\theta - \sin\theta = 0 \Rightarrow k = \tan\theta$$

Hence, $\theta = \arctan k$.

38. **(E)**

This problem can be solved directly by using your calculator. For example,

$$fnInt\left(\frac{1}{\sin(x+\sqrt{x})}, \ x, \ 0, \ 1\right)$$

gives 1.65.

39. **(D)**

$$f(x)=\left(x^2-3\right)^{\frac{2}{3}}$$

$$f'(x)=\frac{2}{3}\left(x^2-3\right)^{-\frac{1}{3}}2x$$

$$=\frac{4x}{3}\left(x^2-3\right)^{-\frac{1}{3}}$$

$f'(x) > 0$ for

    (i) $x>0$ and $x^2-3>0$ or

    (ii) $x<0$ and $x^2-3<0$

(i) $\{x>0\}$ and $\{x^2-3>0\} \Rightarrow$

     $\{x>0\}$ and $\{x<-\sqrt{3}\}$ or $\{x>\sqrt{3}\}$ so $\{x>\sqrt{3}\}$

(ii) $\{x<0\}$ and $\{x^2-3<0\} \Rightarrow$

         $\{x<0\}$ and $\{x^2<3\}$

     $\{x>0\}$ and $\{-\sqrt{3}<x<\sqrt{3}\} \Rightarrow$

         $\{-\sqrt{3}<x<0\}$

Thus $f(x)=\left(x^2-3\right)^{\frac{2}{3}}$ is increasing for x such that

$-\sqrt{3}<x<0$ or $x>\sqrt{3}$

40. **(A)**

$y = \tan u$ with $u = \cos^{-1} x$

therefore, $\dfrac{dy}{dx} = \dfrac{dy}{du}\dfrac{du}{dx}$

$$= (\sec^2 u)\left(\dfrac{-1}{\sqrt{1-x^2}}\right)$$

$$= \dfrac{1}{\cos^2 u}\dfrac{-1}{\sqrt{1-x^2}}$$

$$= \dfrac{-1}{x^2\sqrt{1-x^2}}$$

41. **(B)**

(A) $\log_{\frac{1}{2}} 2 = -1$

$\log_{\frac{1}{\sqrt{2}}} 2 = -2$

(B) $\log_3(2+4) = \log_3 6$

$$= \log_3(2 \times 3)$$

$$= \log_3 2 + \log_3 3$$

True

(C) $\log_{10} 4 = \log_{10} 2^2$

$$= 2\log_{10} 2$$

(D) $\log_{\frac{1}{5}}\left(5\sqrt{5}\right) = \log_{\frac{1}{5}}\left(5^{\frac{3}{2}}\right)$

$$= \log_{\frac{1}{5}}\left[\left(\frac{1}{5}\right)^{-\frac{3}{2}}\right]$$

$$= -\frac{3}{2}$$

(E) $\log_{\frac{1}{2}} 2 - \log_{\frac{1}{2}} 4 = \log_{\frac{1}{2}}\left(\frac{2}{4}\right)$

$$= \log_{\frac{1}{2}}\left(\frac{1}{2}\right) = 1$$

But $\log_{\frac{1}{2}} 2 = -1$

42. **(A)**

$$f(x) = (x^2 - 3)^2$$

$$y = f'(x) = 4x^3 - 12x$$

$$y' = 12(x^2 - 1)$$

$$y'' = 24x$$

$y' = 0$ at $x = 1$. Using y'', we see that the Max. is at $x = -1$.

Therefore, $f'(-1) = 8$ is the Max.

43. **(D)**

You can solve this problem by using your calculator. For example,

$$fnInt\left(\frac{x^2}{e^x}, \ x, \ 0, \ 5\right)$$

which would give 1.75.

44.   **(B)**

Since the curve passes through (4, 7) only when $t = 2$, there is only one tangent line at (4, 7).

$x(t) = t^2$ $y(t) = t^3 - 1$

$x'(t) = 2t$ $y'(t) = 3t^2$

$x'(2) = 4$ $y'(2) = 12$

The slope of the tangent line is

$$m = \frac{y'(2)}{x'(2)} = \frac{12}{4} \Rightarrow \frac{y-7}{x-4} = \frac{12}{4}, \text{ so}$$

$$y - 7 = 3x - 12 \Rightarrow 3x - y = 5.$$

Another way to solve this is to see that

$$y = t^3 - 1 = \left(t^2\right)^{\frac{3}{2}} - 1 = x^{\frac{3}{2}} - 1, \text{ so } y' = \frac{3}{2}x^{\frac{1}{2}}$$

and at the point (4, 7), we have $y' = \frac{3}{2}(4)^{\frac{1}{2}} = 3$, so

$$y - 7 = 3(x - 4) \Rightarrow y = 3x - 5, \text{ or}$$

$$3x - y = 5.$$

45. **(A)**

Use partial fractions:

Let $\dfrac{1}{(x+3)(x+4)} = \dfrac{A}{(x+3)} + \dfrac{B}{(x+4)}$

$1 = A(x+4) + B(x+3)$

$1 = (A+B)x + (4A+3B)$

$0 = A + B$

$1 = 4A + 3B$

$\Rightarrow A = 1 \quad \text{and} \quad B = -1$

SECTION II

1. (A)

Domain $(f) = \{x \mid x \neq \pm 1\}$ because $f(x)$ is undefined when the denominator $1 - x^2 = 0$

$$\Rightarrow x^2 = 0$$

$$\Rightarrow x = \pm 1.$$

(B)

Range $(f) = $ Domain (f^{-1}). To find $f^{-1}(x)$, interchange x and y, then solve for y. We have:

$$x = \frac{y^2 - 4}{1 - y^2}$$

$$x\left(1 - y^2\right) = y^2 - 4$$

$$x - xy^2 = y^2 - 4$$

$$x + 4 = y^2 + xy^2$$

$$= y^2(1 + x)$$

$$\frac{x + 4}{1 + x} = y^2$$

$$\pm\sqrt{\frac{x + 4}{x + 1}} = y$$

$$= f^{-1}(x).$$

Domain $f^{-1} = \{x \mid x \in (-\infty, -4] \cup (-1, +\infty)\}$, so that range $f = \{y \mid y \in (-\infty, -4] \cup (-1, +\infty)\}$.

(C)

We have vertical asymptotes where $f(x)$ is undefined, at $x = 1$ and $x = -1$.

We have horizontal asymptotes at $y = \lim\limits_{x \to \pm\infty} f(x)$

We see $\lim\limits_{x \to \pm\infty} f(x) = \lim\limits_{x \to \pm\infty} \dfrac{x^2 - 4}{1 - x^2}$

$$= \lim_{x \to \pm\infty} \frac{1 - \dfrac{4}{x^2}}{\left(\dfrac{1}{x^2}\right) - 1}$$

$$= -\frac{1}{1}$$

$$= -1,$$

so $y = -1$ is the only horizontal asymptote.

(D)

The critical points occur where $f'(x) = 0$.

$$f'(x) = \frac{\left(1 - x^2\right)(2x) - \left(x^2 - 4\right)(-2x)}{\left(1 - x^2\right)^2}$$

The numerator must be zero, so we have

$$2x - 2x^3 + 2x^3 - 8x = 0$$

$$-6x = 0$$

$$x = 0$$

is the only critical point.

Note: $f'(x) = 0$ is undefined at $x = \pm 1$, but $x = \pm 1$ is not in the domain of f.

2. (A)

$\overline{PA}^2 = 20^2 + x^2$ by the Pythagorean theorem.

$\overline{PA} = \sqrt{400 + x^2}$

Similarly, $\overline{QA} = \sqrt{30^2 + (25-x)^2}$

$$= \sqrt{900 + 625 - 50x + x^2}$$

$$= \sqrt{1,525 - 50x + x^2}$$

(B)

We want to find x which minimizes $\overline{PA} + \overline{QA}$.

Let $f(x) = \overline{PA} + \overline{QA}$

$$= \sqrt{400 + x^2} + \sqrt{1,525 - 50x + x^2}$$

Then $f'(x) = \dfrac{1}{2}(400 + x^2)^{-\frac{1}{2}} 2x + \dfrac{1}{2}(1,525 - 50x + x^2)^{-\frac{1}{2}}(-50 + 2x)$

$$= \frac{x}{\sqrt{400 + x^2}} + \frac{x - 25}{\sqrt{1,525 - 50x + x^2}}$$

$$= \frac{x}{\sqrt{400 + x^2}} + \frac{x - 25}{\sqrt{900 + (25 - x)^2}}$$

To minimize, we set $f'(x) = 0$ and solve for x.

$$0 = \frac{x}{\sqrt{400 + x^2}} + \frac{x - 25}{\sqrt{900 + (25 - x)^2}}.$$

Finding a common denominator:

$$0 = \frac{x\sqrt{900 + (25 - x)^2} + (x - 25)\sqrt{400 + x^2}}{\sqrt{400 + x^2}\sqrt{900 + (25 - x)^2}}$$

The numerator must be zero, so we have

$$0 = x\sqrt{900 + (25 - x)^2} + (x - 25)\sqrt{400 + x^2} \text{ , or}$$

$$x\sqrt{900+(25-x)^2} = (25-x)\sqrt{400+x^2}$$

$$\frac{x}{25-x} = \frac{\sqrt{400+x^2}}{\sqrt{900+(25-x)^2}}$$

(assuming $x \neq 25$).

Squaring both sides, we have

$$\frac{x^2}{625-50x+x^2} = \frac{400+x^2}{900+(25-x)^2}$$

and cross–multiplying gives

$$900x^2 + 625x^2 - 50x^3 + x^4$$

$$= 250,000 - 20,000x + 1,025x^2 - 50x^3 + x^4$$

$$\Rightarrow 500x^2 + 20,000x - 250,000 = 0$$

$$\Rightarrow x^2 + 40x - 500 = 0$$

$$(x+50)(x-10) = 0$$

Therefore, $x = 10, -50$.

We know x is a distance, so it cannot be negative. Hence $x = 10$.

An alternate way to solve the problem is to see that the distance is minimized if the incident angles are equal.

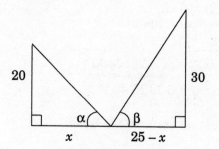

If $\alpha = \beta$, then $\cot\alpha = \cot\beta$

$$\frac{x}{20} = \frac{25 - x}{30}$$

$$30x = 500 - 20x$$

$$50x = 500$$

$$x = 10$$

3. **(A)**

The sine of a sum of two angles is given by $\sin(a + b) = \sin a \cos b + \sin b \cos a$.

So,

$$20\sqrt{5}\sin(311t + \theta) = 20\sqrt{5}\,[\sin(311t)\cos\theta + \sin\theta\cos(311t)]$$

$$= 20\sqrt{5}\left(\frac{\sin(311t)}{\sqrt{5}} + \frac{2\cos(311t)}{\sqrt{5}}\right)$$

$$= 20\sin(311t) + 40\cos(311t) = I(t).$$

(B)

$$I(t) = 20\sqrt{5}\sin(311t + \theta)$$

$$I'(t) = 20\sqrt{5}(311)\cos(311t + \theta) = 0$$

$$\Rightarrow \cos(311t + \theta) = 0$$

$$\Rightarrow 311t + \theta = \frac{\pi}{2} + \pi k,$$

for some integer k.

$$\Rightarrow t = \frac{\dfrac{\pi}{2} - \pi k - \theta}{311}$$

$$\Rightarrow t = \frac{\pi}{622} - \frac{\pi k}{311} - \frac{\theta}{311}$$

Now $I''(t) = -20\sqrt{5}(311)^2 \sin(311t + \theta)$

So $I''\left(\dfrac{\pi}{622} - \dfrac{\pi k}{311} - \dfrac{\theta}{311}\right)$

$$= -20\sqrt{5}(311)^2 \sin\left(\frac{\pi}{2} - \pi k - \theta + \theta\right)$$

$$= -20\sqrt{5}(311)^2 \sin\left(\frac{\pi}{2} - \pi k\right)$$

$$= -20\sqrt{5}(311)^2 \left[\sin\left(\frac{\pi}{2}\right)\cos(-\pi k) + \sin(-\pi k)\cos\left(\frac{\pi}{2}\right)\right]$$

$$= -20\sqrt{5}(311)^2 [1 + 0]$$

$$= -20\sqrt{5}(311)^2 < 0,$$

So we have a maximum by the second derivative test. The maximum value of $I(t)$ occurs at

$$t = \frac{\pi}{622} - \frac{\pi k}{311} - \frac{\theta}{311}$$

and this maximum value is

$$I\left(\frac{\pi}{622} - \frac{\pi k}{311} - \frac{\theta}{311}\right)$$

$$= 20\sqrt{5}\sin\left(\frac{\pi}{2} - \pi k - \theta + \theta\right)$$

$$= 20\sqrt{5}\sin\left(\frac{\pi}{2} - \pi k\right)$$

$$= 20\sqrt{5}\left[\sin\left(\frac{\pi}{2}\right)\cos(-\pi k) + \sin(-\pi k)\cos\left(\frac{\pi}{2}\right)\right]$$

$$= 20\sqrt{5}.$$

4.   (A)

   f is increasing when $f'(x) > 0$. By the chart, we see this occurs between $x = -4$ and $x = 0$, so f is increasing on the interval $[-4, 0]$.

   f is decreasing when $f'(x) < 0$ which occurs on the intervals $(-\infty, -4]$ and $[0, \infty)$.

   (B)

   Vertical asymptotes occur where the function tends to ∞. Here $f(x)$ is undefined at $x = -1, 2$, and

$$\lim_{x \to 2^+} f(x) = \infty, \quad \lim_{x \to 2^-} f(x) = -\infty,$$

$$\lim_{x \to -1^+} f(x) = -\infty, \quad \text{and} \quad \lim_{x \to -1^-} f(x) = \infty,$$

   So, $x = -1$ and $x = 2$ are vertical asymptotes.

   Since $\lim_{x \to \pm\infty} f(x) = 0$, we have $y = 0$ as a horizontal asymptote.

   (C)

   $f(-4) = -\dfrac{2}{3}$ is a local minimum, since $f'(x) < 0$ for $x < -4$ and $f'(x) > 0$ for $x > -4$.

   $f(0) = -6$ is a local maximum, since $f'(x) < 0$ for $x < 0$ and $f'(x) < 0$ for $x > 0$.

(D)

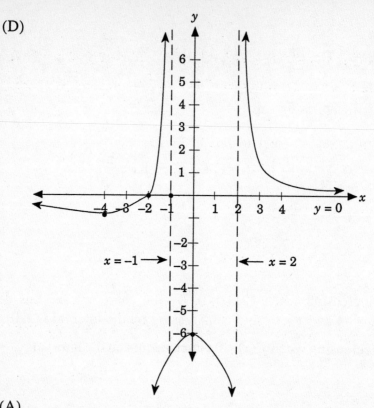

5. (A)

At the point of tangency, x_0,

$$\frac{2}{3}x_0^{\frac{3}{2}} = cx_0 + d \quad \text{and} \quad x_0^{\frac{1}{2}} = c$$

If $x_0 = 2$, then $c = \sqrt{2}$ and $d = -\dfrac{2\sqrt{2}}{3}$

(B)

If $c = 1$, then $x_0 = 1$ if $d = -\dfrac{1}{3}$

(C)

$$\int_0^3 \frac{2}{3}x^{\frac{3}{2}}\,dx = \frac{2}{3}\times\frac{2}{5}\times x^{\frac{5}{2}}\Big|_0^3$$

$$= \frac{4}{15}\times 3\times 3\times\sqrt{3}$$

$$= \frac{12\sqrt{3}}{5}$$

6. **(A)**

Velocity $= v(t) = s'(t) = 112 - 32t$, so $v(3) = 112 - 96 = 16$ ft/sec.

Acceleration $= a(t) = v'(t) = s''(t) = -32$, so $a(3) = -32$ ft/sec.

(B)

Maximum height occurs when $v(t) = 0$.

$$112 - 32t = 0$$

$$\Rightarrow 112 = 32t$$

$$\Rightarrow t = \frac{112}{32} = \frac{7}{2} \text{ seconds.}$$

(C)

The time of impact occurs when $s(t) = 0$ for the second time.

$$0 = 112t - 16t^2 = (112 - 16t)t$$

therefore, $t = \dfrac{112}{16} = 7$ sec.

The velocity at $t = 7$ is $v(7) = s'(7) = 112 - 32(7) = -112$ ft/sec.

(D)

Arc length $= \displaystyle\int_1^{10} \sqrt{1 + (y')^2}\ dx$ for the path of the bug.

$$y = \frac{1}{3}(x^2 - 2)^{\frac{3}{2}}$$

$$y' = \frac{1}{3} \times \frac{3}{2}(x^2 - 2)^{\frac{1}{2}}\, 2x$$

$$= x\sqrt{x^2 - 2}$$

$$(y')^2 = x^2(x^2 - 2)$$

$$= x^4 - 2x^2$$

$$\text{Arc length} = \int_1^{10} \sqrt{1 + x^4 - 2x^2} \; dx$$

$$= \int_1^{10} \sqrt{(x^2 - 1)^2} \; dx$$

$$= \int_1^{10} (x^2 - 1) \; dx$$

$$= \left(\frac{x^3}{3} - x \right) \Big|_1^{10}$$

$$= \frac{1,000}{3} - 10 - \frac{1}{3} + 1$$

$$= 324 \text{ feet.}$$

The path of the projectile = 392 feet, which is longer than the path of the bug.

Advanced Placement Examination in Calculus AB

EXAM VI

ADVANCED PLACEMENT CALCULUS AB EXAM VI

SECTION I

PART A

Time: 55 minutes
28 questions

DIRECTIONS: Each of the following problems is followed by five choices. Solve each problem, select the best choice, and blacken the correct space on your answer sheet. Calculators may not be used for this section of the exam.

NOTE: Unless otherwise specified, the domain of function f is assumed to be the set of all real numbers x for which $f(x)$ is a real number.

1. If $x < 0$ and $f(x) = |x|$ then $f(f(x))$ is equal to:

   (A) x

   (B) $-x$

   (C) $\dfrac{1}{x}$

   (D) $\dfrac{1}{-x}$

   (E) undefined

2. Which one of the following functions satisfies the condition that

   $\displaystyle\int_{-a}^{a} f(x)\,dx = 0$ for any number a?

   (A) $f(x) = x^3 - x^2 + x$

(B) $f(x) = \dfrac{x^4 + x^3}{x}$

(C) $f(x) = x^4 - x^2$

(D) $f(x) = (x + 1)^3 - (3x^2 + 1)$

(E) None of these

3. Find the area enclosed between the graphs of $x + 2 = y^2$ and $y = x$.

(A) $\dfrac{9}{2}$ 　　　　　　　　　　 (D) $\dfrac{26}{6}$

(B) $\dfrac{7}{2}$ 　　　　　　　　　　 (E) None of these

(C) $\dfrac{19}{2}$

4. Let $(-2, g(-2))$ be a relative maximum for $g(x) = 2x^3 + hx^2 + kx - 6$. Use the fact that $\left(-\dfrac{1}{2}, g\left(-\dfrac{1}{2}\right)\right)$ is an inflection point to find the value of $(h - k)$.

(A) 9 　　　　　　　　　　 (B) –9

(C) 15 　　　　　　　　　　 (D) –15

(E) 24

5. $\displaystyle\lim_{x \to 0} \dfrac{\sin x}{|x|} =$

(A) –1 　　　　　　　　　　 (D) $\dfrac{1}{2}$

(B) 0 　　　　　　　　　　 (E) None of these

(C) 1

6. Find the instantaneous rate of change of the area of a circle with respect to the circumference C.

(A) C

(D) $\dfrac{C}{2\pi}$

(B) $\dfrac{C}{2}$

(E) π

(C) $\dfrac{C}{\pi}$

7. $\displaystyle \lim_{x \to 1} \frac{2x-2}{x^3 + 2x^2 - x - 2} =$

(A) 0

(D) $+\infty$

(B) $\dfrac{1}{3}$

(E) $-\infty$

(C) $\dfrac{2}{3}$

8. Determine which of the following is/are (an) asymptote(s) for the graph of $y = \dfrac{e^x}{x}$:

I. $x = 0$

II. $y = 0$

III. $y = x$

(A) I only

(D) I and II

(B) II only

(E) II and III

(C) III only

9. Let $F(x)$ be an antiderivative of $f(x)$. Suppose $F(x)$ is defined by

$$F(x) = \begin{cases} |x| & \text{if } x < 0 \\ -\sin x & \text{if } x \geq 0 \end{cases}$$

Evaluate $[f(b) - f(a)]$ for $a = -\dfrac{\pi}{2}$ and $b = \dfrac{\pi}{2}$.

(A) -1

(D) $\dfrac{\pi+1}{2}$

(B) 0

(E) $\dfrac{\pi+1}{-2}$

(C) 1

10. Let $g(x) = f'(x)$ where $f(x) = \cos(\arcsin x)$. Which one of the following statements is FALSE concerning $g(x)$?

(A) The domain of g is $[-1, 1]$.

(B) The range of g is $(-\infty, +\infty)$.

(C) $\dot{g}$ is a decreasing function.

(D) g is concave down for $x > 0$.

(E) $(0, 0)$ is a point of inflection for $y = g(x)$.

11. Let $f(x) = \sqrt{2-x}$. Then $\lim\limits_{x \to 2^-} f'(x) =$

(A) 0

(D) $+\infty$

(B) 1

(E) $-\infty$

(C) -1

12. Let $f(x) = \dfrac{\frac{1}{x} - x}{\frac{1}{x} + x}$. Then $f'(2.5)$ is approximately:

(A) −0.190

(D) 1.005

(B) 0

(E) None of these

(C) 0.190

13. Let $R = \displaystyle\int_{\frac{1}{\sqrt{2}}}^{1} \frac{2x}{\sqrt{1-x^4}}\, dx$ and find the interval that contains R.

(A) $(-\infty, 0.5]$

(D) $(1.5, 2]$

(B) $(0.5, 1]$

(E) $(2, +\infty)$

(C) $(1, 1.5]$

14. Suppose a particle moves on a straight line with a position function of $s(t) = 3t^3 - 11t^2 + 8t$. In what interval of time is the particle moving to the left on the line?

(A) $(-\infty, 0)$

(D) $\left(\dfrac{4}{9}, 2\right)$

(B) $(0, 1)$

(E) $(2, +\infty)$

(C) $\left(1, \dfrac{8}{3}\right)$

15. Let $f(x) = (x + 2)^3 (3 - 2x)^5 (2x - 1)^{-3} (3x - 4)^{-2}$.

Find $f'(1)$.

(A) −270

(D) 135

(B) −243

(E) None of these

(C) 54

16. $\int \left(\csc^2 x \right) 2^{\cot x}\, dx =$

(A) $\dfrac{2^{\cot x}}{\cot x (\ln 2)} + C$

(B) $\dfrac{2 \csc^2 x}{(\ln 2) \cot x} + C$

(C) $\dfrac{-2^{\cot x}}{\ln 2} + C$

(D) $\dfrac{2^{\cot x} \csc^2 x}{\cot x (\ln 2)} + C$

(E) $\dfrac{1}{\cot x (\ln 2)} + C$

17. Let $f(x) = x^2 + 1$ and $g(x) = \dfrac{1}{x-2}$. Which one of the following statements is <u>FALSE</u>?

(A) $g(f(x))$ is continuous at $x = 2$.

(B) $f(g(x))$ is continuous at $x = 1$.

(C) $g(f(x))$ has two points of discontinuity.

(D) $\lim\limits_{n \to \infty} f(g(x)) = 1$

(E) $D_x[g(f(2))] = -4$

18. Assume $g(x)$ is a continuous function for which:

$g'(x) > 0$ and $g''(x) > 0$ for $x < a$

$g'(x) > 0$ and $g''(x) < 0$ for $x > a$

$g'(x)$ and $g''(x)$ are undefined for $x = a$

Which of the following statements is true about the point $(a, g(a))$?

(A) It is a relative minimum.

(B) It is a relative maximum.

(C) It is a point of inflection.

(D) $y = g(a)$ is an asymptote.

(E) None of these.

19. Use $f(x) = \begin{cases} 2 - x^2 & \text{for } x \geq 0 \\ 2 + x & \text{for } x < 0 \end{cases}$ and find

$$\lim_{h \to 0} \frac{f(x+h) - f(x)}{h}$$

(A) 0   (D) 2

(B) 1   (E) None of these

(C) -1

20. $\lim_{n \to \infty} \left[1 - n \left(\sin \frac{1}{n} \right)^2 \right] =$

(A) 0   (D) ∞

(B) -1 (E) None of the above

(C) 1

21. Let the velocity at time t of a point moving on a line be defined by $v(t) = 2^t \ln 2$ (cm/sec). How many centimeters did the point travel between $t = 0$ and $t = 2$ sec?

(A) 3   (D) $4 \ln 2$

(B) 4   (E) $\frac{5}{2} \ln 2$

(C) $\frac{2}{3} \ln 2$

22. Find the equation of the tangent line to the graph of $y = \dfrac{\ln x}{e^x}$ using $(1, 0)$ as the coordinates of the point of tangency.

    (A) $x - ey - 1 = 0$

    (B) $x + ey - 1 = 0$

    (C) $x - y - 1 = 0$

    (D) $x + y - 1 = 0$

    (E) None of these

23. Find the average value for $y = \dfrac{e^{\sqrt{x}}}{\sqrt{x}}$ in the interval $[1, 4]$.

    (A) 3.114   (D) 103.760

    (B) 34.587   (E) 0.778

    (C) 9.324

24. $\displaystyle\lim_{x \to a} \dfrac{\sqrt[3]{x} - \sqrt[3]{a}}{x - a} =$

    (A) 0   (D) $\dfrac{\sqrt[3]{a}}{3a}$

    (B) $2\sqrt[3]{a}$ (E) None of these

    (C) $\dfrac{3}{2}\sqrt[3]{a^2}$

25. $\displaystyle\lim_{x \to \infty} \dfrac{(\ln x)^2}{x} =$

    (A) ∞ (D) 2

    (B) 1   (E) 0

    (C) $\ln 2$

26. At what value does $f(x) = 4x^5 + 15x^4 + 20x^3 + 10x^2$ have a relative maximum ?

(A) –2   (D) 1

(B) –1   (E) 2

(C) 0

27. The length of the arc given by
    $x = 4\cos^3 t$
    $y = 4\sin^3 t$
    $0 \le t \le \dfrac{\pi}{2}$ is:

(A) $\dfrac{\pi}{2}$ (D) 3

(B) $\dfrac{3\pi}{2}$ (E) 6

(C) 3π

28. Point A moves to the right along the positive x-axis at 7 units per second while point B moves upward along the negative y-axis at 2 units per second. At what rate is the distance between A and B changing when A is at (8, 0) and B is at (0, –6) ?

(A) $\dfrac{32}{5}$ (D) $-\dfrac{22}{5}$

(B) 5   (E) $-\dfrac{32}{5}$

(C) $\dfrac{22}{5}$

PART B

Time: 50 minutes
17 questions

DIRECTIONS: Calculators may be used for this section of the test. Each of the following problems is followed by five choices. Solve each problem, select the best choice, and blacken the correct space on your answer sheet.

NOTES:

1. Unless otherwise specified, answers can be given in unsimplified form.

2. The domain of function f is assumed to be the set of all real numbers x for which $f(x)$ is a real number.

---

29. Let $f(x) = \sin|x|$ and determine which one of the following statements is <u>TRUE</u>:

    (A) $f(x) \geq 0$

    (B) f is an odd function

    (C) $\int_{-\frac{\pi}{4}}^{\frac{\pi}{4}} f(x)\,dx = 0$

    (D) f is symmetric with respect to the line $x = 0$

    (E) f is differentiable at $x = 0$

30. Let $h(x) = \dfrac{f(g(x)) - g(f(x))}{f(x)}$ where $f(x) = x - 1$ and $g(x) = x^2$ and x is any real number. What is the range of h?

    (A) All reals

(B) All reals except 1

(C) Positive reals

(D) Negative reals

(E) None of these

31. Find the volume of the solid of revolution generated when the region enclosed by the graphs of $x = y^2$ and $x = 2y$ is revolved about the y-axis.

(A) 4.189

(D) 4.114

(B) 8.378

(E) −1.269

(C) 13.404

32. Let $f(x) = \sin^2 x \cos^2 2x$. $\int_0^2 f(x)$ equals

(A) 0.715

(D) 0.015

(B) 1.211

(E) 4.782

(C) 3.121

33. $f(x) = \dfrac{2x}{\sqrt{1 - x^4}}$. The minimum of $f'(x)$ is:

(A) 1

(D) 2

(B) 0

(E) 3

(C) −1

34. Let $f(x) = -x + x \ln x$ and calculate $D_x\left[f^{-1}(0)\right]$.

(A) 0

(D) e^{-1}

(B) 1

(E) None of these

(C) e

35. Let $y = u^5$, $\dfrac{du}{dx} = 2$, $\dfrac{d^2u}{dx^2} = -3$, and $\dfrac{d^3u}{dx^3} = 5$.

    Find the value of $\dfrac{d^3y}{dx^3}$ at $u = 1$.

    (A) −20

    (B) −35

    (C) 25

    (D) 145

    (E) None of these

36. Let f be differentiable for all reals with critical values at $x = 6$ and $x = -12$. For what values of x will $f'\left(\dfrac{x}{3}\right) = 0$?

    (A) 0 and −2

    (B) 2 and −4

    (C) −2 and 4

    (D) 6 and −12

    (E) 18 and −36

37. Suppose a particle moves on a straight line with a position function of $s(t) = 3t^3 - 11t^2 + 8t$. The highest velocity with which the particle moves in the negative direction is

    (A) −5.4

    (B) 0

    (C) 2.5

    (D) −4

    (E) 2

38. $\dfrac{\displaystyle\int_0^1 x\,e^x\,dx}{\displaystyle\int_0^1 e^{-x}\,dx} =$

(A) $\dfrac{e}{e-1}$

(D) $\dfrac{e^2}{e-1}$

(B) $\dfrac{e^2+1}{4}$

(E) None of these

(C) $\dfrac{1}{2}$

39. Let $f(x) = \ln(\ln x)$ and find the domain of $f(x)$ in interval notation.

(A) $(0, +\infty)$

(D) $[1, +\infty)$

(B) $[0, +\infty)$

(E) None of these

(C) $(1, +\infty)$

40. Let f be a continuous, one-to-one function such that

$$f(1) = e^{-1}, \quad f^{-1}(1) = 0 \quad \text{and} \quad f'(1) = -2e^{-1}.$$

Which of the following statements are true?

I. f is decreasing

II. f^{-1} is decreasing and one-to-one

III. $D_x\left[f^{-1}\left(e^{-1}\right)\right] = -\dfrac{e}{2}$.

(A) I and II

(D) I, II, and III

(B) I and III

(E) None of these

(C) II and III

41. $\int_0^2 x^x$ is

    (A) 3.27   (D) 1.98

    (B) 2.83   (E) 3.02

    (C) 4.21

42. Let $\alpha = \angle BAC$ in $\triangle ABC$ with $\overline{AB} = c$ and $\overline{AC} = b$, where b and c are constants and $c > b$. Side $\overline{BC}$ changes length as the measure of α changes. Find the instantaneous rate of change of the area of $\triangle ABC$ when $\alpha = \dfrac{\pi}{3}$. Assume the instantaneous rate of change of α is 2.

    (A) $cb\sqrt{2}$ (D) $\dfrac{cb}{\sqrt{2}}$

    (B) $cb\sqrt{3}$ (E) $\dfrac{cb}{2}$

    (C) $\dfrac{cb\sqrt{3}}{2}$

43. $f(x) = \dfrac{e^{\sqrt{x}}}{\sqrt{x}}$. $f'(c) = 0$.   Then c equals

    (A) 3   (D) 2

    (B) 0   (E) 7

    (C) 1

44. As a particle moves along the line $y = 2x + 7$, its minimum distance from the origin is:

(A) $\dfrac{7}{5}$

(D) $\dfrac{\sqrt{5}}{7}$

(B) $\dfrac{7}{5}\sqrt{5}$

(E) $\dfrac{7}{3}\sqrt{5}$

(C) $\dfrac{14}{5}$

45. The base of a solid is the region enclosed by the graph of $x = 1 - y^2$ and the y-axis. If all plane cross sections perpendicular to the x-axis are semicircles with diameters parallel to the y-axis, then the volume is:

(A) $\dfrac{\pi}{8}$

(D) $\dfrac{3\pi}{4}$

(B) $\dfrac{\pi}{4}$

(E) $\dfrac{3\pi}{2}$

(C) $\dfrac{\pi}{2}$

SECTION II

Time: 1 hour and 30 minutes
6 problems*

DIRECTIONS: Show all your work. Grading is based on the methods used to solve the problems as well as the accuracy of your final answers. Please make sure all procedures are clearly shown. For some problems or parts of problems it will be necessary to use a calculator.

NOTES:

1. Unless otherwise specified, answers can be given in unsimplified form.

2. The domain of function f is assumed to be the set of all real numbers x for which $f(x)$ is a real number.

---

1. Let $f(x) = \dfrac{x^2 - 2x + 1}{2 + x - x^2}$ for x in $(-\infty, +\infty)$.

   (A) Find the critical values of f.

   (B) Sketch the graph of f; label local extrema and asymptotes.

   (C) f has one point of inflection at $(p, f(p))$. Find two consecutive integers n and $n + 1$ such that $n < p < n + 1$.

---

* The practice tests in this book incorporate Section II free-response solutions that approximate the content breakdown you will encounter on the AP exam. The overall timing and formatting of the practice tests in this book mirror the actual test; examinees should note, however, that this section is split into two parts on the AP exam. Furthermore, prospective examinees should pay attention to restrictions on calculator use. For details, consult current official College Board materials in print or on the Web.

2. Population growth in a certain bacteria colony is best described by the equation

    $$y = t^2 e^{3t^2} t\sqrt{t}$$

    (A) Find the rate of growth at $t = 1$.

    (B) Find the lowest rate for $t > 0$.

    (C) Find the highest rate for $t > 0$.

3. Let $f(x) = (e^{-\cos x})\sin x$.

    (A) Find $f'(x)$.

    (B) Find $f''(x)$.

    (C) Use parts (A) and (B), together with symmetry and axes intercepts, to sketch the graph of $y = f(x)$. Make sure your graph depicts the correct concavity.

    (D) Evaluate $\int_0^a f(x)\, dx$ where a is the first point of inflection of $f(x)$ in the interval $(0, \pi)$.

4. Find a third degree polynomial function given the following information:

    (i)   The axes intercepts are $(1, 0)$ and $(0, 12)$.

    (ii) Relative maximum at $x = -\dfrac{2}{3}$.

    (iii) Point of inflection at $x = \dfrac{5}{3}$.

    (A) For what values of x is the function positive?

    (B) For what values of x is the derivative of the function positive?

    (C) Find the interval(s) in which the function is concave down.

5. Make a rain gutter from a long strip of sheet metal of width w inches using the following prescribed methods. In each case, find the dimension across the top to maximize the amount of rainwater the gutter can handle.

(A) Bend the metal in the middle to form a V–shaped (isosceles $\triangle$) rain gutter. Find the value of x that maximizes the amount of water the gutter can handle by maximizing the cross–sectional area of the gutter.

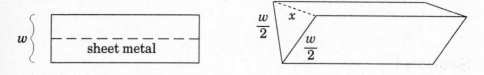

(B) Bend the metal in two places to form an isosceles trapezoid as follows:

Find the value of x that will maximize the amount of water the gutter can handle by maximizing the cross–sectional area of the gutter.

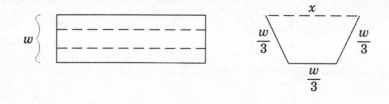

6. Let $f(x)$ be continuous on $[-a, a]$ where $a > 0$, $f(a) = 2$, and $f'(a) = 1$.

(A) Find an equation for the tangent line to $y = f(x)$ at the point $(a, f(a))$.

(B) Suppose $f(x)$ is an odd function, i.e., $f(-x) = -f(x)$, and $F(x)$ is an antiderivative for f. Find $F(a) - F(-a)$. Be sure to show work to justify your conclusions.

(C) If the graph of $f(x)$ lies below the tangent line to $y = f(x)$ at $(a, f(a))$ for all x in $[-a, a]$, then find the area between $y = f(x)$ and the tangent line from $x = -a$ to $x = a$ as a function of a.

ADVANCED PLACEMENT CALCULUS AB EXAM VI

ANSWER KEY

Section I

1.	(B)	12.	(A)	23.	(A)	34.	(B)
2.	(D)	13.	(C)	24.	(D)	35.	(D)
3.	(A)	14.	(D)	25.	(E)	36.	(E)
4.	(C)	15.	(B)	26.	(B)	37.	(A)
5.	(E)	16.	(C)	27.	(E)	38.	(A)
6.	(D)	17.	(E)	28.	(C)	39.	(C)
7.	(B)	18.	(C)	29.	(D)	40.	(D)
8.	(D)	19.	(E)	30.	(E)	41.	(B)
9.	(C)	20.	(C)	31.	(C)	42.	(E)
10.	(A)	21.	(A)	32.	(A)	43.	(C)
11.	(E)	22.	(A)	33.	(D)	44.	(B)
						45.	(B)

Section II

See Detailed Explanations of Answers.

DETAILED EXPLANATIONS
OF ANSWERS

SECTION I

1. **(B)**

$$f(f(x)) = \big|\, |\, x\,|\,\big|$$

$$= |\,x\,|$$

$$= -x \qquad\qquad \text{since } x < 0.$$

2. **(D)**

An odd function will satisfy this condition. None of the functions are odd except

$$f(x) = (x+1)^3 - (3x^2 + 1)$$

$$= (x^3 + 3x^2 + 3x + 1) - (3x^2 + 1)$$

$$= x^3 + 3x$$

$$= -f(-x).$$

Since $f(x)$ is odd, $\displaystyle\int_{-a}^{a} f(x)\,dx = 0$

3. **(A)**

The two curves intersect at $(-1, -1)$ and $(2, 2)$. Therefore,

$$\text{Area} = \int_{-1}^{2} \left[y - \left(y^2 - 2 \right) \right] dy = \left(\frac{y^2}{2} - \frac{y^3}{3} + 2y \right) \Big|_{-1}^{2}$$

$$= \frac{9}{2}.$$

4. **(C)**

$$g(x) = 2x^3 + hx^2 + kx - 6$$

so $\quad g'(x) = 6x^2 + 2hx + k \quad$ and

$$g''(x) = 12x + 2h$$

$$g'(-2) = 0 \Rightarrow$$

$$0 = 24 - 4h + k$$

$$g''\left(-\frac{1}{2} \right) = 0 \Rightarrow$$

$$0 = -6 + 2h \quad \text{so } 3 = h$$

Now $\quad k = -12 \quad$ and $\quad h - k = 3 - (-12) = 15$

5. **(E)**

If $x > 0$, $\quad \lim_{x \to 0^+} \dfrac{\sin x}{|x|} = \lim_{x \to 0^+} \dfrac{\sin x}{x}$

$$= 1$$

If $x < 0$, $\quad \lim_{x \to 0^-} \dfrac{\sin x}{|x|} = \lim_{x \to 0^-} \dfrac{\sin x}{-x}$

$$= -1$$

So, $\quad \lim_{x \to 0} \dfrac{\sin x}{|x|} \quad$ does not exist.

6. **(D)**

$A = \pi r^2$ and

$C = 2\pi r$

$$\Rightarrow \frac{C}{2\pi} = r$$

$$A = \pi \left(\frac{C}{2\pi} \right)^2 = \frac{C^2}{4\pi}$$

so, $\quad \dfrac{dA}{dC} = \dfrac{2C}{4\pi}$

$$= \frac{C}{2\pi}$$

7. **(B)**

$$\lim_{x \to 1} \frac{2x-2}{x^3 + 2x^2 - x - 2} = \lim_{x \to 1} \frac{2(x-1)}{(x-1)(x+1)(x+2)}$$

$$= \lim_{x \to 1} \frac{2}{(x+1)(x+2)}$$

$$= \frac{1}{3}$$

8. **(D)**

$f(x) = \dfrac{e^x}{x} \Rightarrow f$ becomes infinite at $x = 0$, so we have a vertical asymptote at $x = 0$.

Also, $\lim\limits_{x \to -\infty} f(x) = 0$, so there is a horizontal asymptote at $y = 0$.

We see that $\lim\limits_{x \to +\infty} f(x) = +\infty$ so there are no other asymptotes.

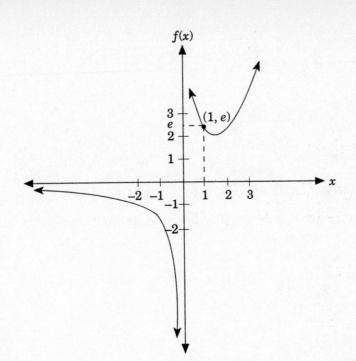

9. **(C)**

$$F(x) = \begin{cases} |x| & \text{if } x < 0 \\ -\sin x & \text{if } x \geq 0 \end{cases}$$

$$f(x) = F'(x) = \begin{cases} -1 & \text{if } x < 0 \\ -\cos x & \text{if } x \geq 0 \end{cases}$$

$$f\left(\frac{\pi}{2}\right) - f\left(-\frac{\pi}{2}\right) = -\cos\frac{\pi}{2} - (-1)$$

$$= 1$$

10. **(A)**

$f(x) = \cos(\arcsin x)$ so

$$g(x) = f'(x) = -\sin(\arcsin x)\frac{1}{\sqrt{1-x^2}}$$

$$= \frac{-x}{\sqrt{1-x^2}}$$

Now $g'(x) = -\left[-\dfrac{1}{2}x\left(1-x^2\right)^{-\frac{3}{2}}(-2x) + \left(1-x^2\right)^{-\frac{1}{2}} \right]$

$$= \dfrac{-1}{\left(1-x^2\right)^{\frac{3}{2}}}$$

Note that the domain of g is $(-1, 1)$ and $g'(x) < 0$.

Therefore, g is a decreasing function defined on $(-1, 1)$

$g''(x) = \dfrac{3}{2}(1-x^2)^{-\frac{5}{2}}(-2x)$

$$= \dfrac{-3x}{(1-x^2)^{\frac{5}{2}}}$$

$\Rightarrow g''(0) = 0,$

so, 0 is an inflection point.

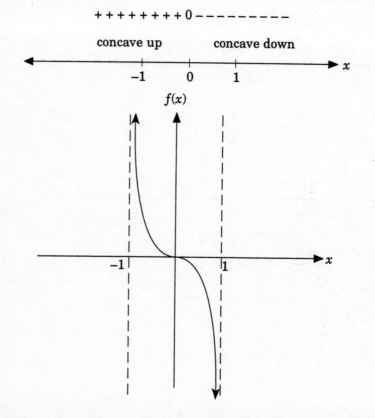

11. **(E)**

If $f(x) = \sqrt{2-x}$ then $f'(x) = \dfrac{-1}{2\sqrt{2-x}}$.

Let $x = 2 - \varepsilon$ with $\varepsilon > 0$. Then

$$\lim_{x \to 2^-} f'(x) = \lim_{\varepsilon \to 0^+} -\frac{1}{2} \times \frac{1}{\sqrt{\varepsilon}}$$
$$\to -\infty$$

12. **(A)**

$$f(x) = \frac{1-x^2}{1+x^2}$$

$$f'(x) = \frac{(1+x^2)(-2x) - (1-x^2)(2x)}{(1+x^2)^2}$$

$$= \frac{-4x}{(1+x^2)^2}$$

$$f'(2.5) = \frac{-4(2.5)}{(1+(2.5)^2)^2}$$

$$\approx \frac{-10}{52.563}$$

$$\approx -0.190$$

13. **(C)**

$$R = \int_{\frac{1}{\sqrt{2}}}^{1} \frac{2x}{\sqrt{1-x^4}}\, dx. \quad \text{Let } u = x^2 \text{ and } du = 2x\, dx$$

$$R = \int_{\frac{1}{\sqrt{2}}}^{1} \frac{du}{\sqrt{1-u^2}}\, dx = \arcsin u \Big|_{\frac{1}{\sqrt{2}}}^{1}$$

$$= \frac{3\pi}{6} - \frac{\pi}{6}$$

$$= \frac{\pi}{3}$$

$$\approx 1.05 \in (1, \ 1.5]$$

14. **(D)**

The particle is moving to the left when $v\ (t) < 0$

$$v(t) = s'(t) = 9t^2 - 22t + 8$$

$$= (9t - 4)(t - 2)$$

$$+ + + + + + + + + + + 0 ------ 0 + + + + + + +$$

right   left   right

$$\underset{-1 \qquad\quad 0 \ \ \frac{4}{9}\ \ 1 \qquad 2 \qquad 3}{\xleftarrow{\hspace{8cm}}} t$$

The particle is moving to the left in $\left(\dfrac{4}{9}, \ 2 \right)$

15. **(B)**

Let $f(x) = (x+2)^3 (3 - 2x)^5 (2x - 1)^{-3} (3x - 4)^{-2}$

$$\ln y = 3\ln(x + 2) + 5\ln(3 - 2x) - 3\ln(2x - 1) - 2\ln(3x - 4)$$

$$\frac{1}{y} y' = \frac{3}{x + 2} + \frac{5(-2)}{3 - 2x} + \frac{-3(2)}{2x - 1} + \frac{-2(3)}{3x - 4}$$

Therefore, $f'(1) = f(1) \left[\dfrac{3}{3} + \dfrac{-10}{1} + \dfrac{-6}{1} + \dfrac{-6}{-1} \right]$

$$= (3^3)(1^5)(1)^{-3}(-1)^{-2}(-9)$$

$$= 27 \times (-9)$$

$$= -243$$

16. **(C)**

$\int (\csc^2 x)\, 2^{\cot x}\, dx$. Let $u = \cot x$ and $du = -\csc^2 x\, dx$

$$-\int 2^u\, du = \frac{-2^u}{\ln 2} + C$$

$$= \frac{-2^{\cot x}}{\ln 2} + C$$

17. **(E)**

Let $f(x) = x^2 + 1$ and $g(x) = \frac{1}{x-2}$.

$$f(g(x)) = f\!\left(\frac{1}{x-2}\right) = \left(\frac{1}{x-2}\right)^2 + 1,$$

which is continuous at $x = 1$

$$\lim_{x \to \infty} f(g(x)) = \lim_{x \to \infty} \left[\left(\frac{1}{x-2}\right)^2 + 1\right]$$

$$= 0^2 + 1$$

$$= 1$$

$$g(f(x)) = g\!\left(x^2 + 1\right) = \frac{1}{x^2 - 1},$$

which is continuous at $x = 2$ and discontinuous at $x = 1$ and -1.

But $D_x\big[g(f(x))\big] = -1(x^2 - 1)^{-2}(2x)$,

and $D_x\big[g(f(2))\big] = -1(2^2 - 1)^{-2}(2)(2)$

$$= -\frac{4}{9}, \text{not} -4.$$

18. **(C)**

Since $g''(x)$ exists in a deleted neighborhood of $x = a$ (although not for $x = a$), and since $g''(x)$ changes sign upon passing through $x = a$, we can conclude that $g(x)$ has a point of inflection at $x = a$.

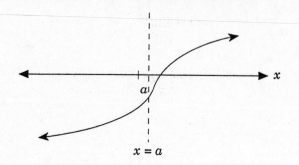

19. **(E)**

As $h \to 0$ through positive values of h, we have $\lim\limits_{h \to 0^+} \dfrac{f(x+h) - f(x)}{h} = -2x.$

However, as $h \to 0$ through negative values, we have $\lim\limits_{h \to 0^-} \dfrac{f(x+h) - f(x)}{h} = 1.$

The discrepancy means that the limit does not exist for $h \to 0$.

20. **(C)**

$$\lim_{n \to \infty}\left[1 - n\left(\sin\frac{1}{n}\right)^2\right] = 1 - \lim_{n \to \infty} n\left(\sin\frac{1}{n}\right)^2.$$

Let $x = \dfrac{1}{n}$.

Then as $n \to \infty$, we see $x \to 0$.

So, $\displaystyle\lim_{n\to\infty}\left[1-n\left(\sin\frac{1}{n}\right)^2\right]=1-\lim_{x\to0}\frac{(\sin x)^2}{x}$

$$=1-\lim_{x\to0}\left[\left(\frac{\sin x}{x}\right)(\sin x)\right]$$

$$=1-\left(\lim_{x\to0}\frac{\sin x}{x}\right)\left(\lim_{x\to0}\sin x\right)$$

$$=1-(1\times0)$$

$$=1-0$$

$$=1.$$

21. **(A)**

The position of the point at time t is given by

$s(t) = \displaystyle\int 2^t\ln2\,dt = 2^t + C$

$s(0) = 1 + C$

$s(2) = 2^2 + C$

distance traveled $= s(2) - s(0) = 3$

22. **(A)**

$y = e^{-x}\ln x$

Therefore, $y' = -e^{-x}\ln x + e^{-x}\times\dfrac{1}{x}$

$$y'(1) = e^{-1}$$

Therefore, the tangent line is $(y-0)=\dfrac{1}{e}(x-1)$ or $x-ey-1=0$

23. **(A)**

Find the average value for $y = \dfrac{e^{\sqrt{x}}}{\sqrt{x}}$ in the interval $[1, 4]$.

Let $u = \sqrt{x}$, so $du = \dfrac{dx}{2\sqrt{x}}$

Average value $= \dfrac{1}{4-1} \displaystyle\int_1^4 \dfrac{e^{\sqrt{x}}}{\sqrt{x}}\, dx$

$= \dfrac{2}{3} \displaystyle\int_1^2 e^u\, du$

$= \dfrac{2e}{3}(e-1)$

≈ 3.114

24. **(D)**

$\displaystyle\lim_{x \to a} \dfrac{\sqrt[3]{x} - \sqrt[3]{a}}{x - a} = \dfrac{\dfrac{1}{3}x^{-\frac{2}{3}}}{1}\bigg|_{x=a}$

$= \dfrac{1}{3}a^{-\frac{2}{3}}$

$= \dfrac{1}{3} \times \dfrac{\sqrt[3]{a}}{a}$

25. **(E)**

$\displaystyle\lim_{x \to \infty} \dfrac{(\ln x)^2}{x} = \dfrac{\infty}{\infty}$, an indeterminate form.

By L'Hôpital's rule, we have $\lim\limits_{x\to\infty}\dfrac{(\ln x)^2}{x}=\lim\limits_{x\to\infty}\dfrac{2(\ln x)x^{-1}}{1}$

$$=\lim\limits_{x\to\infty}\dfrac{2\ln x}{x}$$

$$=\dfrac{\infty}{\infty},$$

still indeterminate.

Applying L'Hôpital's rule again, we have $\lim\limits_{x\to\infty}\dfrac{\frac{2}{x}}{1}=\lim\limits_{x\to\infty}\dfrac{2}{x}$

$$=0.$$

26.   **(B)**

The relative maximum occurs at a critical point. Since the function is a polynomial, its critical points are those points where its derivative is zero.

The derivative is: $f'(x)=20x^4+60x^3+60x^2+20x$

Factor: $f'(x)=20x\left(x^3+3x^2+3x+1\right)$

$$=20x(x+1)^3$$

This is zero at: $x=0$ and $x=-1$

Use the First Derivative Test to see which of these is a relative maximum. Check $f'(x)$ at sample points in each of the intervals bounded by the critical points:

-2 is in $(-\infty,-1)$: $f'(-2)=40>0$,
so $f(x)$ is increasing on $(-\infty,-1)$;

$$-\dfrac{1}{2}\ \text{is in}\ (-1,0)\text{:}\ f'\left(-\dfrac{1}{2}\right)=-\dfrac{5}{4}<0,$$

so $f(x)$ is decreasing on $(-1,0)$;

1 is in $(0,\infty)$: $f'(1)=160>0$
so $f(x)$ is increasing on $(0,\infty)$.

Thus f has a relative maximum at $x = -1$ because $f(x)$ is increasing on $(-\infty, -1)$ and decreasing on $(-1, 0)$.

27.　**(E)**

The arc length formula is:

$$L = \int_0^{\frac{\pi}{2}} \sqrt{\left(\frac{dx}{dt}\right)^2 + \left(\frac{dy}{dt}\right)^2} \, dt$$

Here:

$$\frac{dx}{dt} = \left(12\cos^2 t\right)(-\sin t)$$

$$\frac{dy}{dt} = \left(12\sin^2 t\right)(\cos t)$$

so:

$$\left(\frac{dx}{dt}\right)^2 = 144\sin^2 t \, \cos^4 t$$

$$\left(\frac{dy}{dt}\right)^2 = 144\sin^4 t \, \cos^2 t$$

so:

$$\left(\frac{dx}{dt}\right)^2 + \left(\frac{dy}{dt}\right)^2 = 144\sin^2 \cos^4 t + 144\sin^4 t \, \cos^2 t$$

$$= \left(144\sin^2 \cos^2 t\right)\left(\cos^2 t + \sin^2 t\right)$$

$$= \left(144\sin^2 t \, \cos^2 t\right)(1)$$

so:

$$\sqrt{\left(\frac{dx}{dt}\right)^2 + \left(\frac{dy}{dt}\right)^2} = 12\sin t \, \cos t$$

Thus:

$$L = \int_0^{\frac{\pi}{2}} 12\sin t \, \cos t \, dt$$

$$= 6\sin^2 t \, \Big|_0^{\frac{\pi}{2}}$$

$$= 6(1)^2 - 6(0)^2$$

$$= 6$$

28. **(C)**

Let: $x = |OA|$

$\quad\quad y = |OB|$

$\quad\quad z = |AB|$

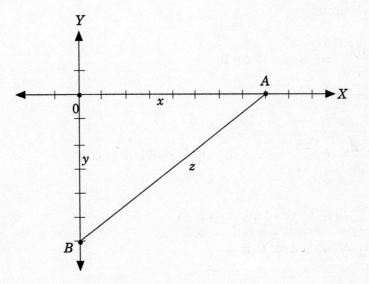

Then x, y, and z are functions of time t, and by the Pythagorean Theorem: $x^2 + y^2 = z^2$

The rates of change of x, y, and z are their derivatives with respect to t:

$$\frac{dx}{dt} = 7$$

$$\frac{dy}{dt} = -2$$

$$\frac{dz}{dt} = ?$$

(Note that $\frac{dy}{dt}$ is negative because the distance $y = |OB|$ is decreasing.)

To find $\frac{dz}{dt}$, differentiate the Pythagorean equation with respect to t:

$$x^2 + y^2 = z^2$$

$$\frac{d}{dt}(x^2 + y^2) = \frac{d}{dt}(z^2)$$

$$2x\frac{dx}{dt} + 2y\frac{dy}{dt} = 2z\frac{dz}{dt}$$

Substitute:

$$2(8)(7) + 2(6)(-2) = 2z\frac{dz}{dt}$$

$$112 - 24 = 2z\frac{dz}{dt}$$

$$2z\frac{dz}{dt} = 88$$

$$z\frac{dz}{dt} = 44$$

Finally, when $x = 8$ and $y = 6$, $z = 10$
(since $x^2 + y^2 = z^2$). Thus:

$$10\frac{dz}{dt} = 44$$

$$\frac{dz}{dt} = \frac{44}{10} = \frac{22}{5}$$

29. **(D)**

$f(x) = \sin|x|$

$f(x) < 0$ for x in $\left(\dfrac{\pi}{2}, \pi\right)$ and f is even, not odd.

$$\int_{-\frac{\pi}{4}}^{\frac{\pi}{4}} f(x)\,dx = 2\int_{0}^{\frac{\pi}{4}} f(x)\,dx \neq 0$$

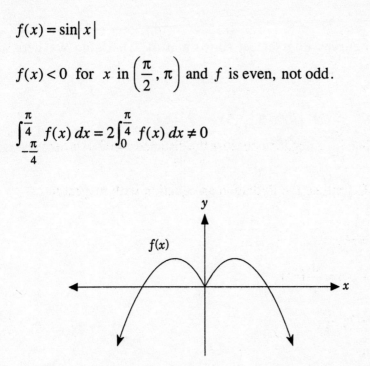

f is symmetric with respect to $x = 0$ since f is even. f is not differentiable at $x = 0$ because the right-hand and left-hand derivatives are $+1$ and -1, respectively.

30. **(E)**

$$h(x) = \frac{f(g(x)) - g(f(x))}{f(x)}$$

$$= \frac{(x^2 - 1) - (x - 1)^2}{x - 1}$$

$$= \frac{(x + 1)(x - 1) - (x - 1)(x - 1)}{(x - 1)}$$

$$= \frac{(x - 1)[(x + 1) - (x - 1)]}{(x - 1)}$$

$$= [x + 1 - x + 1]$$

$$= 2.$$

Since h is a constant function, the range of h is $\{2\}$.

31. **(C)**

The two curves intersect at $(0, 0)$ and $(4, 2)$. Using washers, the volume is

$$\pi\int_0^2 \left[(2y)^2 - (y^2)^2\right] dy = \pi\int_0^2 (4y^2 - y^4) \, dy$$

$$= \pi\left(\frac{4y^3}{3} - \frac{y^5}{5}\right)\Big|_0^2$$

$$= \frac{64\pi}{15}$$

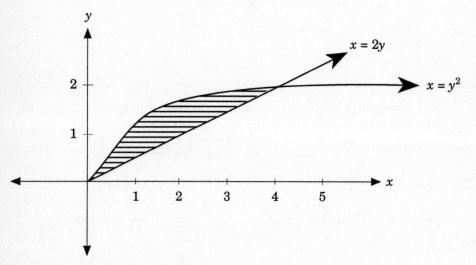

Using shells, the volume is

$$2\pi\int_0^4 x\left(x^{\frac{1}{2}} - \frac{1}{2}x\right) dx = 2\pi\int_0^4 \left(x^{\frac{3}{2}} - \frac{1}{2}x^2\right) dx$$

$$= \frac{64\pi}{15}$$

Calculator: $64 \times \pi \div 15 = \approx 13.404$

32. **(A)**

This is a direct calculator problem. For example,

fnInt ((sin*x* cos2*x*)^2, *x*, 0, 2) can easily give the answer 0.715.

33. **(D)**

Draw the graph $f'(x)$

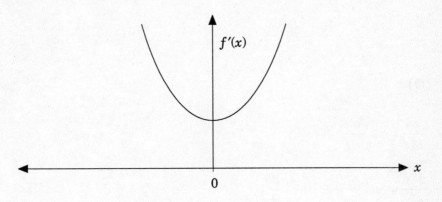

$$f'(x) = 2\frac{\left(1+x^4\right)}{\left(1-x^4\right)^{\frac{3}{2}}}$$

The minimum is clearly at $x = 0$, where $f'(0) = 2$.

Obviously, a minimum exists at $x = 0$. By tracing on the graph to $x = 0$, you find $f'_{min}(x) = 2$.

34. **(B)**

$f(x) = -x + x \ln x$ and $f(e) = -e + e = 0$ so $e = f^{-1}(0)$

Also, $f'(x) = -1 + \dfrac{x}{x} + \ln x = \ln x$.

$$D_x(f^{-1}(x)) = \frac{1}{f'(f^{-1}(x))}$$

$$D_x(f^{-1}(0)) = \frac{1}{f'(f^{-1}(0))}$$

$$= \frac{1}{f'(e)}$$

$$= \frac{1}{\ln e}$$

$$= 1$$

35. **(D)**

$$\frac{dy}{dx} = 5u^4 \frac{du}{dx}$$

$$\frac{d^2y}{dx^2} = 5u^4 \frac{d^2u}{dx^2} + 20u^3 \left(\frac{du}{dx}\right)^2$$

$$\frac{d^3y}{dx^3} = 5u^4 \frac{d^3u}{dx^3} + 20u^3 \frac{du}{dx} \times \frac{d^2u}{dx^2} + 20u^3 \times 2 \times$$

$$\left(\frac{du}{dx}\right) \times \frac{d^2u}{dx^2} + 60u^2 \times \frac{du}{dx} \times \left(\frac{du}{dx}\right)^2$$

$$\frac{d^3y}{dx^3} = 5(1)5 + 20(1)(2)(-3) + 20(1)^3(2)(2)(-3) + 60(1)^2 2(2)^2$$

$$= 25 - 120 - 240 + 480$$

$$= 145$$

36. **(E)**

$f'(6) = 0$ and $f'(-12) = 0$

$f'\left(\dfrac{x}{3}\right) = 0$ when $\dfrac{x}{3} = 6$ or $\dfrac{x}{3} = -12$

so $x = 18$ or $x = -36$

37. **(A)**

Draw the graphs of $s(t)$ and $s'(t)$.

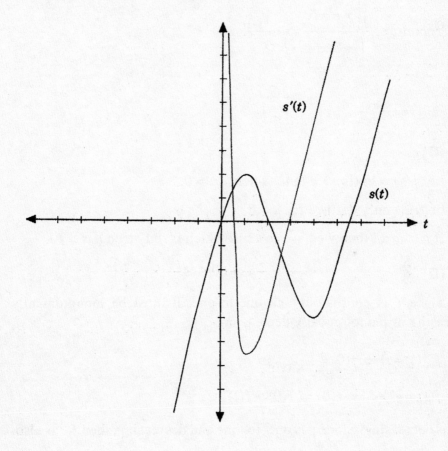

By tracing the most negative $s'(t)$, you get -5.4 at $t = 1.22$.

38. **(A)**

$$\int_0^1 x\, e^x\, dx = x\, e^x \Big|_0^1 - \int_0^1 e^x\, dx = 1,$$

$$\int_0^1 e^{-x}\, dx = -e^{-x} \Big|_0^1$$

$$= -e^{-1} + e^0$$

$$= 1 - e^{-1}$$

Therefore, $\dfrac{\displaystyle\int_0^1 x\, e^x\, dx}{\displaystyle\int_0^1 e^{-x}\, dx} = \dfrac{1}{1 - e^{-1}}$

$$= \dfrac{e}{e-1}$$

39. **(C)**

Let $f(x) = \ln(\ln x) = \ln u$ where $u > 0$.

$\ln(u)$ is only defined for $u > 0$.

If $u = \ln x$, then we have $\ln x > 0$ which is only true if $x > 1$.

40. **(D)**

Since f is continuous and one-to-one, it must be monotonically increasing or monotonically decreasing.

$$f^{-1}(1) = 0 \Rightarrow f(0) = 1$$

$$f(1) = e^{-1} < 1 = f(0) \Rightarrow f(0) > f(1),$$

so f is decreasing. Since f is one–to–one and decreasing, then f^{-1} is also.

$$D_x(f^{-1}(x)) = \frac{1}{f'(f^{-1}(x))}, \qquad \text{so}$$

$$D_x(f^{-1}(e^{-1})) = \frac{1}{f'(f^{-1}(e^{-1}))}$$

$$= \frac{1}{f'(1)}$$

$$= \frac{1}{-2e^{-1}}$$

$$= -\frac{1}{2}e$$

41. **(B)**

   Use the calculator for solving the problem directly. For example,

   fnInt (x^x, x, 0, 2),

   pressing ENTER gives 2.83.

42. **(E)**

   $$\frac{h}{b} = \sin\alpha \quad \text{so} \quad h = b\sin\alpha$$

   $$A = \frac{1}{2}(\text{base} \times \text{height})$$

   $$= \frac{1}{2}cb\sin\alpha$$

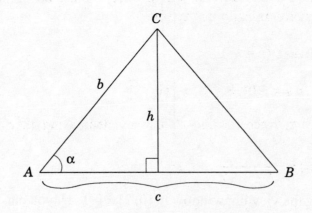

$$\frac{dA}{dt} = \frac{1}{2}cb\cos\alpha\left(\frac{d\alpha}{dt}\right) \Rightarrow \quad \text{at} \quad x = \frac{\pi}{3}$$

$$= \frac{1}{2}cb\cos\left(\frac{\pi}{3}\right)(2)$$

$$= \frac{cb}{2}$$

43. **(C)**

Draw the graphs $f(x)$ and $f'(x)$.

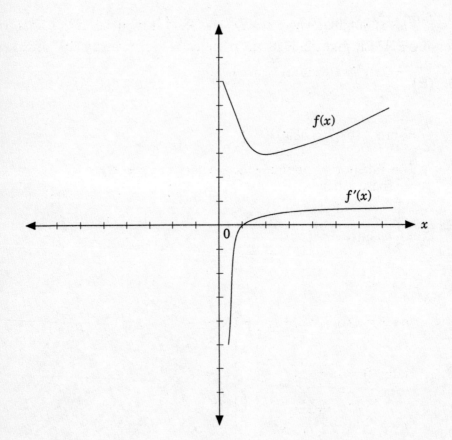

Resetting the viewing window to $[0, 2] \times [-1, 1]$, you can easily find that $c = 1$.

$$f'(x) = \frac{e^{\sqrt{x}}}{2x^{\frac{3}{2}}}\left(\sqrt{x} - 1\right)$$

$f'(x) = 0$ when $\sqrt{x} = 1$, i.e, when $x = 1$.

44.   **(B)**

The distance from a point $P(x, y)$ to the origin $(0, 0)$ is given by:

$$D = \sqrt{x^2 + y^2}$$

This is minimal where $u = D^2 = x^2 + y^2$ is minimal. If $P(x, y)$ is on the given line, then its coordinates x and y satisfy the equation $y = 2x + 7$. Substituting, we have:

$$u = x^2 + y^2$$
$$= x^2 + (2x + 7)^2$$

This function is minimal where its derivative is zero:

$$0 = \frac{du}{dx} = 2x + 2(2x + 7) \cdot 2$$
$$= 10x + 28$$

i.e. $x = -\dfrac{28}{10} = -\dfrac{14}{5}$

and $y = 2x + 7 = 2\left(-\dfrac{14}{5}\right) + 7 = \dfrac{7}{5}$

Here: $D = \sqrt{u} = \sqrt{x^2 + y^2}$

$$= \sqrt{\left(-\frac{14}{5}\right)^2 + \left(\frac{7}{5}\right)^2}$$

$$= \frac{7}{5}\sqrt{5}$$

45. **(B)**

The area of each semicircular cross section is

$$A_x = \frac{1}{2}(\pi y^2) = \frac{\pi}{2}y^2$$

where x is the point on the x-axis locating the cross section and y is the radius of the cross section:

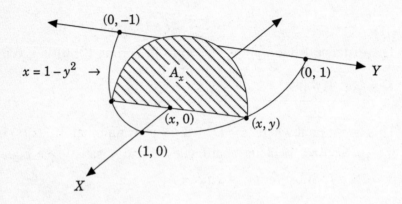

Then the total volume is

$$V = \int_0^1 A_x\,dx$$

$$= \int_0^1 \frac{\pi}{2}y^2\,dx$$

$$= \int_0^1 \frac{\pi}{2}(1-x)\,dx, \text{ since } y^2 = 1-x$$

$$= \frac{\pi}{2}\left[x - \frac{1}{2}x^2\right]_0^1$$

$$= \frac{\pi}{2}\left[\left((1)-\frac{1}{2}(1)^2\right)-\left((0)-\frac{1}{2}(0)^2\right)\right]$$

$$= \frac{\pi}{2}\left[\frac{1}{2}\right]$$

$$= \frac{\pi}{4}$$

SECTION II

1. **(A)**

$$f'(x) = \frac{(-x^2 + x + 2)(2x - 2) - (x^2 - 2x + 1)(-2x + 1)}{(x-2)^2(x+1)^2}$$

$$= \frac{(x-1)\left[-2x^2 + 2x + 4 + 2x^2 - 3x + 1\right]}{(x-2)^2(x+1)^2}$$

$$= \frac{(x-1)(-x+5)}{(x-2)^2(x+1)^2}$$

The critical values are $x = 5, 2, -1$, and 1, since $f'(x)$ at these points is either zero or undefined.

(B)

$$f(x) = \frac{(x-1)^2}{(2-x)(x+1)}$$

```
+ + + + + + + + + + + + + + + + + + 0 - - -    (2 - x)
- - - - - 0 + + + + + + + + + + + + + + + +    (x + 1)
```

```
◄─────────┼────────┼──────┼──────┼──────┼─────►  x
         -1        0       1      2      3
```

$$f'(x) = \frac{(x-1)(-x+5)}{(x-2)^2(x+1)^2}$$

```
(x - 1)    - - - - - - - - - 0 + + + + + + + + + + + + + + + + + + +

(-x + 5)   + + + + + + + + + + + + + + + + + + + + + + + + + + 0 - - -
```

```
         decreasing              increasing          decreasing
◄────────┼────────┼──────✗──────┼──────┼──────┼──────✗───►  x
        -1        0       1      2      3      4       5
```

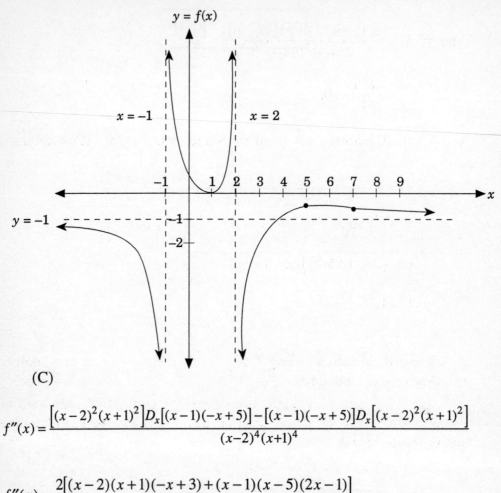

(C)

$$f''(x) = \frac{\left[(x-2)^2(x+1)^2\right]D_x\left[(x-1)(-x+5)\right] - \left[(x-1)(-x+5)\right]D_x\left[(x-2)^2(x+1)^2\right]}{(x-2)^4(x+1)^4}$$

$$f''(x) = \frac{2\left[(x-2)(x+1)(-x+3) + (x-1)(x-5)(2x-1)\right]}{(x-2)^3(x+1)^3}$$

$$f''(x) = \frac{2(x^3 - 9x^2 + 15x - 11)}{(x-2)^3(x+1)^3}$$

The second derivative is zero between 7 and 8 so there is a point of inflection between $n = 7$ and $n + 1 = 8$.

$$f''(7) = \frac{2(7^3 - 9(7^2) + 15(7) - 11)}{(7-2)^3(7+1)^3}$$

$$= \frac{2(-4)}{5^3 8^3} < 0$$

and $f''(8) = \dfrac{2(8^3 - 9(8^2) + 15(8) - 11)}{(8-2)^3(8+1)^3}$

$\qquad = \dfrac{2(45)}{6^3 9^3} > 0,$

so, $f''(x) = 0$ between $x = 7$ and $x = 8$, indicating an inflection point.

2. (A)

$$y = t^2 \exp\!\left(3t^{3.5}\right)$$

$$y' = \left(2t + 10.5t^{4.5}\right)\exp\!\left(3t^{3.5}\right)$$

$$y'(1) = 12.5e^3$$

$$\approx 251$$

(B)

It can be seen from the graph as $t \to 0$, $y' \to 0$. Zero is the limit of y' as $t \to 0$, however, the value is never actually assumed by y' since t never reaches $t = 0$.

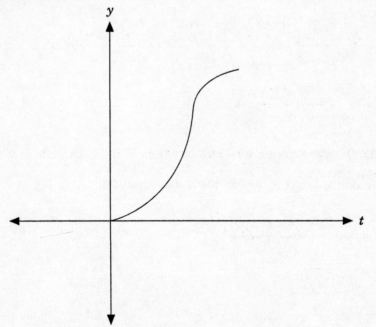

(C)

Obviously, as $t \to \infty$, $y' \to \infty$.

3. (A)

$$f'(x) = \left(e^{-\cos x}\right)(\cos x)) + \sin x\left(e^{-\cos x}\right)\sin x$$

$$= e^{-\cos x}\left[\cos x + \sin^2 x\right]$$

$$= e^{-\cos x}\left[\cos x + (1 - \cos^2 x)\right]$$

(B)

$$f''(x) = e^{-\cos x}\left[-\sin x + 2\cos x + 3x\cos x + \sin^3 x\right]$$

$$= e^{-\cos x}\left[-\sin x + 3\sin x \cos x + \sin^3 x\right]$$

$$= e^{-\cos x}(\sin x)\left(3\cos x + \sin^2 x - 1\right)$$

$$= e^{-\cos x}(\sin x)\left(3\cos x - \left(1 - \sin^2 x\right)\right)$$

$$= e^{-\cos x}(\sin x)\left(3\cos x - \cos^2 x\right)$$

$$= e^{-\cos x}\sin x \cos x(3 - \cos x)$$

(C)

$y' = 0$ when $\cos x + 1 - \cos^2 x = 0$.

We can solve this by the quadratic equation:

$$\cos x = -\frac{1 \pm \sqrt{1 - 4(-1)(1)}}{2(-1)}$$

$$= \frac{1 - \sqrt{5}}{2}.$$

Note that $\cos x = \dfrac{1+\sqrt{5}}{2}$ is not possible because $\dfrac{1+\sqrt{5}}{2} > 1$ and $\cos x$ is always ≤ 1.

So, $x = \arccos\left(\dfrac{1-\sqrt{5}}{2}\right) + 2k\pi \leftarrow$ Location of relative extrema for any integer k.

Let $y'' = 0$ to find points of inflection.

$y'' = 0$ when $\sin x = 0$ or $\cos x = 0$ ($3 - \cos x = 0$ is impossible, as is $e^{-\cos x} = 0$).

$\Rightarrow x = k\pi$ or $x = \dfrac{\pi}{2} + k\pi$ are where the points of inflection are found, for any integer k.

The function crosses the x-axis when $f(x) = e^{-\cos x} (\sin x) = 0$, i.e., when $\sin x = 0$, namely $x = k\pi$, $k =$ any integer.

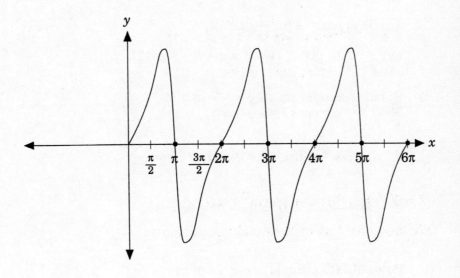

(D)

$$\int_0^{\frac{\pi}{2}} e^{-\cos x} \sin x \, dx = \int_{-1}^0 e^u du \quad \text{where} \quad u = -\cos x, \quad du = \sin x \, dx$$

$$= e^u \Big|_{-1}^0$$

$$= e^0 - e^{-1}$$

$$= 1 - \frac{1}{e}$$

4. (A)

Start with a general third degree polynomial of the form

$$P(x) = ax^3 + bx^2 + cx + d$$

(i)   The intercepts are (1, 0) and (0, 12).

Let $x = 0$ to get $P(0) = 12 = d$

So, $P(x) = ax^3 + bx^2 + cx + 12$

Let $x = 1$ to get $P(1) = 0 = a + b + c + 12$

(ii) Relative maximum at $x = -\frac{2}{3}$ implies

$$P'(x) = 3ax^2 + 2bx + c = 0 \quad \text{when} \quad x = -\frac{2}{3}$$

$$3\left(\frac{4}{9}\right)a - \frac{4}{3}b + c = 0 \Rightarrow 4a - 4b + 3c = 0$$

(iii) Point of inflection at $x = \frac{5}{3}$ implies

$$P''(x) = 6ax + 2b = 0 \quad \text{when} \quad x = \frac{5}{3}$$

$$6\left(\frac{5}{3}\right)a + 2b = 0 \Rightarrow 5a + b = 0$$

Now solve the equations above simultaneously.

$a + b + c = -12$

$4a - 4b + 3c = 0$

$5a + b = 0$

$\Rightarrow 5a = -b$

$a - 5a + c = -12$

$\Rightarrow -4a + c = -12$

$4a + 4(5a) + 3c = 0$

$\Rightarrow 24a + 3c = 0 \Rightarrow 8a + c = 0$

$12a = 12, \quad a = 1, \quad b = -5, \quad c = -12 + 4a = -8.$

The simultaneous solution is $a = 1$, $b = -5$, $c = -8$

so, $P(x) = x^3 - 5x^2 - 8x + 12$

$= (x - 1)(x - 6)(x + 2)$

(A)

$(x + 2)$ $\quad - - - 0 +$

$(x - 6)$ $\quad - 0 + + + + +$

$(x - 1)$ $\quad - - - - - - - - - - - - - - - - - - 0 +$

The polynomial is positive for $-2 < x < 1$ or $x > 6$.

(B)

$P'(x) = 3x^2 - 10x - 8$

$= (3x + 2)(x - 4)$

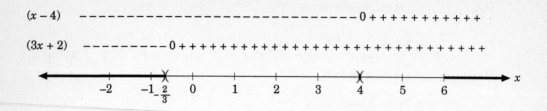

The derivative is positive for $x < -\dfrac{2}{3}$ or $x > 4$.

(C)

$P''(x) = 6x - 10 = 2(3x - 5)$. When $P''(x) < 0$, the function is concave down.

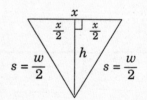

The function is concave down for $x < \dfrac{5}{3}$.

5. (A)

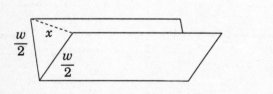

If $s = \dfrac{w}{2}$ then $h^2 = s^2 - \left(\dfrac{x}{2}\right)^2$ for $x \in [0, 2s]$, by the Pythagorean theorem. So the cross-sectional area is

$$A = \frac{1}{2}bh = \frac{1}{2}x\sqrt{s^2 - \frac{x^2}{4}}, \quad \text{so} \quad A^2 = \frac{x^2 s^2}{4} - \frac{x^4}{16},$$

which is an easier function to work with.

The maximum value of a continuous function in a closed interval occurs at the end points or at a critical value. So evaluate the function at 0, $2s$, and any critical values.

To find the critical values, we differentiate A^2 with respect to x:

$$2AA' = \frac{s^2}{4}2x - \frac{4x^3}{16} = \frac{x}{4}(2s^2 - x^2)$$

Set $A' = 0$ to find critical value(s). If $A' = 0$ then $x = 0$ or $2s^2 - x^2 = 0$. $x = 0$ makes no constructive sense, so $x = s\sqrt{2}$.

Evaluate A at the endpoints and critical point to get:

x	A
0	0
$2s$	0
$s\sqrt{2}$	$\dfrac{s^2}{2}$

The maximum amount of water is handled when

$$x = s\sqrt{2} = \frac{w\sqrt{2}}{2}$$

(B)

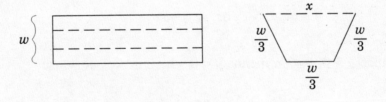

If $a = \dfrac{w}{3}$ then $h^2 = a^2 - y^2$ for $y \in [0, a]$, by the Pythagorean theorem.

$$A = \frac{1}{2}h(2y+2a) = \frac{2}{2}\sqrt{a^2-y^2}\,(y+a)$$

$$= (y+a)\sqrt{a^2-y^2}\,.$$

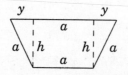

Taking the derivative of A with respect to y, we have

$$A' = (y+a)\frac{1}{2}(a^2-y^2)^{-\frac{1}{2}}(-2y) + \sqrt{a^2-y^2}$$

$$= (a^2-y^2)^{-\frac{1}{2}}\left[-y^2-ay+a^2-y^2\right]$$

$$= \frac{(-2y^2-ay+a^2)}{\sqrt{a^2-y^2}}$$

The maximum value of a continuous function in a closed interval occurs at a critical value or its endpoints. So evaluate the function at 0 and a and any critical values. We find critical values as follows:

If $A' = 0$ then $-2y^2 - ay + a^2 = 0$

$$(-2y+a)(y+a) = 0$$

$$\Rightarrow y = \frac{a}{2} \quad \text{or} \quad y = -a\,.$$

Since $a > 0$, $y = -a$ means $y < 0$ which makes no sense.

So $y = \frac{a}{2}$ is a critical value. We then have:

y	A
0	a^2
a	0
$\dfrac{a}{2}$	$\dfrac{3a^2\sqrt{3}}{4} > a^2$

So the maximum amount of water is handled when $y = \dfrac{a}{2}$, which

means $x = a + 2y = a + a = 2a = \dfrac{2w}{3}$.

6. (A)

$y - y_1 = m(x - x_1)$ so

$y - 2 = 1(x - a)$

$y = x - a + 2$

(B)

The integral of an odd function over an interval symmetric about the origin (say, from $x = -a$ to $x = a$) must vanish.

We start with:

$$\int_{-a}^{a} f(a) - f(-a) = \int_{-a}^{a} f(x)\, dx$$

as given, and then split integral into two parts whose values add up to zero.

$$\int_{-a}^{a} f(x)\, dx = \int_{-a}^{0} f(x)\, dx + \int_{0}^{a} f(x)\, dx$$

We must rewrite the first integral on the right. We use the change of variable $u = -x$

$x = -u$ therefore $dx \rightarrow -du$

$x = 0 \rightarrow u = 0$

$x = -a \rightarrow u = a$

$f(x) \rightarrow f(-u) = -f(a)$

The integral becomes

$$-\int_{-a}^{0} f(-x)\, dx \Rightarrow \int_{-a}^{0} -f(u)\,(-du)$$

$$= \int_{a}^{0} f(u)\,(du)$$

$$= \int_{0}^{a} f(u)\,(du)$$

or, equivalently, $-\int_{0}^{a} f(x)\, dx$. Hence, we see that

$$\int_{-a}^{a} f(x)\, dx = 0$$

(C)

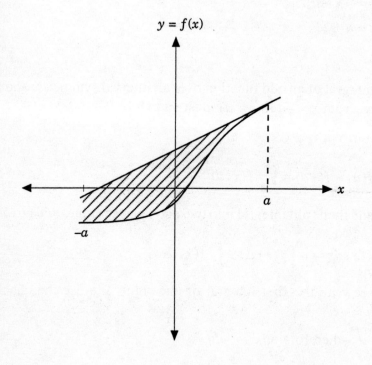

$$A = \int_{-a}^{a} \left[(x - a + 2) - f(x) \right] dx$$

$$= \left[\frac{x^2}{2} + (2 - a)x - F(x) \right]\Big|_{-a}^{a}$$

$$= \left[\frac{a^2}{2} + (2 - a)a - F(a) \right] - \left[\frac{(-a)^2}{2} + (2 - a)(-a) - F(-a) \right]$$

$$= 2a(2 - a) - F(a) + F(-a)$$

$$= 2a(2 - a)$$

since $F(-a) = F(a)$

Advanced Placement Examination in Calculus AB

ANSWER SHEETS

AP Calculus AB
Test 1

1. Ⓐ Ⓑ Ⓒ Ⓓ Ⓔ
2. Ⓐ Ⓑ Ⓒ Ⓓ Ⓔ
3. Ⓐ Ⓑ Ⓒ Ⓓ Ⓔ
4. Ⓐ Ⓑ Ⓒ Ⓓ Ⓔ
5. Ⓐ Ⓑ Ⓒ Ⓓ Ⓔ
6. Ⓐ Ⓑ Ⓒ Ⓓ Ⓔ
7. Ⓐ Ⓑ Ⓒ Ⓓ Ⓔ
8. Ⓐ Ⓑ Ⓒ Ⓓ Ⓔ
9. Ⓐ Ⓑ Ⓒ Ⓓ Ⓔ
10. Ⓐ Ⓑ Ⓒ Ⓓ Ⓔ
11. Ⓐ Ⓑ Ⓒ Ⓓ Ⓔ
12. Ⓐ Ⓑ Ⓒ Ⓓ Ⓔ
13. Ⓐ Ⓑ Ⓒ Ⓓ Ⓔ
14. Ⓐ Ⓑ Ⓒ Ⓓ Ⓔ
15. Ⓐ Ⓑ Ⓒ Ⓓ Ⓔ
16. Ⓐ Ⓑ Ⓒ Ⓓ Ⓔ
17. Ⓐ Ⓑ Ⓒ Ⓓ Ⓔ
18. Ⓐ Ⓑ Ⓒ Ⓓ Ⓔ
19. Ⓐ Ⓑ Ⓒ Ⓓ Ⓔ
20. Ⓐ Ⓑ Ⓒ Ⓓ Ⓔ
21. Ⓐ Ⓑ Ⓒ Ⓓ Ⓔ
22. Ⓐ Ⓑ Ⓒ Ⓓ Ⓔ
23. Ⓐ Ⓑ Ⓒ Ⓓ Ⓔ

24. Ⓐ Ⓑ Ⓒ Ⓓ Ⓔ
25. Ⓐ Ⓑ Ⓒ Ⓓ Ⓔ
26. Ⓐ Ⓑ Ⓒ Ⓓ Ⓔ
27. Ⓐ Ⓑ Ⓒ Ⓓ Ⓔ
28. Ⓐ Ⓑ Ⓒ Ⓓ Ⓔ
29. Ⓐ Ⓑ Ⓒ Ⓓ Ⓔ
30. Ⓐ Ⓑ Ⓒ Ⓓ Ⓔ
31. Ⓐ Ⓑ Ⓒ Ⓓ Ⓔ
32. Ⓐ Ⓑ Ⓒ Ⓓ Ⓔ
33. Ⓐ Ⓑ Ⓒ Ⓓ Ⓔ
34. Ⓐ Ⓑ Ⓒ Ⓓ Ⓔ
35. Ⓐ Ⓑ Ⓒ Ⓓ Ⓔ
36. Ⓐ Ⓑ Ⓒ Ⓓ Ⓔ
37. Ⓐ Ⓑ Ⓒ Ⓓ Ⓔ
38. Ⓐ Ⓑ Ⓒ Ⓓ Ⓔ
39. Ⓐ Ⓑ Ⓒ Ⓓ Ⓔ
40. Ⓐ Ⓑ Ⓒ Ⓓ Ⓔ
41. Ⓐ Ⓑ Ⓒ Ⓓ Ⓔ
42. Ⓐ Ⓑ Ⓒ Ⓓ Ⓔ
43. Ⓐ Ⓑ Ⓒ Ⓓ Ⓔ
44. Ⓐ Ⓑ Ⓒ Ⓓ Ⓔ
45. Ⓐ Ⓑ Ⓒ Ⓓ Ⓔ

AP Calculus AB
Test 2

1. Ⓐ Ⓑ Ⓒ Ⓓ Ⓔ   24. Ⓐ Ⓑ Ⓒ Ⓓ Ⓔ
2. Ⓐ Ⓑ Ⓒ Ⓓ Ⓔ   25. Ⓐ Ⓑ Ⓒ Ⓓ Ⓔ
3. Ⓐ Ⓑ Ⓒ Ⓓ Ⓔ   26. Ⓐ Ⓑ Ⓒ Ⓓ Ⓔ
4. Ⓐ Ⓑ Ⓒ Ⓓ Ⓔ   27. Ⓐ Ⓑ Ⓒ Ⓓ Ⓔ
5. Ⓐ Ⓑ Ⓒ Ⓓ Ⓔ   28. Ⓐ Ⓑ Ⓒ Ⓓ Ⓔ
6. Ⓐ Ⓑ Ⓒ Ⓓ Ⓔ   29. Ⓐ Ⓑ Ⓒ Ⓓ Ⓔ
7. Ⓐ Ⓑ Ⓒ Ⓓ Ⓔ   30. Ⓐ Ⓑ Ⓒ Ⓓ Ⓔ
8. Ⓐ Ⓑ Ⓒ Ⓓ Ⓔ   31. Ⓐ Ⓑ Ⓒ Ⓓ Ⓔ
9. Ⓐ Ⓑ Ⓒ Ⓓ Ⓔ   32. Ⓐ Ⓑ Ⓒ Ⓓ Ⓔ
10. Ⓐ Ⓑ Ⓒ Ⓓ Ⓔ   33. Ⓐ Ⓑ Ⓒ Ⓓ Ⓔ
11. Ⓐ Ⓑ Ⓒ Ⓓ Ⓔ   34. Ⓐ Ⓑ Ⓒ Ⓓ Ⓔ
12. Ⓐ Ⓑ Ⓒ Ⓓ Ⓔ   35. Ⓐ Ⓑ Ⓒ Ⓓ Ⓔ
13. Ⓐ Ⓑ Ⓒ Ⓓ Ⓔ   36. Ⓐ Ⓑ Ⓒ Ⓓ Ⓔ
14. Ⓐ Ⓑ Ⓒ Ⓓ Ⓔ   37. Ⓐ Ⓑ Ⓒ Ⓓ Ⓔ
15. Ⓐ Ⓑ Ⓒ Ⓓ Ⓔ   38. Ⓐ Ⓑ Ⓒ Ⓓ Ⓔ
16. Ⓐ Ⓑ Ⓒ Ⓓ Ⓔ   39. Ⓐ Ⓑ Ⓒ Ⓓ Ⓔ
17. Ⓐ Ⓑ Ⓒ Ⓓ Ⓔ   40. Ⓐ Ⓑ Ⓒ Ⓓ Ⓔ
18. Ⓐ Ⓑ Ⓒ Ⓓ Ⓔ   41. Ⓐ Ⓑ Ⓒ Ⓓ Ⓔ
19. Ⓐ Ⓑ Ⓒ Ⓓ Ⓔ   42. Ⓐ Ⓑ Ⓒ Ⓓ Ⓔ
20. Ⓐ Ⓑ Ⓒ Ⓓ Ⓔ   43. Ⓐ Ⓑ Ⓒ Ⓓ Ⓔ
21. Ⓐ Ⓑ Ⓒ Ⓓ Ⓔ   44. Ⓐ Ⓑ Ⓒ Ⓓ Ⓔ
22. Ⓐ Ⓑ Ⓒ Ⓓ Ⓔ   45. Ⓐ Ⓑ Ⓒ Ⓓ Ⓔ
23. Ⓐ Ⓑ Ⓒ Ⓓ Ⓔ

AP Calculus AB
Test 3

1. Ⓐ Ⓑ Ⓒ Ⓓ Ⓔ
2. Ⓐ Ⓑ Ⓒ Ⓓ Ⓔ
3. Ⓐ Ⓑ Ⓒ Ⓓ Ⓔ
4. Ⓐ Ⓑ Ⓒ Ⓓ Ⓔ
5. Ⓐ Ⓑ Ⓒ Ⓓ Ⓔ
6. Ⓐ Ⓑ Ⓒ Ⓓ Ⓔ
7. Ⓐ Ⓑ Ⓒ Ⓓ Ⓔ
8. Ⓐ Ⓑ Ⓒ Ⓓ Ⓔ
9. Ⓐ Ⓑ Ⓒ Ⓓ Ⓔ
10. Ⓐ Ⓑ Ⓒ Ⓓ Ⓔ
11. Ⓐ Ⓑ Ⓒ Ⓓ Ⓔ
12. Ⓐ Ⓑ Ⓒ Ⓓ Ⓔ
13. Ⓐ Ⓑ Ⓒ Ⓓ Ⓔ
14. Ⓐ Ⓑ Ⓒ Ⓓ Ⓔ
15. Ⓐ Ⓑ Ⓒ Ⓓ Ⓔ
16. Ⓐ Ⓑ Ⓒ Ⓓ Ⓔ
17. Ⓐ Ⓑ Ⓒ Ⓓ Ⓔ
18. Ⓐ Ⓑ Ⓒ Ⓓ Ⓔ
19. Ⓐ Ⓑ Ⓒ Ⓓ Ⓔ
20. Ⓐ Ⓑ Ⓒ Ⓓ Ⓔ
21. Ⓐ Ⓑ Ⓒ Ⓓ Ⓔ
22. Ⓐ Ⓑ Ⓒ Ⓓ Ⓔ
23. Ⓐ Ⓑ Ⓒ Ⓓ Ⓔ

24. Ⓐ Ⓑ Ⓒ Ⓓ Ⓔ
25. Ⓐ Ⓑ Ⓒ Ⓓ Ⓔ
26. Ⓐ Ⓑ Ⓒ Ⓓ Ⓔ
27. Ⓐ Ⓑ Ⓒ Ⓓ Ⓔ
28. Ⓐ Ⓑ Ⓒ Ⓓ Ⓔ
29. Ⓐ Ⓑ Ⓒ Ⓓ Ⓔ
30. Ⓐ Ⓑ Ⓒ Ⓓ Ⓔ
31. Ⓐ Ⓑ Ⓒ Ⓓ Ⓔ
32. Ⓐ Ⓑ Ⓒ Ⓓ Ⓔ
33. Ⓐ Ⓑ Ⓒ Ⓓ Ⓔ
34. Ⓐ Ⓑ Ⓒ Ⓓ Ⓔ
35. Ⓐ Ⓑ Ⓒ Ⓓ Ⓔ
36. Ⓐ Ⓑ Ⓒ Ⓓ Ⓔ
37. Ⓐ Ⓑ Ⓒ Ⓓ Ⓔ
38. Ⓐ Ⓑ Ⓒ Ⓓ Ⓔ
39. Ⓐ Ⓑ Ⓒ Ⓓ Ⓔ
40. Ⓐ Ⓑ Ⓒ Ⓓ Ⓔ
41. Ⓐ Ⓑ Ⓒ Ⓓ Ⓔ
42. Ⓐ Ⓑ Ⓒ Ⓓ Ⓔ
43. Ⓐ Ⓑ Ⓒ Ⓓ Ⓔ
44. Ⓐ Ⓑ Ⓒ Ⓓ Ⓔ
45. Ⓐ Ⓑ Ⓒ Ⓓ Ⓔ

AP Calculus AB
Test 4

1. Ⓐ Ⓑ Ⓒ Ⓓ Ⓔ
2. Ⓐ Ⓑ Ⓒ Ⓓ Ⓔ
3. Ⓐ Ⓑ Ⓒ Ⓓ Ⓔ
4. Ⓐ Ⓑ Ⓒ Ⓓ Ⓔ
5. Ⓐ Ⓑ Ⓒ Ⓓ Ⓔ
6. Ⓐ Ⓑ Ⓒ Ⓓ Ⓔ
7. Ⓐ Ⓑ Ⓒ Ⓓ Ⓔ
8. Ⓐ Ⓑ Ⓒ Ⓓ Ⓔ
9. Ⓐ Ⓑ Ⓒ Ⓓ Ⓔ
10. Ⓐ Ⓑ Ⓒ Ⓓ Ⓔ
11. Ⓐ Ⓑ Ⓒ Ⓓ Ⓔ
12. Ⓐ Ⓑ Ⓒ Ⓓ Ⓔ
13. Ⓐ Ⓑ Ⓒ Ⓓ Ⓔ
14. Ⓐ Ⓑ Ⓒ Ⓓ Ⓔ
15. Ⓐ Ⓑ Ⓒ Ⓓ Ⓔ
16. Ⓐ Ⓑ Ⓒ Ⓓ Ⓔ
17. Ⓐ Ⓑ Ⓒ Ⓓ Ⓔ
18. Ⓐ Ⓑ Ⓒ Ⓓ Ⓔ
19. Ⓐ Ⓑ Ⓒ Ⓓ Ⓔ
20. Ⓐ Ⓑ Ⓒ Ⓓ Ⓔ
21. Ⓐ Ⓑ Ⓒ Ⓓ Ⓔ
22. Ⓐ Ⓑ Ⓒ Ⓓ Ⓔ
23. Ⓐ Ⓑ Ⓒ Ⓓ Ⓔ

24. Ⓐ Ⓑ Ⓒ Ⓓ Ⓔ
25. Ⓐ Ⓑ Ⓒ Ⓓ Ⓔ
26. Ⓐ Ⓑ Ⓒ Ⓓ Ⓔ
27. Ⓐ Ⓑ Ⓒ Ⓓ Ⓔ
28. Ⓐ Ⓑ Ⓒ Ⓓ Ⓔ
29. Ⓐ Ⓑ Ⓒ Ⓓ Ⓔ
30. Ⓐ Ⓑ Ⓒ Ⓓ Ⓔ
31. Ⓐ Ⓑ Ⓒ Ⓓ Ⓔ
32. Ⓐ Ⓑ Ⓒ Ⓓ Ⓔ
33. Ⓐ Ⓑ Ⓒ Ⓓ Ⓔ
34. Ⓐ Ⓑ Ⓒ Ⓓ Ⓔ
35. Ⓐ Ⓑ Ⓒ Ⓓ Ⓔ
36. Ⓐ Ⓑ Ⓒ Ⓓ Ⓔ
37. Ⓐ Ⓑ Ⓒ Ⓓ Ⓔ
38. Ⓐ Ⓑ Ⓒ Ⓓ Ⓔ
39. Ⓐ Ⓑ Ⓒ Ⓓ Ⓔ
40. Ⓐ Ⓑ Ⓒ Ⓓ Ⓔ
41. Ⓐ Ⓑ Ⓒ Ⓓ Ⓔ
42. Ⓐ Ⓑ Ⓒ Ⓓ Ⓔ
43. Ⓐ Ⓑ Ⓒ Ⓓ Ⓔ
44. Ⓐ Ⓑ Ⓒ Ⓓ Ⓔ
45. Ⓐ Ⓑ Ⓒ Ⓓ Ⓔ

AP Calculus AB
Test 5

1. Ⓐ Ⓑ Ⓒ Ⓓ Ⓔ
2. Ⓐ Ⓑ Ⓒ Ⓓ Ⓔ
3. Ⓐ Ⓑ Ⓒ Ⓓ Ⓔ
4. Ⓐ Ⓑ Ⓒ Ⓓ Ⓔ
5. Ⓐ Ⓑ Ⓒ Ⓓ Ⓔ
6. Ⓐ Ⓑ Ⓒ Ⓓ Ⓔ
7. Ⓐ Ⓑ Ⓒ Ⓓ Ⓔ
8. Ⓐ Ⓑ Ⓒ Ⓓ Ⓔ
9. Ⓐ Ⓑ Ⓒ Ⓓ Ⓔ
10. Ⓐ Ⓑ Ⓒ Ⓓ Ⓔ
11. Ⓐ Ⓑ Ⓒ Ⓓ Ⓔ
12. Ⓐ Ⓑ Ⓒ Ⓓ Ⓔ
13. Ⓐ Ⓑ Ⓒ Ⓓ Ⓔ
14. Ⓐ Ⓑ Ⓒ Ⓓ Ⓔ
15. Ⓐ Ⓑ Ⓒ Ⓓ Ⓔ
16. Ⓐ Ⓑ Ⓒ Ⓓ Ⓔ
17. Ⓐ Ⓑ Ⓒ Ⓓ Ⓔ
18. Ⓐ Ⓑ Ⓒ Ⓓ Ⓔ
19. Ⓐ Ⓑ Ⓒ Ⓓ Ⓔ
20. Ⓐ Ⓑ Ⓒ Ⓓ Ⓔ
21. Ⓐ Ⓑ Ⓒ Ⓓ Ⓔ
22. Ⓐ Ⓑ Ⓒ Ⓓ Ⓔ
23. Ⓐ Ⓑ Ⓒ Ⓓ Ⓔ

24. Ⓐ Ⓑ Ⓒ Ⓓ Ⓔ
25. Ⓐ Ⓑ Ⓒ Ⓓ Ⓔ
26. Ⓐ Ⓑ Ⓒ Ⓓ Ⓔ
27. Ⓐ Ⓑ Ⓒ Ⓓ Ⓔ
28. Ⓐ Ⓑ Ⓒ Ⓓ Ⓔ
29. Ⓐ Ⓑ Ⓒ Ⓓ Ⓔ
30. Ⓐ Ⓑ Ⓒ Ⓓ Ⓔ
31. Ⓐ Ⓑ Ⓒ Ⓓ Ⓔ
32. Ⓐ Ⓑ Ⓒ Ⓓ Ⓔ
33. Ⓐ Ⓑ Ⓒ Ⓓ Ⓔ
34. Ⓐ Ⓑ Ⓒ Ⓓ Ⓔ
35. Ⓐ Ⓑ Ⓒ Ⓓ Ⓔ
36. Ⓐ Ⓑ Ⓒ Ⓓ Ⓔ
37. Ⓐ Ⓑ Ⓒ Ⓓ Ⓔ
38. Ⓐ Ⓑ Ⓒ Ⓓ Ⓔ
39. Ⓐ Ⓑ Ⓒ Ⓓ Ⓔ
40. Ⓐ Ⓑ Ⓒ Ⓓ Ⓔ
41. Ⓐ Ⓑ Ⓒ Ⓓ Ⓔ
42. Ⓐ Ⓑ Ⓒ Ⓓ Ⓔ
43. Ⓐ Ⓑ Ⓒ Ⓓ Ⓔ
44. Ⓐ Ⓑ Ⓒ Ⓓ Ⓔ
45. Ⓐ Ⓑ Ⓒ Ⓓ Ⓔ

AP Calculus AB
Test 6

1. Ⓐ Ⓑ Ⓒ Ⓓ Ⓔ
2. Ⓐ Ⓑ Ⓒ Ⓓ Ⓔ
3. Ⓐ Ⓑ Ⓒ Ⓓ Ⓔ
4. Ⓐ Ⓑ Ⓒ Ⓓ Ⓔ
5. Ⓐ Ⓑ Ⓒ Ⓓ Ⓔ
6. Ⓐ Ⓑ Ⓒ Ⓓ Ⓔ
7. Ⓐ Ⓑ Ⓒ Ⓓ Ⓔ
8. Ⓐ Ⓑ Ⓒ Ⓓ Ⓔ
9. Ⓐ Ⓑ Ⓒ Ⓓ Ⓔ
10. Ⓐ Ⓑ Ⓒ Ⓓ Ⓔ
11. Ⓐ Ⓑ Ⓒ Ⓓ Ⓔ
12. Ⓐ Ⓑ Ⓒ Ⓓ Ⓔ
13. Ⓐ Ⓑ Ⓒ Ⓓ Ⓔ
14. Ⓐ Ⓑ Ⓒ Ⓓ Ⓔ
15. Ⓐ Ⓑ Ⓒ Ⓓ Ⓔ
16. Ⓐ Ⓑ Ⓒ Ⓓ Ⓔ
17. Ⓐ Ⓑ Ⓒ Ⓓ Ⓔ
18. Ⓐ Ⓑ Ⓒ Ⓓ Ⓔ
19. Ⓐ Ⓑ Ⓒ Ⓓ Ⓔ
20. Ⓐ Ⓑ Ⓒ Ⓓ Ⓔ
21. Ⓐ Ⓑ Ⓒ Ⓓ Ⓔ
22. Ⓐ Ⓑ Ⓒ Ⓓ Ⓔ
23. Ⓐ Ⓑ Ⓒ Ⓓ Ⓔ

24. Ⓐ Ⓑ Ⓒ Ⓓ Ⓔ
25. Ⓐ Ⓑ Ⓒ Ⓓ Ⓔ
26. Ⓐ Ⓑ Ⓒ Ⓓ Ⓔ
27. Ⓐ Ⓑ Ⓒ Ⓓ Ⓔ
28. Ⓐ Ⓑ Ⓒ Ⓓ Ⓔ
29. Ⓐ Ⓑ Ⓒ Ⓓ Ⓔ
30. Ⓐ Ⓑ Ⓒ Ⓓ Ⓔ
31. Ⓐ Ⓑ Ⓒ Ⓓ Ⓔ
32. Ⓐ Ⓑ Ⓒ Ⓓ Ⓔ
33. Ⓐ Ⓑ Ⓒ Ⓓ Ⓔ
34. Ⓐ Ⓑ Ⓒ Ⓓ Ⓔ
35. Ⓐ Ⓑ Ⓒ Ⓓ Ⓔ
36. Ⓐ Ⓑ Ⓒ Ⓓ Ⓔ
37. Ⓐ Ⓑ Ⓒ Ⓓ Ⓔ
38. Ⓐ Ⓑ Ⓒ Ⓓ Ⓔ
39. Ⓐ Ⓑ Ⓒ Ⓓ Ⓔ
40. Ⓐ Ⓑ Ⓒ Ⓓ Ⓔ
41. Ⓐ Ⓑ Ⓒ Ⓓ Ⓔ
42. Ⓐ Ⓑ Ⓒ Ⓓ Ⓔ
43. Ⓐ Ⓑ Ⓒ Ⓓ Ⓔ
44. Ⓐ Ⓑ Ⓒ Ⓓ Ⓔ
45. Ⓐ Ⓑ Ⓒ Ⓓ Ⓔ

REA's Test Prep Books Are The Best!

(a sample of the <u>hundreds of letters</u> REA receives each year)

" My students are finding your *AP Calculus AB* book very useful. "
Teacher, Danbury, CT

" This actually works! REA's 6 AP [Calculus AB] practice exams are just great. "

" The 6 tests RE   Calculus AB] test. "

" Your book   ore complete than
anything   e them all! "

" Compared to the other books that my fellow students had, your book was
the most useful in helping me get a great score. "
Student, North Hollywood, CA

" Your book was responsible for my success on the exam, which helped me get
into the college of my choice... I will look for REA the next time I need help. "
Student, Chesterfield, MO

" Just a short note to say thanks for the great support your book gave me in
helping me pass the test... I'm on my way to a B.S. degree because of you! "
Student, Orlando, FL